TOUCHING PARCHMENT

Touching Parchment

How Medieval Users Rubbed, Handled, and Kissed Their Manuscripts

Vol. 1: Officials and Their Books

Kathryn M. Rudy

©2023 Kathryn M. Rudy

This work is licensed under an Attribution-NonCommercial 4.0 International (CC BY-NC 4.0). This license allows you to share, copy, distribute and transmit the text; to adapt the text for non-commercial purposes of the text providing attribution is made to the authors (but not in any way that suggests that they endorse you or your use of the work). Attribution should include the following information:

Kathryn M. Rudy, *Touching Parchment: How Medieval Users Rubbed, Handled, and Kissed Their Manuscripts. Vol. 1: Officials and Their Books*. Cambridge, UK: Open Book Publishers, 2023, https://doi.org/10.11647/OBP.0337

Copyright and permissions for the reuse of many of the images included in this publication differ from the above. This information is provided in the captions and in the list of illustrations. Every effort has been made to identify and contact copyright holders and any omission or error will be corrected if notification is made to the publisher.

Further details about CC BY-NC licenses are available at http://creativecommons.org/licenses/by-nc/4.0/

All external links were active at the time of publication unless otherwise stated and have been archived via the Internet Archive Wayback Machine at https://archive.org/web

Digital material and resources associated with this volume are available at https://doi.org/10.11647/OBP.0337#resources

ISBN Paperback: 978-1-80064-959-0
ISBN Hardback: 978-1-80064-960-6
ISBN Digital (PDF): 978-1-80064-961-3
ISBN Digital ebook (epub): 978-1-80064-962-0
ISBN Digital ebook (azw3): 978-1-80064-963-7
ISBN XML: 978-1-80064-964-4
ISBN HTML: 978-1-80064-965-1
DOI: 10.11647/OBP.0337

Cover Charles V swearing an oath on an open book being held by a bishop, Paris, 1365. London, British Library, Cotton Ms. Tiberius B VIII/2, fol. 46v. image reproduced with kind permission from The British Library.
Cover design by Jeevanjot Kaur Nagpal

Contents

Acknowledgments	vii
Abbreviations	xv
PART I: Introduction	**xvii**
1. Feeling One's Way Through the Book	1
I. Structure of the Book	4
II. Damage	5
III. A Haptic Approach	10
2. Ways of Touching Manuscripts	29
I. Inadvertent Wear	29
II. Targeted Wear	32
Part II: Books and Authority	**45**
3. Swearing on Relics and Gospels	51
I. Swearing on Gospels	54
II. Proffering the Book	69
4. Kissing: From Relics to Manuscripts	81
I. Kissing Missals	85
II. A Brief History of the Missal	86
III. Transformations of the Book	108
IV. Printed Canon Pages	118
5. Swearing: From Gospels to Legal Manuscripts	123
I. Last Judgment Imagery for Reinforcing Obligation	125
II. Local Government: Customary Law Books	137
III. The University: Old Proctors' Book	154
IV. The Inquisition: Inquisitor's Manual	160

6. Performances Within the Church	167
I. Choral Manuscripts	167
II. Books and Holy Water	176
III. Grand Obituary of Notre-Dame in Paris	186
Conclusion: The Gloves Are Off	213
Coda	223
Index	225
Bibliography	227
Illustrations	239

Acknowledgments

I am touched by the generosity of individuals and institutions that made this study possible. A Major Research Grant from the Leverhulme allowed me to read, write, travel, play idea-generating games, and most importantly, to take some risks. Several institutions have granted me fellowships that have afforded me opportunities to develop ideas about touching manuscripts in conversation with their members. Back in 2000 at the Center for Advanced Study in the Visual Arts in Washington, DC, Barry Flood and Zoë Strother first coaxed these ideas from their kernel. The ideas then developed during residencies at the Internationales Kolleg für Kulturtechnikforschung und Medienphilosophie (IKKM) at the Bauhaus-Universität Weimar, where Lorenz Engell and Bernhard Siegert created a stimulating and edgy atmosphere. They encouraged me to think about objects as a series of operations. In Weimar I had particularly fruitful conversations with Moritz Hiller and Katharina Rein. Meanwhile, my former research assistant, Leif Weitzel, not only scraped hundreds of images of missals for me (from the internet, not with a blade), but also helped build an enormous loom in my office in the Palais Dürckheim.

I am grateful to the Netherlands Institute for Advanced Study in Amsterdam, which not only provided access to scholars and libraries, but also hosted my fiftieth birthday party. At the Institut für Realienkunde des Mittelalters und der frühen Neuzeit in Krems an der Donau (Austria), Isabella Nicka, Thomas Kühtreiber, and Heike Schlie provided emulable models of collegiality and taught me the art of the coffee break. Serving as the Wanley Fellow at the Bodleian Library in Oxford gave me access to some of the greatest minds and filthiest books in the world. I am grateful for joyous exchanges with David Rundle, Emma Smith, Elizabeth Leach, Karl Kügle, Henrike Lähnemann, Jaś Elsner, and Martin Kauffmann. I will remember Nigel Palmer, who sadly died during the preparation of this volume, as enthusiastically supportive. During my sojourn at the Getty Research Institute, Rheagan Martin and Beth Morrison in the Getty manuscripts department identified several relevant items that would have otherwise passed me by. Numerous conversations with Nancy Turner, the famed manuscript conservator at the Getty, have proved invaluable. I am grateful to Maria Fredericks, Drue Heinz Book Conservator at the Thaw Conservation Center at The Morgan Library & Museum, for friendly chats about curtains in manuscripts. During stays in New York, conversations with Kathryn Smith, Ittai Weinryb, and Ivan Gaskell provoked thoughts. At Yale I had particularly fruitful talks with Ray Clemens, Jackie Jung, Christiane Gruber (during a seminar we led together at Yale), and Mitch Merback, who was hanging around at the time. Academia would thrive if everyone who worked on materiality and craft could attend Tactics & Praxis events at the University of Cambridge, steered by Louise Haywood, Georgina Evans, and Isabelle McNeill. On the continent, I enjoyed spending time at Radboud in Nijmegen, where Maaike van Berkel, László Munteán, Shari Boodts, Hanneke van Asperen, Willy Piron, and Johan Oosterman always made me feel welcome. One of my favorite intellectual gatherings took place in Stockholm, where Jonatan Pettersson brought together fascinating scholars at the Sjöfartshuset, including Vincent Debiais, Benjamin Pohl, Leah Tether, Mary Franklin Brown, Stefka Georgieva Eriksen, and Keith Busby. My research partner, Eileen Tisdall (brilliant pollen analyist) and I emjoyed the joyous and lively exchange. I am grateful to Karin Gludovatz for the splendid invitation to come to the Freie Universität in Berlin, where this book received its final sentences. As such, this book has been partially funded by the Deutsche Forschungsgemeinschaft (DFG, German Research Foundation) under Germany's Excellence Strategy in the context of the Cluster of Excellence Temporal Communities: Doing Literature in a Global Perspective (EXC 2020–Project ID 390608380).

Some of the ideas in this volume culminated in *Sensational Books*, an exhibition at the Bodleian. Delayed by two years because of covid, the show finally opened in May 2022. Presenting manuscripts to the public so that they could imagine handling, licking, and sniffing them was immensely rewarding, and I am grateful to the people who made that happen, including Sallyanne Gilchrist, Maddy Slaven, Jo Maddocks, and Richard Ovenden, and my marvelous co-curator Emma Smith.

Conversations with many other people have enriched this study, including Klaas van der Hoek, Irene van Renswoude, Marlene Hennessey, Maria Theisen, Monica Seidler-Hux, Rysiek Kukczycki, Kate Gerry, Ron Akehurst, Miri Rubin, Matthew Champion, Erik Kwakkel, Megan Holmes, Ed van der Vlist, Sonja Drimmer, Hanno Wijsman, Dominique van Wijnsberghe, Julian Luxford, Gia Toussaint, Rosalind Brown-Grant, David Ganz, Verena Schulz, Agnès Bos, Jack Hartnell, Sherry Lindquist, Hanna Vorholt, Andrea Pearson, Rory Loughnane, Ryan Perry, Doug Mortlock, Peter Kidd, Emily Rose, Suzanne Paul, James Freeman, Sandra Hindman, Laura Light, Anders Winroth, and Patricia Simons. From time to time Emily Guerry appears as if by magic in the UK or France, and then says fascinating things.

I am grateful to Paul Binski and Stella Nair for introducing me to the work of Paul Connerton; to Berthold Kress for help interpreting information pertaining to the collegiate church of St Severin in Cologne; to Reima Välimäki for telling me about the inquisitor's manual in Linz; to Joshua O'Driscoll at the Morgan Library for showing me the Arenberg Gospels under UV light; to Jos Biemans, for leading me to the Gospels of St Amand in Cologne; to Kasper van Ommen and Harm Beukers from the University of Leiden for telling me about the surgical manuscripts splashed in blood. They don't appear in this book, because studying them involved developing completely different methods of analysis, and they will form their own separate study. My special thanks go to Lisa Regan, Katharine Ridler, and Julia Faiers, who read and commented on the text at various stages of development. James Marrow helped me to arrange the ideas. I am grateful to him for his close reading and for encouraging me to work harder and write more clearly, as he has done since we met in 1992.

Of the manuscripts discussed and reproduced in this book, I have consulted nearly all of them in the flesh over a 20-year period, with a few exceptions. The remainder I have studied as digital proxies. Research for this volume (and the three that will follow it) therefore required many research trips. The School of Art History at the University of St Andrews kindly gave me a research budget that enabled me to study manuscripts in France, Belgium, and The Netherlands; and I am grateful to the various institutions that have invited me to come give talks about my research. In nearly every case, I was able to extend my stay to peruse collections, including those at Princeton, Leiden, Manchester, Cambridge, Chicago, New York, London, York, Melbourne, Zurich, Turku, and Bergen.

Visiting the manuscripts in this study has given me immense pleasure, as did meeting their keepers, including Hendrik Strelow at the Schnütgen in Cologne and Charlotte Denoël at the BnF. My thanks go to Lianne van Beek at Erfgoed 's-Hertogenbosch, who was generous with time and resources, as were the staff at the Noordbrabants Museum. Many people have kindly supplied me with images, including Remco Sleiderink, Louis Swinkels and Yvette Driever at the Museum Het Valkhof, Tina Oelbrandt in Linkebeek, and Tina Bode at the Old Synagogue in Erfurt.

My colleagues at St Andrews have facilitated my long absences and have given me much to think about. I am grateful to Alistair Rider, Andrew Horn, Anna Grasskamp, Billy Rough, Brendan Cassidy, Catherine Spencer, Elsje van Kessel, Emily Savage, Francesca Borgo, Hollie Buttery, Jeremy Howard, Julian Luxford, Karen Brown, Kate Cowcher, Laura Moretti, Lenia Kouneni, Linda Goddard, Luke Gartlan, Marika Knowles, Natalia Sassu Suarez Ferri, Natalie Adamson, Nicole Meehan, Ruth Ezra, Sam Rose, Shona Kallestrup, Stephanie O'Rourke, and Yusen Yu. These arrangements, and this book, would not have been possible without the support staff at St Andrews, including Graeme Hyland, Jo Fitchet, Lynn Ayton, Andrew Demetrius, and Dawn Waddell. At the St Andrews Institute for Mediaeval Studies, Margaret Connolly, Justine Firnhaber-Baker, Rachel Hart, and John Hudson have contributed in numerous ways. I never thought I'd be saying this, but I have a fond affection for my senior management at St Andrews, especially my Principal and Vice-chancellor, Professor Dame Sally Mapstone DBE FRSE (who alone appears here with her titles and postnomials); Provost Frank Lorenz Müller; Master Lorna Milne; and my former Vice-Principal for Research, Derek Woolins. They put research-friendly policies in place.

Closest to my heart are the Wonderfuls: Elizabeth Sandoval, Julia Faiers, Cecilia Mazzocchio, Roisin Astell, Suzette van Haaren, Anna de Bruyn, Kristen Herdman, Larissa van Vianen, Irene van Renswoude, Molly Proud, Kate Hodgson, Marie Hartmann, and Fergus Bovill.

If it weren't for the people in medieval manuscript studies, I would have done something else with my life, perhaps pursued a career in race-car driving or poodle training. My friends and colleagues have kept me on the path of studying medieval manuscripts, and I have only occasionally regretted it.

This book is dedicated to Robert Hillenbrand:
friend, exemplar, and mensch.

Abbreviations

BKB	Brussels, Koninklijke Bibliotheek
BnF	Paris, Bibliothèque national de France
HKB	The Hague, Koninklijke Bibliotheek
LBL	London, British Library
OBL	Oxford, Bodleian Library
ÖNB	Vienna, Österreichische Nationalbibliothek
IRHT-CNRS	Institut de recherche et d'histoire des textes-Le Centre national de la recherche scientifique

PART I
INTRODUCTION

1. Feeling One's Way Through the Book

Anyone who has examined considerable numbers of medieval European books—in museums, libraries' special collections, archives, and in the homes of private collectors—will have noticed that they rarely survive into the modern era unscathed. Candle wax, water, and fire can disfigure books dramatically. Repeated handling can result in more subtle damage to images, parchment or paper folios, stitching, or bindings; this includes applying grease or dirt through bodily contact, abrading material by repeatedly touching it, poking holes by sewing on objects, and degrading the fibers of parchment, paper, leather, and thread by repeatedly bending and unbending them. These activities leave traces that reveal how people have interacted with books. Heavy use is visible in dirty surfaces, tattered stitching, frayed edges, and deformed material.

Consider an opening from a missal made in Angers (Fig. 1).[1] The imagery in the spread has become murky and mottled, stained and smeared, especially at the center of each of the framed illuminations, with Christ's legs dissolving into the wooden vertical of the cross, John's robe blending into the featureless topography, and Christ's loved ones rendered faceless. The lower corners of both folios were so sullied and damaged that a modern restorer replaced them with crisp white parchment. This manuscript was probably made for Jean Michel's investiture as Bishop of Angers in 1439. The bishop's coat of

---

1   Angers, Archives départementales de Maine-et-Loire, Ms. J(001) 4138, Fol. 196v (quater)-197r (quinques). Since the foliation misses the entire canon, these folios are referred to as 196, 196bis, 196ter, 196quater, 196quinquies, 197, etc. It has been fully digitized: https://bvmm.irht.cnrs.fr/mirador/index.php?manifest=https://bvmm.irht.cnrs.fr/iiif/1334/manifest. Its bibliography is maintained here: http://initiale.irht.cnrs.fr/codex/5771

arms, featuring three large nails, flanks the images in the opening. The decoration testifies to a bespoke and precious manuscript, while the abrasion testifies to something utilitarian and work-a-day.

Fig. 1 Opening from a Missal for the Use of Angers at the Canon, 1439? Angers, Archives départementales de Maine-et-Loire, J(001) 4138, fol. 196v (quater)-196r (quinquies). Cliché: IRHT-CNRS

Although the Angers Missal has been exhibited internationally,[2] curators often exclude damaged manuscripts from exhibitions, and cataloguers rarely describe this damage or illustrate it in plates. Institutions regularly digitize only the "museum-quality" manuscripts and miniatures in their collections, leaving the others to languish in obscurity; the importance of these institutional decisions cannot be underestimated, as increasingly, scholars' access to medieval manuscripts is mediated through digital proxies.[3] At the pre-publication layout stage, scholarly authors banish

---

2   The manuscript was exhibited in *Anjou—Sevilla. Tesoros de arte, Exposicion organizada por la Comisaria de la Ciudad de Sevillla para 1992 y el Conseil Général de Maine-et-Loire, Real Monasterio de San Clemente, 25 de Junio2 de Agosto* (Tabapress, 1992).

3   Literature about the stakes of digitizing medieval manuscripts grows weekly. For a recent perspicacious study, see Johanna Green, "Digital Manuscripts as Sites of Touch: Using Social Media for 'Hands-On' Engagement with Medieval Manuscript

images of tattered manuscripts from books and articles, and editors have been known to crop out damaged edges in documentary photographs. Yet these signs of wear reveal much about how people interacted with their manuscripts, and as such, they hold a rich record of a book's past. Noticing, categorizing, and studying these forms of damage are the subjects of this multi-volume book.

Although one could approach these questions from the perspective of a conservator who is responsible for stabilizing books, or a restorer seeking to reverse signs of wear, I am approaching the matter from the perspective of an art historian who asks: Why does the image look the way it does? In considering the image in its material context, I also ask: Why do the page and the volume look the way they do? I am observing and analyzing, not intervening. As part of a future project, I will use laboratory equipment that extends human vision and applies metrics, but for the present preliminary study, I rely solely on my own (bespectacled) sight, sound, and touch. Although many of the figures in this book present images from manuscripts, I have tried to treat the miniatures in their bookish contexts. It has often been necessary to make or commission new photography in order to capture entire books rather than cropped images within them. I am interested in how people interacted with images, decoration, and text in the past, but those elements are part of a larger context—namely, the manuscript as a whole—and individual manuscripts were involved in a collective response. My interest telescopes from the image to the page, to the book, to its community of users, and finally to the constellation of objects with which it was used. This approach implies that meaning-making takes place as much in the reception as in the production, and that the user or users could co-produce the image. Moreover, the image was not stable, but subject to loss, abrasion, and even repainting.

It is, of course, not possible for one person to systematically examine every damaged manuscript, nor do I pretend to have done so. But I have examined manuscripts for signs of wear for well over a decade. I began identifying manuscripts that had been deliberately touched in 2007, when I gave a public lecture on this topic at the Koninklijke Bibliotheek in The Hague. Since then, I have visited hundreds of repositories of

---

Materiality," *Archive Journal* (September 2018). http://www.archivejournal.net/?p=7795.

medieval manuscripts and collected hundreds of thousands of digital photographs. More than 900 of the photographs document interpretable marks of wear. From that set, I selected manuscripts that would populate the typology outlined in these pages, without overwhelming readers with redundant examples. Many come from collections in Northern Europe and the UK, where I have spent much of the last 25 years. I intended to demonstrate that such deliberate touching is a pan-European phenomenon, and I hope that further studies by regional specialists can begin to specify distinctive local and chronological nuances.

Some of these ideas first appeared in my Dirty Books project, in which I measured levels of grime in the margins of fifteenth-century prayer books in order to discover which parts of the book had been used and which ignored.[4] The current study analyzes different kinds of grime, as well as abrasion, generated from a variety of user activities. Since this book reflects 25 years of research into manuscripts in repositories across Europe, North America, and Europe, it has been necessary for me to select some examples and exclude others. I am also working on projects in other media related to this current body of work. These include a picture book containing many more examples of damage, but with only a thin aspic of text to hold them together. I am also creating a series of videos to capture moving images of manuscripts, which can document some signs of wear more eloquently than still images and printed prose can.

I. Structure of the Book

This is the first of multiple volumes. In Part I of the current volume, I introduce a haptic approach to studying European medieval manuscripts that were made and used between ca. 1100 and ca. 1500. What can signs of wear, in the context of the book's contents and social function, reveal about how the object was used in rituals? In this first chapter, I provide an overview of the approach, which draws on archeology, anthropology, and linguistics, as well as on studies of memory. I attempt to answer

---

4   The current study expands my earlier work on this topic: see Kathryn Rudy, "Dirty Books: Quantifying Patterns of Use in Medieval Manuscripts Using a Densitometer," *Journal of Historians of Netherlandish Art*, 2.1 (Summer, 2010), and idem, "Kissing Images, Unfurling Rolls, Measuring Wounds, Sewing Badges and Carrying Talismans: Considering Some Harley Manuscripts Through the Physical Rituals They Reveal," *eBLJ* special volume: Proceedings from the Harley Conference, British Library, 29–30 June 2009 (2011).

a question frequently asked by audiences when I have discussed this material publicly: *How does one know when the damage occurred?*

In Chapter 2, I categorize the various kinds of traces visible in manuscripts, which correspond to respective ways of handling those books. This taxonomy, illustrated with examples, operates throughout the rest of the volume and in the future volumes, as well. The subsequent chapters make plain the great variety of meanings, emotions, and rituals involving book-touching. Each of these chapters treats a group of manuscripts used in a particular context, for it was the ritual setting that drove how books were handled.

Chapters 3 and 4 investigate rituals governed by priests and bishops. In the context of official ceremonies, two kinds of manuscripts played central roles during ecclesiastical rituals: Gospel manuscripts and missals. Carrying out codified rituals required touching these books in ostentatious ways. Such rituals were adapted for other contexts, in which oath-taking and official legal and civic pronouncements took place; these will be taken up in Volume 2.

In Chapter 6 I consider rituals other than the Mass that took place in churches, and dwell for some time on one manuscript—the Grand Obituary of Notre-Dame—whose signs of wear reveal the tactile aspects of funerary memorial practices. It is noteworthy here that the manuscript's wear was caused during memorial services for several celebrated members of the church and each one is different: there was no single ritual but rather the individual obituaries engendered slightly different micro-cultures of book-touching.

Although the subject of this study is ostensibly books, it is really about people, and it will demonstrate how people who had roles as officials (abbots, priests, members of the high nobility) used books in theatrical ways that reinforced their authority.

II. Damage

In proposing that a variety of practices by users caused different kinds of damage to medieval manuscripts, I endeavor in this study to reveal how early owners interacted with their books.[5] Such users were not

---

5   In building this argument, I am drawing on several important studies that interpret damage in manuscripts. Michael Camille did so in a sustained way in "Obscenity under Erasure: Censorship in Medieval Illuminated Manuscripts," In *Obscenity:*

being subversive, but by touching the folios or even specific images, they were using their books in a perfectly sanctioned way. As I hope to show, different gestures of handling the manuscript resulted in patterns of wear distinct enough to be distinguishable: setting a dry finger onto an image and then lifting it will mar the book differently from stroking it; touching with a wet finger will liquefy some of the water-soluble paint in a way that a dry finger will not; touching paint that is adhering to a semi-porous material (such as parchment) yields a different pattern of damage than touching paint on a non-porous material (such as gold leaf) or a highly porous material (such as rag-based paper); touching the book with the mouth and face will deposit facial oil which may affect the translucency of the page, but not reconstitute the water-based paint; and one person touching the book many times will yield a different pattern than many people each touching it once. Throughout this study I will consider signs of wear with respect to these and other variables, further inflected by social contexts.

Because I hold as axiomatic that the parchment surface provides clues as to how people behaved with their books, manuscripts and their signs of wear are my primary evidence, although I occasionally refer to other medieval hand-held objects. Stains, marks, and compounded inadvertent smears of dirt in books reveal important aspects of how they

---

Social Control and Artistic Creation in the European Middle Ages, edited by Jan M. Ziolkowski (Brill, 1998), pp. 139–54. Camille had also noted kissing as a ritual that degraded manuscripts, although he was more interested in theorizing (and dating) late medieval censorship. Gil Bartholeyns, Pierre-Olivier Dittmar, and Vincent Jolivet, "Des Raisons de Détruire une Image," *Images Revues* 2 (2006), argue that the mechanisms for destroying an image in a manuscript could include iconoclasm, idolatry, the expunging of evil (which is distinct from iconoclasm), or repeated gestures. I agree and am expanding and further nuancing the categories. John Lowden has applied use-wear analysis in a brief but insightful article and acknowledged that lay people kissed manuscripts and rubbed images of saints, in his keynote address at the conference "Treasures Known and Unknown," held at the British Library Conference Centre, 2–3 July 2007, British Library. Lowden paved the way in seeing certain forms of destruction as a legitimate form of use, rather than strictly censorship or iconoclasm. See also Erik Kwakkel, "Decoding the Material Book: Cultural Residue in Medieval Manuscripts" in *The Medieval Manuscript Book: Cultural Approaches*, eds. Michael Van Dussen and Michael Johnston (Cambridge University Press, 2015), pp. 60–76; although this text does not address use wear, it does show how codicological features can be read. Cormack Bradin and Carla Mazzio ask a similar set of questions of early modern printed books in *Book Use Book Theory 1500–1700* (University of Chicago Library, 2005), http://pi.lib.uchicago.edu/1001/dig/pres/2011-0098.

were used, and even what people hoped to gain by using them. How did readers activate their bodies in the ritual of reading? Can a pattern of wear be discerned within a particular book, or across a group of books? Were the marks formed by love? Desire? Hatred? Habit? Were these micro-performances with hands and fingers done publicly or privately? Did books help to achieve group cohesion and identity, and if so, how? What of their hopes and desires are revealed in their habits and rituals?

Previous scholars have discussed beholders' desires to destroy images—that is, to commit iconoclasm—but they have not paid enough attention to other forms of degradation and the methods by which the surfaces of objects were altered, whether deliberately or inadvertently.[6] Likewise, marks made by readers wielding quills—including annotations, glosses, and reading notes—have been studied,[7] but until now, marks made by readers' hands alone—which can also significantly change the surface of the page—have gone largely uncharted. And yet questions of surface are omnipresent in art history. Ever since Giorgio Vasari (1511–1574), the notion of the communicability of the surface of the object in its own right—through brushstroke and style—is at the center of connoisseurship. On the strength of this we credit works of art to particular artists—attributions that, at times, are worth millions. Why,

---

6 Iconoclasm and allied forms of erasure have been treated elsewhere—by David Freedberg globally, and by Michael Camille and Horst Bredekamp for the medieval period: David Freedberg, *The Power of Images: Studies in the History and Theory of Response* (University of Chicago Press, 1989); David Freedberg, "The Fear of Art: How Censorship Becomes Iconoclasm," *Social Research* 83.1 (2016), pp. 67–99; Michael Camille, "Obscenity under Erasure: Censorship in Medieval Illuminated Manuscripts," in *Obscenity: Social Control and Artistic Creation in the European Middle Ages*, edited by Jan M. Ziolkowski (Brill, 1998), pp. 139–54; Horst Bredekamp, *Kunst als Medium sozialer Konflikte: Bilderkämpfe von der Spätantike bis zur Hussitenrevolution* (Suhrkamp, 1975). Although not specifically about iconoclasm, Madeline Harrison Caviness, *Visualizing Women in the Middle Ages: Sight, Spectacle, and Scopic Economy* (University of Pennsylvania Press, 2001) presents examples of erasure and censorship, treated from a feminist perspective, different from that of Camille. Scholars of Persian and Islamic traditions have noticed multiple and contradictory motivations for deliberately destroying images; see Christiane Gruber, "In Defense and Devotion: Affective Practices in Early Modern Turco-Persian Manuscript Paintings," in *Affect, Emotion, and Subjectivity in Early Modern Muslim Empires: New Studies in Ottoman, Safavid, and Mughal Art and Culture*, edited by Kishwar Rizvi (Brill, 2017), pp. 95–123.

7 For a lively illustrated introduction, with further references, see Irene O'Daly, "Leiden, UB, GRO 22," *The Art of Reasoning in Medieval Manuscripts* (Dec. 2020), https://art-of-reasoning.huygens.knaw.nl/gro22.

then, can we not equally consider surface degradation and the stories it can tell us about how objects were used? In so doing, I am still asking: "Why does the image look the way it does?," an essential question for any art historian, but focusing on function instead of production. The beholder/reader co-produces the image alongside the scribe and illuminator, putting on the "finishing touches," as it were.

Paradoxically, art historians have usually placed more truth value in texts than in images. For example, an art historian can more confidently attribute an early modern painting when armed with a contract or inventory from a contemporary archive than when looking closely at the painting itself. Whereas archives will divulge occasional documents that confirm interpretations about artistic production, their materials are nearly silent on questions of degradation and abrasion, outside sparse instructions to priests to kiss the book or sprinkle holy water, which may splash on it. Nevertheless, medieval writers occasionally emphasized the utilitarian qualities of the objects around them. That objects were subjected to intense, often ritualized handling in the Middle Ages is confirmed by Boncompagno da Signa (c. 1170–1240) in his book *On Memory* (*Rhetorica novissima*).

> I claim it as established that all books that have been written, or have existed in every region of the earth, all tools, records, inscriptions on wax tablets, epitaphs, all paintings, images, and sculptures; all crosses, of stone, iron, or wood set up at the intersections of two, three, or four roads, and those fixed on monastic houses, placed on top of churches, of houses of charity and bell towers; pillories, forks, gibbets, iron chains, and swords of justice that are carrid before princes for the sake of instilling fear; eye extractions, mutilations, and various tortures of bandits and forgers; all posts that are set up to mark out boundaries; all bell-peals, the clap of wooden tablets in Greek churches, the calls to prayer from the mosques of the Saracens; the blarings of horns and trumpets; all seals; the various dress and tokens of the religious and the dead; alphabets; the insignia of harbors, boats, travelers' inns, taverns, fisheries, nets, messengers, and various entertainers; knights' standards, the insignia of arms, and armed men; Arabic numerals, astrolabes, clocks, and the seal on a papal bull; the marks and points on knucklebones, varieties of colors, memorial knots, supports for the feet, bandages for the fingers, the lead seals in the staves of penitents; the small notches that seneschals, administrators, and stewards make in sticks when they pay out or receive household expenses; the slaps that bishops give to adults during sacramental anointings; the blows given to boys to preserve the events of

history in their memories; the nods and signals of lovers; the whispers of thieves; courteous gifts and small presents—all have been devised for the purpose of supporting the weakness of natural memory.[8]

Most of these noisy actions that Boncompagno so graphically evokes involve enacting rituals with objects, either seldom and ceremonial or mundane and quotidian. These actions form the "intangible cultural heritage" in which memory and values are stored and transmitted, and yet, the instructions for using these objects are rarely written down. This may be because ritualized actions—such as slapping boys, notching sticks, signalling to lovers, and indeed making gestures with the paintings in manuscripts—are largely transmitted through social copying and repetition, and the actions are only written down or codified when they are threatened from the outside (with extinction), as the cultural historian Jan Assmann has convincingly argued.[9]

It is not possible to rely on historical meta-texts to study degradation. Only occasionally do instructions such as rubrics indicate that a reader must, say, plant a kiss. Instead, I am primarily using visual evidence to support my claims. Throughout my research I have kept an open mind about possible explanations for the patterns of wear in manuscripts; most solutions are unlikely to find corollaries in textual records. For example, I have found no documents that describe medieval users touching their books with a wet finger. To bring the varieties of degradation, and the correlative gestures that caused them, into view, I have laid out various kinds of touching that can be identified in manuscripts and have categorized them below (in *Ways of Touching*); this forms the basis of the rest of this study. Implicit in my approach is that different kinds of touching cause different kinds of damage. A meta-goal is to produce a taxonomy of the types of damage that result from users handling manuscripts, and to improve our ability to distinguish them. The taxonomy appears as a series of nested and hierarchical categories at the end of this study.

---

8   *On Memory* (*Rhetorica novissima*, VIII, 13), translated by Sean Gallagher in *The Medieval Craft of Memory: An Anthology of Texts and Pictures*, edited by Mary Carruthers and Jan M. Ziolkowski, p. 111.

9   Jan Assmann, *Cultural Memory and Early Civilization: Writing, Remembrance, and Political Imagination* (Cambridge University Press, 2011), esp. pp. 81–87.

III. A Haptic Approach

Mark-making in manuscripts occurred deliberately when scribes, painters, and illuminators applied words, images, and decoration to the book, but also accidentally when votaries handling their folios inadvertently deposited fingerprints, skin, dirt, spittle, wax, and other detritus. I consider these signs of use as readable, interpretable information that can help to construct object biographies. They record some of the past users' actions. Whereas most historians use texts as sources for writing history, in this project I follow Gustaaf Renier (1892–1962) in seeking traces of the past in the present.[10] Rather than pursue the historian's texts or the art historian's images, I place human signs of wear—which form a particular kind of trace—at the center of the study. A user could touch different areas of the same manuscript with a variety of techniques and intentions.

While a single use of an object may forever change it—for example, when red wine spills on a white altar cloth, when the swinging sword of Thomas of Canterbury's executioner dents the blade and chips the altar, or when a thorn from the Crown of Thorns is snapped off in a gifting ceremony to a dignitary—most of the changes to durable objects are gradual and result from the cumulative effects of ritualized actions. Repeated actions cause wear, and that wear can be interpreted to understand the actions that gave rise to it in the first place.

Signs of wear in medieval objects abound, and they tell much of the story of how use changed those objects. Natural materials from which medieval objects were usually made tend to deteriorate. Unlike our own era's glass and steel architecture, which does not show signs of wear, pre-modern buildings comprised stone, wood, and brick.[11] Anyone who

---

10 Gustaaf Johannes Renier, *History, Its Purpose and Method* (Allen and Unwin, 1950), *passim*; Peter Burke, *Eyewitnessing: The Uses of Images as Historical Evidence* (Cornell University Press, 2001, reprinted 2008), p. 13 and *passim*, draw on these ideas. Ann-Sophie Lehmann, "Taking Fingerprints: The Indexical Affordances of Artworks' Material Surfaces," in *Spur der Arbeit: Oberfläche und Werkprozess*, edited by Magdalena Bushart and Henrike Haug (Böhlau Verlag, 2018 (2017)), pp. 199–218, demonstrates why surfaces and fingerprints are essential to forging and understanding meaning.

11 Pallasmaa has written about the dire implications of non-organic building materials in modern architecture: Juhani Pallasmaa, *The Eyes of the Skin: Architecture and the Senses* (Academy Editions, 1996); *The Thinking Hand: Existential and Embodied Wisdom in Architecture* (Wiley, 2009).

has walked up the marble steps of an old building knows how centuries of footfall erode the stone. Likewise, the cumulative steps of thousands of pilgrims in Canterbury Cathedral wore a trough around what must have been a glistening, ornate shrine to Thomas Becket. After Henry VIII obliterated the shrine, only the trough remained. On a smaller scale, many hand-held objects were made of materials of animal origin (antler, bone, amber, leather, skin, parchment, wool, silk, or even marble, which after all also consists of once-living material); such materials often last a long time, but sooner or later reveal signs of wear.[12]

This study concerns the physical rituals that users employed with their books, and my methodology is conceptually congruous with my subject. Applying use-wear analysis extends my previous work, in which I used a densitometer to measure fingerprints and wear on individual pages to find out which pages of their prayer books votaries read and looked at, and which they ignored.[13] Here I have abandoned numerical values and spreadsheets and use only sight, touch, and hearing to make these observations: a well-worn folio has less elasticity, less "snap" than a fresh one; turning damaged parchment folios sounds different from turning pristine ones. I have not tasted any folios, although late medieval users may have done so.[14]

---

12   This study joins others in interpreting medieval objects through their materials. See Lorraine Daston, *Things That Talk: Object Lessons from Art and Science* (Zone Books, 2008); Caroline Walker Bynum, *Christian Materiality: An Essay on Religion in Late Medieval Europe* (Zone Books, 2011); Martha Rosler et al., "Notes from the Field: Materiality," *The Art Bulletin* 95.1 (2013), pp. 10–37; Christy Anderson, Anne Dunlop, and Pamela H. Smith, eds, *The Matter of Art Materials, Practices, Cultural Logics, c.1250–1750* (Manchester University Press, 2016). According to James Elkins, "It is one of the common self-descriptions of art history that it pays attention to materiality, to the embodied, physical presence of the artwork. But it only does so in a limited way… [M]ost texts on painting written by art historians treat pictures as images," From James Elkins, "On Some Limits of Materiality in Art History," *31: Das Magazin des Instituts für Theorie* [Zürich] 12 (2008), pp. 25–30.

13   Kathryn M. Rudy, "Dirty Books: Quantifying Patterns of Use in Medieval Manuscripts Using a Densitometer," *Journal of Historians of Netherlandish Art* 2.1(2010).

14   Rachel Fulton, "Taste and See that the Lord is Sweet' (Ps. 33:9): The Flavor of God in the Monastic West," *The Journal of Religion* 86.2 (2006), pp. 169–204. The Sensory Turn has made inroads in manuscript studies, as evidenced by Theresa Zammit Lupi, "Books as Multisensory Experience," *Tracing Written Heritage in a Digital Age*, edited by Ephrem Ishac, Thomas Casandy and Theresa Zammit Lupi (Harrassowitz, 2021), pp. 21–31. For the development of the sensory turn in the humanities, see Richard G. Newhauser, "The Senses, the Medieval Sensorium, and

Every mark that users left in their books through kiss or touch stemmed from a particular moment when they touched that book. Marking the book and leaving traces also produced a specific sensory experience.[15] With reciprocal effects, the act of touching changes not only the object but also the person who touches it, perhaps to fulfill a vow, prayer, oath, or other speech act. Book tactility engaged the pile of velvet, the lumps and knobs of leather glued to the cut edges of book blocks, decorative cut-outs and blind-stamped leather covers, sewn-in badges, and curtains. A book was made richer through such variety of materials. In this study I concentrate on how users handled books, those three-dimensional, multi-faceted objects that usually combined texts and images in a physical structure scaled to the human body. When relevant, other kinds of objects (panel paintings, relics, sculptures) enter my discussion. As bearers of the Word in a culture dominated by Christianity, manuscripts possessed a special charge within late medieval culture. Yet they could not, for the most part, be ensconced in locked chests or fully protected from exposure, because manuscripts only make sense when handled: they must be opened to divulge their surfaces and contents.[16] The codex constitutes a haptic medium, like clothing, certain liturgical objects, processional carts, storage boxes, or animated sculptures, whose meaning only comes into being during manipulation.[17]

Sensing (in) the Middle Ages," in *Handbook of Medieval Culture* (Vol. 3), edited by Albrecht Classen (De Gruyter, 2015), pp. 1559–75.

15 For an excellent overview of the understanding of the senses in the middle ages, see the introductory essay by Fiona Griffiths and Kathryn Starkey in the volume they co-edited: *Sensory Reflections: Traces of Experience in Medieval Artifacts* (De Gruyter, 2018). https://doi.org/10.1515/9783110563443. As Bernard of Clairvaux discusses (and as the essays in this volume show), the five corporeal senses were joined by five spiritual senses. Medieval people would have experienced objects with a combination of all ten senses.

16 Exceptions include rituals in which the book remains closed, as discussed by Eyal Poleg, "The Bible as Talisman: Textus and Oath-Books," in *Approaching the Bible in Medieval England* (Manchester Medieval Studies) (Manchester University Press, 2013), pp. 59–107.

17 For approaches to manipulable objects other than manuscripts, see Sarah Blick and Laura Deborah Gelfand, eds, *Push Me, Pull You: Imaginative and Emotional Interaction in Late Medieval and Renaissance Art* (2 vols) (Brill, 2011); and Adrian W. B. Randolph, *Touching Objects: Intimate Experiences of Italian Fifteenth-Century Art* (Yale University Press, 2014).

A. Methods

Use-wear analysis, which arose from the discipline of archeology, has informed my methods and those of some other art historians.[18] For example, Anthony Cutler studied the added sheen and loss of surface detail on Byzantine ivories to discover how they were handled.[19] Like parchment, ivory derives from animals and therefore wears down after repeated holding. As Cutler points out, often the lower corners of ivory plaques are shiny and abraded, because the thumbs worked away the surface during repeated acts of holding/beholding. (In the taxonomy discussed below, these are *inadvertent signs of wear*.) This abrasion reveals something important about how beholders used such ivories: they held and manipulated them as embodied actors. In identifying such abraded ivories, Cutler also underscores the intensity of their use. By extension, such signs of wear point to the necessity of these items in culture—as functional, practical, and vital objects.

Using and keeping old objects in circulation for a long time, and copying them accurately, helped to ensure conservatism in devotional practice. Manuscripts provided anchors for the words uttered in rituals. They tied present performance with the sacred past and maintained continuity. As Paul Connerton shows, the transmission of culture demands rituals, and the carrying out of rituals demands ceremonial objects. Objects themselves provide the best witnesses to the rituals that have been performed on them (if those rituals do not outright destroy them). Likewise, ritual actions preserve collective memory.[20] The incorporated (bodily) memory that Connerton posits stands in

---

18 For an example of such an approach, applied to stone objects made 6000 years ago, see Richard Fullagar and Rhys Jones, "Usewear and Residue Analysis of Stone Artefacts from the Enclosed Chamber, Rocky Cape, Tasmania," *Archaeology in Oceania* 39, 2 (2004), pp. 79–93. Archeologists continue to explore how materials affect cognition; see Lambros Malafouris, *How Things Shape the Mind: A Theory of Material Engagement* (MIT Press, 2013).

19 Anthony Cutler, *The Hand of the Master: Craftsmanship, Ivory, and Society in Byzantium (9th-11th Centuries)* (Princeton University Press, 1994), esp. pp. 23–25, 29. Considering signs of wear in ivories as clues to their original function has an older scholarly tradition: Louis Serbat, "Tablettes à écrire du XIVe siècle," *Mémoires de la Société nationale des Antiquaires de France* 73 (1913, published 1914), 301–13, p. 309, notes that the detached pages of an ivory booklet were once connected, as one can see from signs of abrasion caused by the thong hinges.

20 Paul Connerton, *How Societies Remember* (Cambridge University Press, 1989).

opposition to inscribed (written) memory, although both come together in the manuscripts I discuss; many of the uses toggle between treating the manuscript as a text- and image-carrier and regarding it as a sacred or charged object.

Most rituals require a place demarcated as special; some demand ritualized words (which, if formal, in a foreign language, or mysterious amplifies their power); some need ritual objects, while others rely on a particular set of codified behaviors. So much the better if the objects are transfigured during these manipulations. For example, through loving actions the supplicant could physically alter the object of desire, which would record the nature of the ritual in the object's accumulated signs of wear. In this regard, it is useful to consider *How to Do Things with Words*, in which the philosopher J. L. Austin outlines speech-act theory.[21] Instead of insisting that meaning is generated entirely from words' content, Austin proposes that some kinds of meaning can be generated from the contexts in which words are uttered. Specifically, there are certain kinds of language—speech acts—which perform specialized tasks or meanings by their very utterance. In contrast to most normal declarative sentences, a speech act changes the world in some way: for example, "You are now wife and wife," "I pardon you," "This is the body of Christ." These words, spoken by someone who has the authority to speak them—a justice of the peace, the president of the United States, and an ordained priest, respectively—and possibly accompanied by certain ritual actions (such as signing a marriage certificate, making a public broadcast and filing appropriate paperwork, or raising the Corpus Christi) effect significant changes. Ceremonial language with unconventional or foreign words and antiquated grammar often marks speech acts as distinct from regular speech. In relation to my study, many medieval speech acts required touching books in particular ways in order to achieve a permanent perceived change with legal, religious, or cultural *gravitas*.

Ways of handling books could be considered a "technique of the body," a term coined by Marcel Mauss, who recognized that everyday actions such as swimming, walking, and sleeping are always

---

21 J. L. Austin, *How to Do Things with Words*, The William James Lectures (Clarendon Press, 1962).

contextualized in social settings.[22] Walking through a market will be different from walking down a country lane, and even sleeping (whether on the ground in a circle, or under covers in a bed with a pillow) is not "natural" but learned. Consequently, people from different cultures and backgrounds sleep and walk differently. Social settings can equally affect behavior. I apply this idea to manuscript handling by considering the various sites in which reading takes place with prescribed sets of actions. Various people—bishops, priests, judges, deacons, abbesses, dukes, and lay believers, to name but a few—learned techniques of the body that involved and incorporated books. The handling of books in the late Middle Ages occurred in a range of contextually specific ways, which constitute practices of behaving with a culturally important object (the book), whose techniques originated with persons of authority, and whom others imitated. The contexts of use are therefore paramount: Who handles books, under what conditions, with what solemnity, and yielding what results?

A single parchment book could become part of someone's daily and habituated devotional activities, and therefore bear signs of daily ritual. Once people started consuming printed books, many owned several rather than one, and their devotional rituals might be spread out among several different volumes. Proportional to the total number of printed books produced, few heavily worn examples have survived. Manuscripts in particular, because of their longevity and singularity, were protagonists and mediators in structures of control. Such structures were enacted through rituals that included a priest celebrating Mass at an altar; a prolector (someone who publicly reads at court, a role that will be explored in Volume 2);[23] various lay and religious people swearing an oath; students learning from books in school; lay people using books in church, sometimes under the guidance of a confessor. People learned to use their books by imitating the practices of figures in authority, through events that took place in particular locations—at a church (high altar, side altar, nave, church yard), on a street in the

---

22 Reprinted in Marcel Mauss, "Techniques of the Body," in *Incorporations*, edited by Jonathan Crary and Sanford Kwinter (Zone, 1992), pp. 455–77.
23 Joyce Coleman defines and discusses the term *prolector* in *Public Reading and the Reading Public in Late Medieval England and France* (Cambridge University Press, 1996).

context of a procession, in a place of learning (I hesitate to use the word *classroom*, an anachronism), in a convent (chapter house, refectory), at court, at the city hall, courthouse, in front of the west portal of a cathedral, or at a shrine or chapel. These settings engendered different kinds of book touching. At each of these locations, a select audience witnessed a figure in authority handling a book, and in each of these settings, I argue, that person dramatized the performance of ritual in ways that left traces in the books they used.

In these spaces of authority, officials intentionally touched the books to teach or present beliefs about the world; viewers then demonstrated participation by following their lead. This was part of enacting a social order, in which the book had meaning in terms of the ways it bound people together around faith, the law, and political systems. Christianity's rituals relied on the authority of the written word. Books therefore figured prominently in its rituals, both as texts that provided scripts and as props that promoted the idea of the Word as divine *logos* (John 1:1). Priests, bishops, and other ecclesiastical officials brandished books publicly and in so doing demonstrated how to handle them. Books also took center stage at court, where public readings took place as a form of entertainment. Readers who recited texts put themselves with their props—(illuminated) manuscripts—on display as authorities on book handling. The courthouse provided another locus where the book—with its function to hold laws, records, and oaths in perpetuity—was publicly manipulated in ways meant to underscore the cultural and political weight of a legal written code. Scribes transmitted knowledge through copied texts, just as readers transmitted rituals through copied gestures.[24]

---

24 Doctors created mobile spaces of authority when, during consultations with patients, they handled almanacs, phlebotomy and urine charts, and other accoutrements that demonstrated their mastery of medical and astronomical knowledge. I have not been able to demonstrate that their patients copied doctors' gestures in their own books, although they may have done so, especially since calendars, zodiacal diagrams, and lists of Egyptian days are sometimes copied into private prayer books. See Karen Eileen Overbey and Jennifer Borland, "Diagnostic Performance and Diagrammatic Manipulation in the Physician's Folding Almanacs," in *The Agency of Things in Medieval and Early Modern Art: Materials, Power and Manipulation*, edited by Grazyna Jurkowlaniec, Ika Maryjaszkiewicz and Zuzanna Sarnecka (Routledge, 2018), pp. 144–56.

In some cases, particular gestures were required of the audience, which turned audience members into actors. They performed on a stage that involved persons in authority, particular scripted actions, and ritual objects (including books). An analogous public practice—kissing an icon—structured one way in which Byzantine believers used images, as there was considerable social pressure to take one's osculation in turn.[25] Likewise, certain legal and religious rituals demanded audience participation, such as placing a hand on an image. In many of these situations, the book was not the only ritual object present, but served within a constellation of objects, which might also include an altar, lectern, pax, aspergillum, rod, canopy, bier, crucifix, tympanum depicting the Last Judgment, or indeed, an icon. Marks of wear incurred during devotion—both targeted and inadvertent—can equally be observed in manuscripts used during public rituals. Such marks therefore provide us with insight into the ways that groups used touch ritually as well.

The number of deliberately touched manuscripts is so vast that the phenomenon warrants a social explanation. Certain ways in which books were touched publicly—during a performance or ritual—came to resemble ways in which books were handled privately. I am proposing two main forms of behavioral transmission, horizontal and vertical. My premise is that audiences watched authority figures handling books in public settings (such as Mass, where the priest kissed the book) and then adapted some of those behaviors in the use of their personal books of hours and prayer books. Figures in authority—including teachers, confessors, priests, monks, and civic leaders—presented themselves as models. The wealthy laity, who brought their books to church in the later Middle Ages, also put some of their books to use in public settings. Their performances were on display and copied by others. In short, believers were imitative. While their ultimate exemplar was Jesus, they also imitated saints, priests, and each other.

Horizontally, owners of prayer books across peer groups learned and normalized ways of handling manuscript prayer books and books of hours. The similarities in how particular images are touched, such as coffins at the Mass of the Dead in books of hours, is so systematic as to

---

25 Robert S. Nelson, "The Discourse of Icons, Then and Now," *Art History* 12 (1989), pp. 144–57, shows how images in manuscripts project into, and interact with, the viewer, who sometimes kisses them.

make it unlikely that individuals simultaneously invented this form of book handling in "private devotional" isolation, but rather that ways of touching manuscripts formed a shared practice which, moreover, helped to establish social bonds. (This idea will be taken up in Volume 3.)

Most of the material under scrutiny comes from the later Middle Ages, until the Protestant Reformation and the printing press changed Christians' relationship with religious authority and with books. Two kinds of manuscripts—the Gospel manuscript (also known as the evangeliary) and the missal—stand at the heart of this study and therefore form the backbones of Chapters 3 and 4. This is because a sea-change occurred in the twelfth century, when the missal was born out of combined elements from the evangeliary, epistolary, and sacramentary. The missal presented a compendium of all the texts a priest would need to conduct Mass (but without the choral parts, which were copied into separate books for use by the chorus). Simultaneously with these changes, Mass became more theatrical and its associated gestures grew larger. The act that sealed the most important ritual in the Latin church—transubstantiation, the turning of the bread into the flesh of Christ through words (the primary Christian speech act)—became more adamantly punctuated with a gesture: kissing. This gesture came to be copied in all kinds of other rituals and adapted for various contexts. This idea, that rituals and gestures of book handling migrate outward and downward into different social contexts, fuels much of the discussion in the book, as well as the argument in Volume 2.

A working hypothesis drives this study: that contexts of book handling produced different ways of touching manuscripts, which resulted in different forms of wear. Traditionally, much of the damage in books has been ascribed to iconoclasm, but that only accounts for two categories of damage. Specifically, users can destroy an image because they object to *all* images—that is, to the act of representation itself—or they attack an image because they abhor the subject depicted.[26] Iconoclasts in the second category, confronting particular figurative images, often mutilated faces and gouged out eyes: they *defaced* them. In

---

26 The medieval liturgical scholar William Durandus (1230–1296) lists the biblical injunctions against image-making. See *The* Rationale divinorum officiorum *of William Durand of Mende: A New Translation of the Prologue and Book One*, trans. Timothy M. Thibodeau (Columbia University Press, 2007), pp. 32–33.

medieval manuscripts, some hostile attacks left their traces in the form of rubbed devils and smeared baddies, or of images of St Thomas of Canterbury obliterated in the post-Reformation maelstrom.[27] My few examples are disproportionate with the immense number of medieval images that have been assaulted in these ways.

Leaving iconoclasm aside, here I examine other behaviors and motivations which left distinctively different patterns of wear. For example, book users expressed extreme veneration of images—what one could call *iconophilia*—through physical contact: positive emotions accompanied some users' intensely corporeal relationships with books. *Why* one touched a book inflected *how* one touched: with the hand or the mouth; with the whole hand or just a finger; and with a finger that could be wet or dry. One could use a sharp instrument for poking (usually for iconoclasm), or a blade for scraping (possibly in an extreme form of iconophilia). One could gesture lightly or rub up and down vigorously. One person could touch a single image hundreds of times, or hundreds of people could touch an image once, and the resulting patterns of wear will differ. The actors, the type of book, the location, and the users' emotions all contextualize modes of handling. Different ways of touching medieval manuscripts manifest themselves in visibly distinct forms of wear. I have recorded different forms of wear to avoid labeling all damage as "iconoclasm."

B. When Did the Damage Occur?

When studying the signs of wear in medieval manuscripts, one persistent question is *when* the damage occurred. Camille addresses this in an article about erasures of sexualized images in manuscripts, and he concludes that much of this kind of sanitation of manuscripts occurred

---

27 Important work has been written about illuminations of St Margaret that have been touched violently, including: Jennifer Borland, "Violence on Vellum: St. Margaret's Transgressive Body and Its Audience," in *Representing Medieval Genders and Sexualities in Europe: Construction, Transformation, and Subversion, 600–1530*, edited by Elizabeth L'Estrange and Alison More (Ashgate, 2011), pp. 67–87; Josepha Weitzmann-Fiedler, "Zur Illustration der Margaretenlegende," *Münchner Jahrbuch der bildenden Kunst* 3.17 (1966), pp. 17–48. See also John Lowden's web-published lecture, "Treasures Known and Unknown in the British Library," particularly the section on the *Passio* of St Margaret (https://www.bl.uk/catalogues/illuminatedmanuscripts/TourKnownB.asp).

in the fifteenth century, rather than at the hands of priggish Victorians; he contends that Europeans were developing a sense of privacy in the late fifteenth century that amounted to a form of prudery.[28] One rarely has proof, only evidence, of when damage occurred; however, one can consider the following observations, which suggest that use-wear damage was often performed early in the life cycles of manuscripts.

Those who keep their books in pristine states, by definition, leave few traces behind; those who value utility over preservation often find multiple ways to interact physically with a book. One can identify three different categories of user-generated additions. Certain kinds of manuscripts, such as necrological calendars, are designed with plenty of blank space to be filled in with the names of the dead. To fill them up is to use them in the manner intended. Other manuscripts have blank parchment at the ends of quires, of which users took advantage to add texts. Into prayer books and missals, they could inscribe more prayers or new Masses onto flyleaves as prayers developed and feast days accrued. (This happened, for example, in Paris, Bib. Ste Genevieve Ms. 97, where a fifteenth-century hand has added a text for the feast of St Elizabeth; Fig. 2). Students could react to the contents by drawing manicules or inscribing other comments in textbooks. Someone even added images of punishments to a fifteenth-century copy of *Tractatus de Maleficiis*, or Treatise on Evil Deeds.[29] Owners could also take advantage of the blank areas in the book to add birth, death, and marriage information (which is often dated), to let a child use a blank page to practice writing ABCs, to make inventories or shopping lists. Thirdly, users could add physical material to the book, such as parchment paintings, additional leaves, or

---

28 Michael Camille writes: "The number of times one comes across erasure of male and female genitals in manuscripts suggests that it was a widespread phenomenon in the later Middle Ages, that is, sometime in the period when these images were still circulating as functional objects and before they became collectable curiosities or valuable works of art in the nineteenth century," in "Obscenity Under Erasure: Censorship in Medieval Illuminated Manuscripts," *Obscenity: Social Control and Artistic Creation in the European Middle Ages*, edited by Jan M. Ziolkowski, pp. 139–54 (Brill, 1998), at p. 147.

29 Philadelphia, Free Library of Philadelphia, Rare Book Department, LC 14 23. See Kathryn M. Rudy, "Adding Images to the Book as an Afterthought," *Reactions: Medieval/Modern*, edited by Dot Porter (University of Pennsylvania Libraries, 2016), pp. 31–42. Erik Kwakkel's essay in this volume, "Filling a Void: The Use of Marginal Space in Medieval Books," pp. 19–28, presents fascinating examples of written additions.

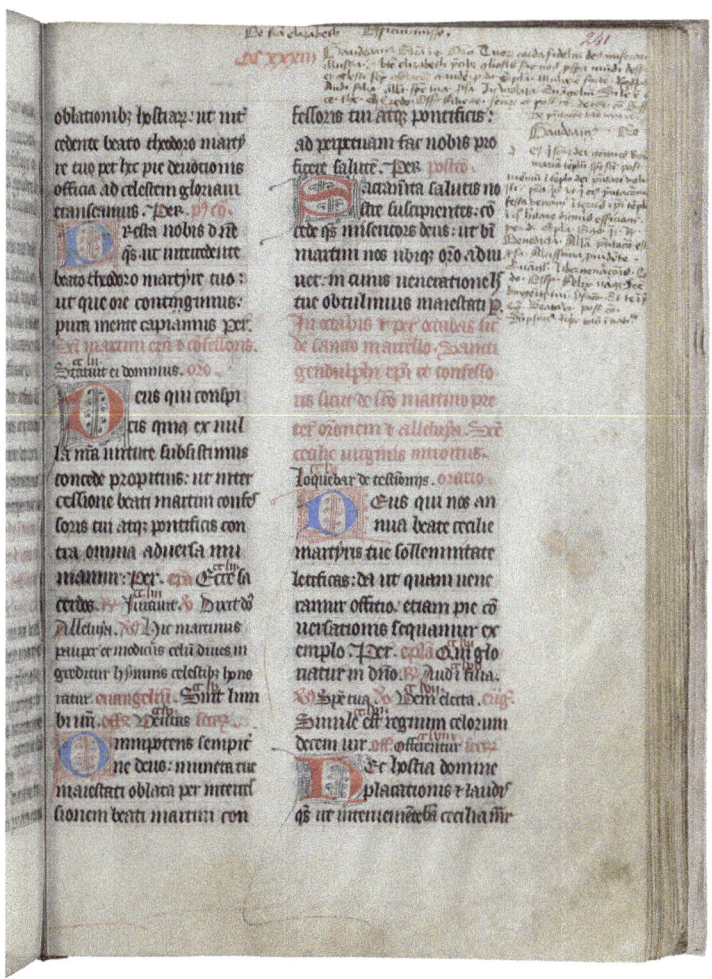

Fig. 2 Folio from a missal, with a Mass for St Elizabeth added in a fifteenth-century hand. Paris, Bibliothèque Sainte-Geneviève, Ms 97, fol. 241r. Cliché: IRHT-CNRS

entire quires.[30] They could glue or sew two-dimensional objects to its folios to transform it into a treasure chest. They could sew curtains above

---

30   For parchment paintings—that is, independent sheets added later to manuscripts—see Kathryn M. Rudy, *Postcards on Parchment: The Social Lives of Medieval Books* (Yale University Press, 2015).

miniatures, to add a layer of ritual, to introduce more precious materials into the book, and to protect the image. Manuscripts with these sorts of additions often have other signs of wear, indicating many interactive events. Personal prayer books could serve as comfort objects with which the owner would spend considerable time, poring and lingering over the content, stroking and riffling the folios.

Someone who handles a book frequently is likely to use it in multiple ways, adding images, texts, and physical material, not to mention grime and fingerprints. Thus, the dates of additions often coincide with periods of heavy use. In the case of Ms. Lat. Liturg. d. 7 (discussed below; see Figs 4–5), the damage must be medieval, because it pre-dates the medieval repair. And the damage from use coincides with the textual additions, which are made in a late medieval hand. In some manuscripts that bear needle holes from now-missing curtains above miniatures, the curtains may have been added as a response to partial damage of the book through touching: a protective textile, it was calculated, would prevent further damage. Those who used their books intensively and frequently also caused damage to the books' spines, which afforded them the opportunity to incorporate new images and quires at rebinding. Many medieval manuscripts in pre-modern bindings are often in their second or third binding. Rebinding often coincides with, or immediately follows, an intense period of use.

In the case of the missal for Angers mentioned above, it may have been bishop Jean Michel who wrote notes on the blank back of the Crucifixion, detailing how to acknowledge the Passion for each day of the week (Angers, Archives départementales de Maine-et-Loire, J[001] 4138, fol. 196r, Fig. 3). Jean Michel, or whoever wrote the instructions, considered the manuscript a utilitarian object that would help him to carry out the celebration and enactment of the death and resurrection of Jesus over a series of days. These added notes—plus the grime on many of the book's lower corners and the targeted touching of the illuminations of Christ Crucified and God Enthroned—help to build a coherent use-wear portrait of the manuscript, which coalesces around the added script, and which is typical of a mid-fifteenth-century hand.

Because scripts change over time, most readers could not read old manuscripts without specialized training. Proponents of Carolingian script attempted to overcome this problem by imposing a script designed

Fig. 3 Opening in a missal for the Use of Angers, before the Canon, 1439(?). Angers, Archives départementales de Maine-et-Loire, J(001) 4138, fols 195v-196r. Cliché: IRHT-CNRS

to be pan-European and standardized, but even that failed. Consider the *Aratea* manuscript in Leiden University (Ms. Voss. lat. Q. 79), an astrological text written in the ninth century based on a Hellenistic Greek source. Although it was copied in clear Carolingian rustic capitals with few abbreviations and regular spacing, someone in the thirteenth century apparently could not easily read the script and therefore felt the need to re-transcribe all the texts in a gothic hand in the margins, with even wider spaces between letters, but using capital and lower-case letters.[31] This implies that older manuscripts would have limited utility as readable documents, outside a circumscribed group of scholars. It seems likely, then, that scripts remained in regular circulation for only a short period, and that regular lay book readers would not necessarily be

---

31 Ranee Katzenstein and Emilie Savage-Smith, *The Leiden Aratea: Ancient Constellations in a Medieval Manuscript*. (J. Paul Getty Museum, 1988), pp. 6–7. Erik Kwakkel makes the point that certain readers preferred certain scripts and had difficulty deciphering others in: "Decoding the Material Book: Cultural Residue in Medieval Manuscripts," *The Medieval Manuscript Book: Cultural Approaches*, eds. Michael Van Dussen and Michael Johnson (Cambridge University Press, 2015), pp. 60–76, at p. 69.

able to read much earlier scripts. People who used manuscripts to access their texts either did so close to the time when they were made or else were trained for that task.

Third, the person most receptive to the content and design choices found within a particular manuscript is the one who commissioned it. The default here is that most wear by abrasion happens during a manuscript's period of highest functional utility, early in its existence. In other words, utility correlates with tactility.[32] However, in cases studied here, I note instances in which the date of the damage is especially ambiguous or unknowable.

In his *Making and Effacing Art*, Philip Fisher articulates a shift in handling and display as an object moves from utilitarian value to museum value. Taking an ancient sword as an example, Fisher considers its original function in the hands of the warrior who wields it in battle. After the warrior's death, the sword becomes a sacred object that will "summon and transmit the spirit of the warrior," but is used only in ceremonies (such as healing rituals) that might involve touching the sword.[33] After the society suffers defeat and the sword becomes part of the booty acquired by the victors, it becomes an object of wealth, and concomitant with this function, it is suitably displayed. In each of these contexts, the sword has meaning in a community of objects, first clustered with shields and protective gear in its warrior context; then alongside priestly costumes in its sacred context; and eventually with jewels and carpets in its treasure context. In a final stage, a new civilization appropriates the sword and puts it in a museum, where it is classified and preserved. In this context, it is studied and compared with other examples, which represents a fourth kind of "cultural heritage" value.[34]

Such shifting values apply not only to hypothetical swords, but also to real manuscripts. Over time, the function of many medieval books changed, often from utility to nostalgia. In the case of prayer books, owners might continue to use a book to record birth, death, and marriage information even if they retire it from daily ritual devotion. The prayer

---

32 I owe this phrase to Erik Inglis.
33 Philip Fisher, "Art and the Future's Past," in *Making and Effacing Art: Modern American Art in a Culture of Museums* (Harvard University Press, 1991), p. 5.
34 ibid, p. 5.

book could become an heirloom and family record. Whether later family members still used it as a prayer book would depend on their abilities to read the antiquated script, and whether a shift in devotional habits had rendered it obsolete. Later, it might become an object of historical and monetary value to a modern collector, such as Harley, Morgan, or Getty, or a European royal family, and from there enter a museum or national library, where preservation might be paramount, but other values—such as displaying industrialists' wealth or promoting national pride—might also operate. In this model, the bulk of the use-wear—which is related to its religious or performative functions—will have occurred early in an object's history.

One could point to exceptions to this trend: namely, manuscripts that were degraded in the modern era by post-medieval collectors. One can think of the illuminated volumes that were dismantled to be mounted in albums, manuscripts left in display cases until their bindings froze open, and manuscripts pawed by generations of cultural tourists. One would not be surprised if such handlers skipped the text pages and turned straight to the pictures, just as modern viewers might do when leafing through a digital version of a manuscript posted online. The most celebrated manuscripts often attract the most attention, and that very attention leads to their degradation. Although I remain cognizant of these forms of modern degradation, they are not my subject in this study. The wear I am interested in studying occurred in the pre-modern period, when the bulk of the utility-motivated damage took place.

Certain book types had more stability and therefore longevity than others: a thirteenth-century Paris Bible could stay relevant for centuries, because the text did not change, and its readers would have been learned men who could navigate the highly abbreviated and diminutive Gothic script. In contrast, a missal might well become obsolete when new feasts came into existence; up to a certain point, clerics could inscribe new feasts on the empty pages at the end of the book to keep the manuscript up to date. As long as additions were being made, the book was presumably still in use. Events including the Protestant Reformation created situations in which some books quickly lost their ritual relevance but took on historical value, if they were kept at all. Inversely, manuscripts collected for their historical value lose their utilitarian value. The more collectors value a book as a "museum piece," the less they want to risk damaging the painting (although cutting the painting out altogether was not always seen as damaging the book, but as a means of preserving and displaying the illumination). If manuscripts generally moved along a continuum from utility when they were new, to preservation when they were old, then it is reasonable to propose that most of the utility-related marks of wear were incurred early in books' histories.

A significant exception to this model is the Gospel manuscript. Because the text was considered to have been written by the Four Evengelists, it did not change. Unlike other book types, it could have a very long career without growing obsolete: no new feasts, prayers, or laws needed to be added to it. Insofar as it served as a symbol of the Word of God, the Gospel manuscript had many roles for which it did not need to be read. For that reason, its antiquated script did not render it illegible, for its legibility was not required. On the contrary, an antiquated script and decoration could render it more powerful, closer to the origin. Gospel manuscripts could be made for a monastic library as a book to study, but that is not the concern of the current investigation. What interests me are Gospel manuscripts made for the altar, to fulfil a role in a performance. As altargoods, they could have a function more like relics than other books had, as discussed below in Chapters 3 and 4.

In light of the progressive resocialization of most books (except Gospel manuscripts), consider the shifting functions of medieval manuscripts: when new, they provided text to read and images to gaze upon. They were designed for immediate and compelling needs, often to the specifications of a particular recipient. As hand-crafted objects, they were not designed for the use of subsequent owners, although later owners could upgrade and personalize them. My previous work on use-wear analysis suggests that second owners who upgraded manuscripts paid most attention to the very sections that they had added themselves.[35] That stands to reason, since those added sections represented items that owners so fiercely desired that they were willing to go to great lengths to have the new parts added. Adding a quire, for example, would entail obtaining the parchment, hiring a scribe, incorporating the new material and rebinding the entire book. It is no wonder that added sections are often the most heavily thumbed.

---

35 Kathryn Rudy, *Piety in Pieces: How Medieval Readers Customized Their Manuscripts* (Open Book Publishers, 2016), p. 203 and *passim*, https://doi.org/10.11647/OBP.0094.

All of this raises several questions. How did different forms of handling manifest on the page? How can one distinguish forms of handling to make this a useful category of historical inquiry? In what ways can signs of wear—and not just words, images, and decoration on the page—be legible and interpretable? In order to consider these questions, I distinguish among categories of damage by producing a typology, because creating new knowledge depends upon noticing patterns and forging categories for understanding. Some examples that follow exhibit patterns of wear wrought by regular, hard use. These patterns are different from the abrasion incurred when users purposely touched specific passages of ink, paint, or parchment. The typology I propose will, I hope, bring clarity to a complex field of analysis, allow one to gain some control over it, and lead to narratives about the handling of books by medieval users that make internal sense within individual book-objects and across groups of books.

2. Ways of Touching Manuscripts

My typology of manuscript damage is divided into two large designations: I. *inadvertent wear*; and II. *targeted wear*, with further varieties of damage falling beneath these two headings. These categories then operate throughout the rest of the book and in the subsequent volumes. Wear resulted from explicit physical attention to the objects and people depicted in manuscripts, but also to some words and even types of decoration. Often this attention was targeted not at the whole figure but at a particular detail, such as the face, hands, or feet, or in the case of words, an initial. Targeted wear accumulates, so that multiple acts of reading/handling wear down an image, soften its outlines, and erode paint layers. Targeted wear, like inadvertent wear, can result from habituated actions, and much of it arises from two opposing feelings: veneration or belligerence. Layered onto these two categories are two sets of motivations, although these might overlap or be indistinguishable: the actions resulting from strong emotions, or from codified ritual.[1]

I. Inadvertent Wear

Owners inadvertently left signs of their presence simply by handling their books vigorously over time. A primitive choir breviary made in the last quarter of the thirteenth century in Provence has been so vigorously handled that the moisture from and contact with the user's hands have caused the lower corner of the book to become friable and disintegrate (OBL, Ms. Lat. Liturg. d. 7; Fig. 4).[2] In a whole section from folios 83

---

1   Andrew H. Chen, in *Flagellant Confraternities and Italian Art, 1260–1610: Ritual and Experience* (Amsterdam University Press, 2018), convincingly argues that ritual tempers and shapes emotion.
2   S.J.P. Van Dijk, *Handlist of Latin Liturgical Manuscripts in the Bodleian Library*, 8 vols. (typescript 1957–1960), *Service Books*, p. 242. According to Van Dijk, in the fourteenth century the book belonged to Apt cathedral. Among the fifteenth-century additions in the calendar (6v) is the name of Casper de Chatillinge.

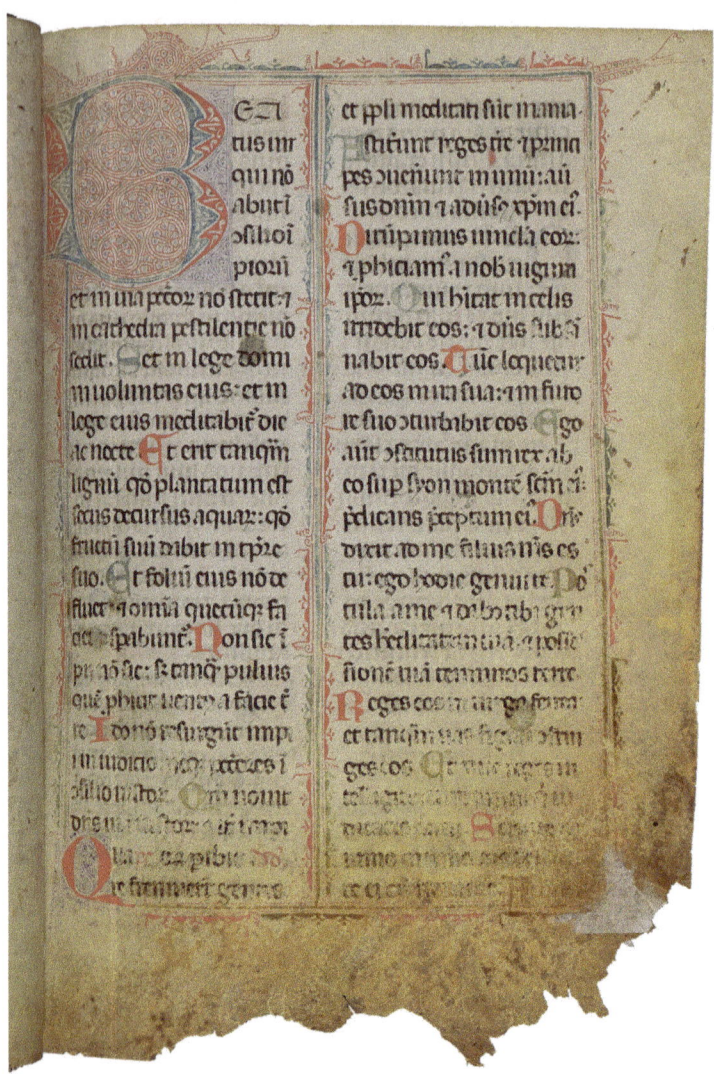

Fig. 4 Heavily worn folio in a choir breviary, at the incipit Beatus vir. Oxford, Bodleian Library, Ms. Lat. Liturg. d. 7, fol. 41r.

to 91, these damaged corners were cut away and new ones pasted in (Fig. 5). A medieval scribe has rewritten the texts onto those corners in an old-fashioned script to try to match the rest of the page. But even the replacement areas were so vigorously handled that they degraded, yellowed, and became brittle with moisture damage (presumably moisture from sweaty hands). More texts, in the form of entire quires, were also added in the fourteenth and fifteenth centuries. These repairs and additions indicate that the manuscript was in continuous use for several hundred years; its users repaired it to keep it functional even as it gradually disintegrated.[3] In the modern era, the manuscript was owned by John Th. Payne, a London bookseller, and then sold at Sotheby's on 30 April 1857. Trying to mask the extensive wear and discoloration, someone, possibly Mr. Payne, guillotined the book block and then gilded its edges before rebinding the volume.

Fig. 5 Opening in a choir breviary, with replaced corners. Oxford, Bodleian Library, Ms. Lat. Liturg. d. 7, fol. 88v-89r.

---

3   See Rudy, *Piety in Pieces* (2016), https://doi.org/10.11647/OBP.0094.

II. Targeted Wear

The way damage looks on the page usually allows one to distinguish between targeted and inadvertent wear. Whereas inadvertent wear is often confined to the edges of the page, to the margin, or to the upper layer of surface (from such causes as splashes of holy water, wine, rainwater, or wax), targeted wear often appears in the middle of the page and digs down into the layers. Targeted wear requires a motive, a desire to interact with a word, image, part of an image, or a shape (such as a decorative form). Here I do not explore the technical analysis of chemicals or paint solubility (other than to note that tempera and ink are water soluble), but rely entirely on the senses—specifically, close visual, tactile, and auditory perception. Parchment that has been wetted re-dries in such a way that it can change a book's acoustics, just as repeatedly bending and unbending can soften parchment, and abrasion can change the surface texture, making it either shinier or more velvety.

Consider the following ways in which users could touch books, which can explain the patterns of wear found in late medieval manuscripts.

Depositing Wax

In the previous section, I proposed that wax stains constituted a form of inadvertent wear, part of the vicissitudes of handling books in the vicinity of lighted candles. However, readers could also deposit wax on purpose. An example appears in a twelfth-century manuscript containing Augustine's commentary on Psalms CXIX-CL (OBL, Ms. Bodl. 241; Fig. 6 and Fig. 7).[4] It belonged to Reading Abbey, where monks would have read the text aloud in the refectory. Hundreds of carefully placed wax stains dot the margins.[5] They largely correspond to the textual divisions and are distinct from the "nota" signs inscribed in pen in the margins. Photographing the folios in raking light reveals how the wax caused distortions in the parchment, and it also reveals how several spots of wax (near the capital S and B, respectively) were scraped off, probably with a fingernail. The monk reading the collation may have signalled where

---

4   Otto Pächt and J. J. G. Alexander, *Illuminated Manuscripts in the Bodleian Library Oxford* (Vol. 2), edited by J. J. G. Alexander (Clarendon Press, 1966–1973), p. 119.
5   There are also some places where the candle spilled hot wax accidentally.

the next day's reading was to begin by depositing a ball of soft wax in the margin, and then scraping the wax off when he next progressed through the reading. In other words, the blobs of wax functioned like temporary place markers. This phenomenon is difficult to detect, since monks would scrape the wax off after use, and the residue is nearly invisible under traditional photography.

Fig. 6 Folio of Augustine's commentary on Psalms from Reading Abbey, with wax stains, photographed in raking light. Oxford, Bodleian Library, Ms. Bodl. 241, fol. 33v

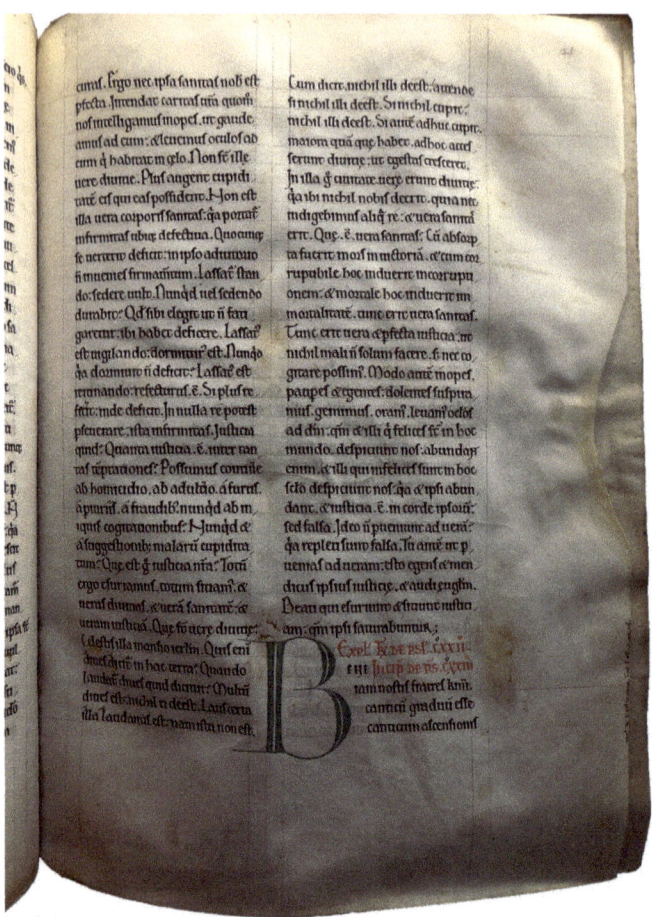

Fig. 7 Folio of Augustine's commentary on Psalms from Reading Abbey, with wax stains. Oxford, Bodleian Library, Ms. Bodl. 241, fol. 24r

Ritualized Kissing

Users often kissed books. Sometimes the object of the kiss was the entire book (in which case the book could be closed) and sometimes it was an image, word, or letter within the book (which necessitated opening the book). Persons in authority performed this technique according to types of books and places within them (as when priests kissed missals). Moisture from the mouth could deform the parchment, weaken it, and make it wrinkle. Parchment that has been kissed may become tacky, so that it adheres to whatever surface touches it. This could result in paint transfer onto the facing page. Furthermore, paint that has been moistened through kissing can become smeared or streaky. Another of the by-products of kissing is inadvertent application of facial oils to the parchment. This can cause parchment to become darkened, shiny, and/or translucent.

Touching with a Wet (Kissed) Finger to Transport a Kiss

Just as a pax can carry the kiss from a priest's mouth to his congregation, his finger could also carry a kiss from his mouth to the book. In effect, the finger mediated between the breath of a priest and the Word of God, as inscribed on the surface of the manuscript. In several examples, one can discern the whorls of a fingerprint stamped onto the manuscript; this could only have resulted from touching the book with a wet finger.

Many wet-touched initials appear in religious service books (such as Bodley missal Canon. Liturg. 344, for which see Figs 49–50). Officiants performed this gesture in order to venerate the Word of God while preserving the script: they often limited their touching to the oversized beginning letters. An initial stands for the text as a whole. A single wet-touching alone could mark the painted image; this partly depends on the water solubility of the inks and paints used. Although I cannot always distinguish the wear of wet lips from the wear of a wet finger, I suspect that readers preferred the finger when aiming at a small target. When wetting their fingers and books in this way, perhaps users sought to physicalize their emotional bonds with the Word or the figure behind the image depicted. Perhaps they wanted to forge a link between their breath and the book's words.

Touching a *Book Cover* with a Dry Hand

Besides opening a book, other motivations exist for touching it: to carry it ceremoniously, affirm one's adherence to a book-based dogma, or swear an oath. Oath-swearing was sometimes performed on a closed book, and sometimes on an open one. Such acts recognize the book's cultural *gravitas* and treat the book—which contains the Word of God—as a relic.

Touching a *Mark* (Image, Text, or Decoration Within a Book) with a Dry Hand

Touching a mark with a dry hand implies a desire to be in physical proximity to an image, word, or decoration. Touching it with a finger, rather than with the whole hand, changes the gesture, making it more precise, so that one might only touch the depicted face or hem, a detail of the decoration, or a particular word in a text. This form of touching might also externalize one's progress through a text. While a single event of touching may not register on the surface, repeated acts will dislodge the ink, paint, or gold, while depositing dirt and oil, so that its cumulative effects register a reader's presence in the book. Those touching it could reach into the book lying open on a lectern; they could have their eyes on a page other than the one they were touching, or they could touch a book that was proffered to them. These situations will result in different patterns of wear.

Among this kind of cumulative wear, one can identify two subsets: a single individual touching the same image many times, or many people touching a particular image once. These activities result in different kinds of wear: an individual who touches a book repeatedly does so out of habit, and therefore touches it the same way each time. This results in neat, localized paint loss. In contrast, when large numbers of people each touch a painting once, they tend to do so differently from one another. They are not acting out of personal habit, but according to conventions adopted by particular groups of people. They might place the hand on an image to swear an oath upon the figure represented. Touching the image binds them with both the image and other members of this group. Because each act of touching is unique, the paint loss from these cumulative acts usually falls over a wider area and has an indistinct edge. Some beholders feel confident enough to touch the eyes depicted in the images with full contact; others touch the hem, or just lightly touch the represented chin. The motivation in play here is to publicly proclaim group membership, physically declaring one's allegiance—frequently in a public setting.

Touching a Mark (Image, Text, or Decoration) with a Body Part Other Than the Hand

Some rituals call for the pressing of a manuscript to the body as a medicinal aid. The body part may be the forehead, or the abdomen of a woman in labor, for example. Most of these forms of touch depend on belief in the apotropaic power of manuscripts and amount to the practice of sympathetic magic. They are performed for the benefit of the person who is touching the book. The feeling involved here might be both despair and hope. Examples of this kind of touching will be taken up in Volumes 2 and 3.

Dramatizing with a Finger

Someone has touched the apostles and Mary at the scene of the Ascension of Christ in a Roman missal written in ca. 1380–1420 in Church Slavonic and Croatian (Fig. 8).[6] This missal is illuminated with relevant pictorial subjects and not simply a Crucifixion image, as many late medieval missals are (as discussed below in Chapter 4). The book's user, presumably a priest or bishop, has not only touched the figures' hems and faces with a wet finger—with special attention to the Virgin in blue—but he has also traced the path of their gaze upward as they watch Christ disappear into the firmament.

Erasing/Rubbing Out with a Finger

Whereas dramatizing with a finger usually involves a single quick gesture, erasing with a finger involves a back-and-forth motion. Its purpose is to rub out the representation, and thereby to demonstrate one's moral position toward it. Devils, torturers, and other antagonists often receive this treatment, as do specific body parts: users often attack the heads and faces of figures to destroy them (as opposed to the feet, which seem only to be kissed in reverence). This act allows viewers to rise in anger and hatred, and to expunge the devil by attacking

---

6   For a catalogue description and a full digitization of the Croatian missal (Ljubljana, National and University Library, Ms. 162), see https://www.nuk.uni-lj.si/sites/default/files/dokumenti/2015/katalog_rokopisov.pdf

Fig. 8 Folio from a missal, with the Ascension of Christ, ca. 1380–1420. Ljubliana, The National and University Library of Slovenia, Ms. 162, fol. 102r. Public domain image provided by Narodna in univerzitetna knjižnica

his picture. In some cases, beholders are merely taking cues from the Virgin, who was said to deface the devil.[7] Whereas the destruction of

---

7   Deirdre Jackson, "Virgin, Devil, Bishop, King: Nicola Pisano's Pulpit in Siena and Alfonso X's Cantigas de Santa Maria," *Illuminating the Middle Ages: Tributes to Prof. John Lowden from His Students, Friends and Colleagues* (Vol. 79 of the Library of the Written Word series), edited by Laura Cleaver, Alixe Bovey and Lucy Donkin, (Brill, 2020), pp. 259–75.

figural forms from veneration often accumulates over many reading events, destruction from negation can be accomplished in an instant. While a person who touches an image for dramatic effect may not intend to destroy it, someone who touches it to erase it does so with destruction as his or her goal.

Sewing Curtains to the Page

In the interiors of their books, owners could sew curtains over an image, a word, or an entire page. As Christine Sciacca argues, the primary reason for medieval users to sew in curtains was to protect metallic pigment, to use the silk as interleaving material, but also to cover an image. Unveiling the illumination would result in a ceremonial moment of revelation.[8] Veiling directs attention to a particular area of the book by temporarily obscuring it; unveiling ritualizes a gesture effected in parallel with reading. Sewing curtains into a manuscript involved two acts of piety. First, to place a particular image under a veil was to dress it in a luxury "jacket" that marked it as special, an act which elevated prized manuscripts to the level of relics.[9] Second, each act of lifting the curtain created a ritual of veneration. The initial sewing and the later manipulation both cause targeted wear, and the two activities each leave telltale traces: the first leaves rows of needle holes, even when the curtain itself has been removed. The second causes a cumulative, often dark, scuff on the image or its frame where the thumb makes repeated contact. The sewing process brings about secondary rubbing, not on the image but near it.[10] The practice of sewing curtains into manuscripts was not uncommon: in the Morgan Library alone, no fewer than 13 manuscripts have curtains or needle holes that imply missing curtains, many of them luxury Gospel manuscripts.[11] Needle holes also appear at

---

8   See Christine Sciacca, "Raising the Curtain on the Use of Textiles in Manuscripts," in *Weaving, Veiling, and Dressing: Textiles and Their Metaphors in the Late Middle Ages* (Medieval Church Studies), edited by Kathryn M. Rudy and Barbara Baert (Brepols, 2007), pp. 161–90.
9   Sciacca makes this point, p. 163.
10 For an example (London BL, Harley Ms. 2966), see Kathryn M. Rudy, "Kissing Images" (2011).
11 According to Corsair (http://corsair.themorgan.org/index.html), the manuscripts in the Morgan Library with current or former curtains are G.24; G.44 (curtains removed, housed separately); G.48; M.1149; M.311; M.440; M.708; M.709; M.710;

the tops of many full-page miniatures in books of hours; these will be taken up in Volume 3.

Other Kinds of Sewing

Users could sew protrusions, such as leather or parchment knots, or textile or parchment tabs, to the fore-edge to create a permanent bookmark. Their presence implies an overt use of the sense of touch (and not just the senses of sight and proprioception) to navigate through the leaves.

Parchment makers also repaired holes in parchment by suturing them. Scribes often interact with these holes, as with one scribe who continued the stitches to create a triangular face that seems to be sewn to the page (Fig. 9). To experience them fully, one would have to touch them.

***

All these forms of touching demonstrate that medieval manuscripts could inspire a wide range of interactions, not merely reading and viewing. The abrading gestures could occur with wet or dry techniques, directly with the body or mediated by instruments, by one person or by many, and on a continuum from spontaneous to premeditated. These variations produced different marks on the page and corresponded to diverse situations and states of mind. Among these intersection possibilities, one can observe a strong correlation between those readers who added objects to their manuscripts such as images, badges, and curtains, and those who regularly and heavily handled their books. That being the case, a single manuscript might exhibit wear from several of the categories outlined above. (Case studies of manuscripts that received multiple, complex forms of touching will appear in Volume 4.)

Distinguishing targeted wear from regular hard use can sometimes be difficult; of the dozens of examples of targeted wear considered in

---

M.711; M.780; M.833; M.939. I thank Maria Fredericks for alerting me to the rich textiles in the Morgan's manuscript collection. See Morgan Simms Adams, "Identifying Evidence of Textile Curtains in Medieval Manuscripts in the Morgan Library & Museum," *Suave Mechanicals: Essays on the History of Bookbinding* (Vol. 6), (The Legacy Press, 2020), pp. 2–61.

Fig. 9 Margin in a missal with a repair, from a missal from the Knights Hospitallers, Southern Germany, 1469. 's-Heerenberg, The Netherlands, Collection Dr. J. H. van Heek, Huis Bergh Foundation, Ms. 15. Image © The Huis Bergh Foundation, CC BY 4.0

this study, most are quite clear, but a few are ambiguous. When seeking to untangle the causes of various forms of wear, I have asked of each example: How did the medieval person hold this book? What was the context of use—where and with what community of objects was the manuscript used? Was this book placed on a lectern, prie-dieu, or altar, or was it held in the hands? Could the excessive wear have been the result of regular handling? Is there a pattern of targeted wear across several folios in the manuscript (which would further suggest that the wear had been administered intentionally)? Do the patterns of wear across the entire book result from the use of the book in a ritual? Does other circumstantial evidence corroborate that the damage occurred in the Middle Ages rather than in the post-medieval period?

Occasionally one finds stray marks or signs of wear in manuscripts that are difficult to interpret: Are they traces of targeted wear or not? One such example is provided by a fingerprint on the face of a man building the Tower of Babel (Fig. 10). I doubt that this fingerprint represents an act of targeted wear, because no larger pattern of repeated wear appears in this manuscript; it seems unlikely that this anonymous figure would have elicited a sufficiently strong response to motivate a viewer to deliberately touch the image. My working assumption is that targeted wear would always have been linked to emotional motivation, and ought to make coherent sense within the context of a given volume. In the case of the Tower of Babel, I suspect that we are encountering the mark of a stray wet finger. In short, some signs of wear resist unambiguous interpretation, and I do not assume that every fingerprint, stain, and smudge in a given manuscript was purposefully aimed at a particular image.

Fig. 10 Tower of Babel, from *Guiard des Moulins, Grande Bible Historiale Complétée*, written and illuminated in Paris, 1371–1372. The Hague, Meermanno Museum, Ms. 10 B 23, fol. 19r

PART II
BOOKS AND AUTHORITY

Liturgical manuscripts—such as Gospels and missals—both betokened and maintained the authority of the officials who used them. In a Christian context, these volumes were understood to contain divinely sourced texts. By extension, their users had the imprimatur of divine sanction. In the words of the medieval historian of the liturgy, William Durand (c. 1230–1296): "The codex of the Gospels is also placed on the altar, since the Gospel was published by Him, that is, Christ, and He still provides testimony to us."[1] These manuscripts were used in ceremonies as props for authenticating speech acts, in J. L. Austin's formulation (See Chapter 1). The repeated performances centered on the book and conducted at altars formed the Ur rituals that were adapted at other kinds of rituals discussed later in this study, since the ways in which church officials handled missals and Gospels had an enormous impact on how other book-centered ceremonies were configured, and how, ultimately, the laity treated its books (as I will demonstrate in Volume 2).

It is especially worthwhile to study rituals involving missals and Gospels because they strongly influenced rituals in other domains. Jacques Le Goff has shown how ceremonies in one domain can influence those conducted in another, and he looked specifically at how the ritual of vassalage borrowed from the ritual of the liturgy.[2] Like the Mass- and Gospel-oriented oath-taking ceremonies, the vassalage ceremony required three components: utterances, gestures, and props. These consist of an uttered statement wherein the vassal accedes to accepting the lord (which is an example of a speech act); a gesture, or better, a "reciprocity of gestures" between lord and vassal, wherein the vassal places his hands inside those of the lord, signifying that the vassal will serve the lord, while reciprocally, the lord will protect the vassal. This gesture is depicted in a historiated initial at the start of a fourteenth-century French copy of the *Constitutiones feudorum cum glossis*, now in

---

[1] *The* Rationale divinorum officiorum *of William Durand of Mende: A New Translation of the Prologue and Book One*, trans. Timothy M. Thibodeau (Columbia University Press, 2007), p. 42.

[2] Jacques Le Goff, "Le rituel symbolique de la vassalité," Pour un autre Moyen Age: Temps, travail et culture en Occident (Gallimard, 1977); English trans. "The Symbolic Ritual of Vassalage," *Time, Work and Culture in the Middle Ages*, trans. Arthur Goldhammer (University of Chicago Press, 1980), pp. 237–87. Eric Palazzo, emphasizing the centrality of the liturgy, repeats the point in "Art and Liturgy in the Middle Ages."

Vienna (Fig. 11).[3] The miniature emphasizes the men's inequality, with the lord larger, seated, and with his head extending beyond the upper frame, while the vassal is smaller, kneeling, and with his foot outside the lower bounding frame, as if to suggest that he is stepping upward from below.[4] The miniaturist has enlarged their hand gestures at the center of the miniature and framed them against a plain gold background so that they are easily legible. Central to the painter's concerns is to show that the lord envelopes the vassal's hands. In the second part of the ceremony, the vassal would place his hand on a liturgical manuscript or a relic and swear that he would not injure the lord. By undergoing this ceremony, a vassal became a "man of mouth and hands," signifying that he had sworn with uttered statements and appropriate hand gestures. Ceremonies in other domains of late medieval practice followed the same formula of utterance-gesture-prop. That prop was often a book, an object that was charged with such values as accumulated history, divine provenance, and tradition; in short, with authority.

In the following chapters, I investigate other related medieval rituals, which likewise depend on three symbolic categories of speech, gesture, and objects, in which those objects are books. In the period under scrutiny, "religious" and "secular" are false distinctions, with the Church permeating every aspect of life, and the Church's ceremonies shaping other forms of ritualized conduct and providing both the backdrop (often an altar), and the props (Gospel manuscripts, liturgical or para-liturgical manuscripts, or images such as the canon plates associated with them) for a variety of rituals. To do this, I will employ four kinds

---

3   Vienna, ÖNB, Cod. 2262, Fol. 174v. The manuscript is a compilation from the fourteenth century, with three texts bound together in the fifteenth century. The initial (Fol. 174v) prefaces the *Constitutiones feudorum cum glossis* (Fols 174v-196r), written in France, possibly Avignon, as suggested by H. J. Hermann, *Die westeuropäischen Handschriften und Inkunabeln der Gotik und der Renaissance mit Ausnahme der Niederländischen Handschriften. 2. Englische und französische Handschriften des XIV. Jahrhunderts* (Beschreibendes Verzeichnis der illuminierten Handschriften in Österreich. VIII. Band: Die illuminierten Handschriften und Inkunabeln der Nationalbibliothek in Wien) (Verlag von Karl W. Hiersemann, 1936), pp. 121–22.

4   In discussing this image, I wish to show that some lord-vassal relationships were forged as this image intimates, but I am not implying the existence of a universal "feudal system," which was a term and concept only introduced in the seventeenth century. See Elizabeth A. R. Brown. "The Tyranny of a Construct: Feudalism and Historians of Medieval Europe," *The American Historical Review* 79, 4 (1974), pp. 1063–88.

Fig. 11 Incipit of the *Constitutiones feudorum cum glossis*. France, 14th century. Vienna, Österreichische Nationalbibliothek, cod. 2262, fol. 174v.

of evidence: instructions for handling books in various ceremonies (prescriptive texts), Durandus's commentaries on ritual (descriptive texts), images of such ceremonies taking place, and marks in surviving manuscripts that had been used in such rituals. The first kind of evidence survives in the form of rubrics that provide instructions for carrying out certain gestures. One problem with this category is summarized by the great historian of the liturgy, Andrew Hughes, who writes: "Much of liturgical practice was so much a part of everyday custom, known to all, that it did not need to be explained or prescribed, or, therefore, written down."[5] In other words, manuscripts for Mass and office assumed that their users had been steeped in liturgical conduct and therefore did not require the actions expected of them to be spelled out. Of the second category, Durandus wrote an interpretation of church ritual that is helpful for parsing late medieval understanding of church furnishings, liturgical garb, and the gestures of ceremonies.[6] Regarding the third category, images of ceremonies taking place are always fictionalized and idealized renditions of events but may nonetheless prove useful when asking the question: How did medieval people interact with their books?[7] Visual depictions of various ceremonies sometimes appear in the very manuscripts used to perform those ceremonies. The final category of evidence—use-wear evidence—plays the largest role in the current study. As I have explained above, I bring an often-overlooked kind of evidence to the fore, wherein manuscripts self-document their own utility.

---

5   Andrew S. Hughes, *Medieval Manuscripts for Mass and Office a Guide to Their Organization and Terminology* (University of Toronto Press, 1995), p. xxiv. This position echoes that of Jan Assmann, *Cultural Memory and Early Civilization: Writing, Remembrance, and Political Imagination* (Cambridge University Press, 2011), esp. pp. 81–87.

6   *Rationale IV: On the Mass and Each Action Pertaining to It*, trans. Timothy M. Thibodeau. Corpus Christianorum in Translation (CCT 14) (Brepols, 2013). In the fifteenth century a German-language guide to the Mass was written, a "Meßerklärung." A copy from 1471 survives in Berlin, Staatsbibliothek, Ms. Germ. Fol. 1287, for which see Peter Jörg Becker and Eef Overgaauw (eds.), *Aderlass und Seelentrost. Mittelalterliche Handschriften und Inkunabeln aus Berliner Sammlungen*, Exh. Cat. (Mainz Zabern, 2003), Cat. 117, pp. 227–29. Although I will not take this up in the current study, a comparison between this text and that of Durand could make a useful PhD thesis.

7   The illustrated *ordo* is therefore an important category of visual evidence. These are ceremonial records, the most richly illuminated of which has been discussed by Carra Ferguson O'Meara, in *Monarchy and Consent. The Coronation Book of Charles V of France. British Library MS Cotton Tiberius B. VIII* (Harvey Miller, 2001), in which the author argues that the representation of the coronation ceremony is never neutral. For Charles V, the representational choices were politically charged.

3. Swearing on Relics and Gospels

Sometime before January 1078, Manasses I of Gournay, Archbishop of Reims (ca. 1069–1080) ignored a summons to come to Poitiers. Hugh of Die, the papal legate for France, was angered by this and deposed the archbishop. In response, Manasses traveled to Rome and appealed directly to the pope, Gregory VII. The pope restored Manasses to his office on the condition that he swear on the relics of St Peter that he would respond to all future summonses.[8] By uttering the words while touching the bones of the first pope, Manasses would have increased the *gravitas* of his words. According to Christian belief, relics formed a direct conduit to the living saint who dwelled in heaven. A man might swear on a particular saint's remains that he was telling the truth, that he was willing to accept the responsibility of a given office, or to show his fidelity to a particular leader. Relics authenticated and witnessed declarations.

The idea of swearing "on" something predates Christianity and is related to Old Testament ideas of testifying by placing one's hand on one's testes. This refers to the original covenant of circumcision and assumes that all oath-swearers are men. Eventually, the object on which Christians swore shifted—in part, no doubt, because they were not ceremonially circumcised, and so this gesture had a diluted meaning in a Christian culture, since Christians did not overtly express a covenant with God through the male genitalia. The Christian concept also draws on ancient Israeli oaths involving a self-curse, i.e., that "harm will befall

---

8   *Letters of (and Concerning) Manasses I, Archbishop of Reims, and Hugh, Bishop of Die and Papal Legate, to Pope Gregory VII (r. 1077–1080)*, trans. by John S. Ott: http://www.web.pdx.edu/~ott/manasses/index.html

me if I do such and such." The Old Testament describes various kinds of oaths, enforced by God.[9]

Oath-swearing took place in a variety of contexts in the Middle Ages. Many people swore on relics during the "Peace of God" movement, which had started in 975 when Bishop Guy of Le Puy called knights and armed peasants to a nearby field and asked them to swear an oath to maintain peace. This act curbed the pillaging of churches in the area. Thereafter other towns would use their relics to draw crowds and to enforce similar large-scale oaths. This practice spread from southern France into Burgundy. Public displays of relics often resulted in miracles, which in turn encouraged larger crowds and audiences.[10] Crowds at such events would have witnessed a range of ritualized gestures as oaths were sworn and relics handled. With relics used in this way before numerous crowds and audiences, their function of supplying a divine presence to oaths was sealed in convention and in literature. As Lothar Kolmer has shown, written sources from the eighth through the thirteenth centuries specify, either descriptively or prescriptively, oaths sworn on relics.[11] The Bayeaux Tapestry (made in the 1070s) and four of the illustrated copies of the *Sachsenspiegel* (made in the 1330s and discussed below in Chapter 5) depict individuals swearing oaths on a reliquary.

Related to oaths and similarly endorsed by divine presence were vows, such as marital vows and monastic vows. Both oaths and vows were promissory in character. Non-promissory oaths also operated, as in jurisprudence: during a legal proceeding, an individual could testify "under oath" to the character of the accused, for example. Such a statement does not make promises about the future but asserts the truth of a narrative describing the past. While oaths, vows, and witness statements had different contexts, they shared features in the Christian European Middle Ages, in that they all constituted speech acts uttered with elevated, non-quotidian language, and often involved props that

---

9   For an overview with a bibliography, see https://www.jewishvirtuallibrary.org/oath
10 Kathleen G. Cushing, *Reform and the Papacy in the Eleventh Century: Spirituality and Social Change* (Manchester University Press, 2005), pp. 39–41; Daniel F. Callahan, "The Peace of God and the Cult of the Saints in Aquitaine in the Tenth and Eleventh Centuries," *Historical Reflections / Réflexions Historiques* 14.3 (1987), pp. 445–66.
11 Lothar Kolmer, *Promissorische Eide im Mittelalter* (M. Lassleben, 1989), p. 237, no. 22.

bridged the physical and supernatural worlds. As such, they all relied on religious magic—that is, the supernatural forces that would punish those who swore false oaths, perjured themselves, or failed to live up to their vows. These punishments could befall the false oath-swearer immediately, but it was morely likely that they would appear later, at the Last Judgment.[12] Therefore, the effectiveness of oaths rested on the parties' credulity—in this case, in a Christian afterlife.

With this supernatural context in mind, one can see why medieval Christians swore oaths on certain objects that bridged the divide between the earthly and heavenly realms. In the twentieth century, Philipp Hofmeister—who was both a Benedictine monk at the abbey of Neresheim and a professor of canon law at the University of Munich—traced the shift in oath-swearing ceremonies over the Christian Middle Ages.[13] Swearing an oath was a particular kind of speech act, which followed established scripts, involved bodily gestures, and required witnesses as well as props. Relics were an ideal conduit with heaven and added solemnity to an utterance. From the sixth century onward, Gospel manuscripts (containing the texts purportedly written by Matthew, Mark, Luke, and John) came to fulfill this role, because scripture was understood to contain the Word made flesh, and therefore to embody divine presence. In 529 the Code of Justinian—a book that codified Roman law under the Emperor Justinian I of Constantinople—even stipulated that public officials swear oaths on Gospel manuscripts, although the reach of this book beyond Byzantium was limited.[14] It is clear from the Ordo discussed below that many ceremonies in Western Europe codified the use of relics instead. For several centuries, either Gospel manuscripts or relics could be used as objects on which to swear oaths, and often both were used together. As Hofmeister shows, in the fourteenth and fifteenth centuries in particular, the many relics of the True Cross scattered across Europe were employed in such rituals, with

---

12   For a full and articulate overview of the magical qualities of Christian oath-swearing, see Lothar Kolmer, *Promissorische Eide im Mittelalter* (M. Lassleben, 1989), pp. 225–36.

13   Philipp Hofmeister, *Die christlichen Eidesformen. Eine liturgie- und rechtsgeschichtliche Untersuchung* (Zink, 1957); for a discussion of Justinian, see pp. 36–67.

14   For a discussion of Justinian, see Hofmeister (1957), pp. 39–40; and Ganz (2017), p. 94. For a discussion of the Code's transmission, see Charles M. Radding and Antonio Ciaralli, *The Corpus Iuris Civilis in the Middle Ages: Manuscripts and Transmission from the Sixth Century to the Juristic Revival* (Brill, 2007), pp. 133–68.

the subject instructed to place one hand on the Cross relic and the other on the Gospels.[15]

As a general trend, however, from the tenth century—when the Peace of God took place—until the fourteenth century, relics became less prominent and Gospel manuscripts became more commonly used. Kolmer attributes the waxing use of the Gospel to the increasing importance of the written word in general, and of the Word of God in particular. The punishment for failing to keep an oath would be meted out by God, and the Gospel was understood to be directly bound to God, whereas the saints (as approximated by their relics) functioned as middlemen.[16] In the late fourteenth and fifteenth centuries, as I will show below, new manuscripts were made for oath-swearing. This new genre contained inchoate civic legal codes and oaths, and upon these books individuals swore civic oaths. Oath-taking rituals further expanded to include organizations such as brotherhoods and universities (for which, see Chapter 5).[17] Finally, personal prayer books often contain marks of wear indicating that they have been used for swearing oaths (discussed in Volume 3). These later book types borrow imagery—as well as the gestures for using that imagery in the context of a speech act—from missals and Gospel manuscripts. Each new object for oath-swearing builds upon the previous objects' imagery—and its gestural language—to maintain historical continuity and the authority that accompanies age.

I. Swearing on Gospels

According to legend, Charlemagne put three fingers on the image of St John in the Vienna Coronation Gospels during his coronation ceremony on Christmas Day, 800.[18] However, Lawrence Nees points out that much of the story about Charlemagne's coronation was only invented in retrospect: the story supplied "foregrounding of the distant

---

15 For examples, see Hofmeister, *Die christlichen Eidesformen*, pp. 62–67.
16 Kolmer, p. 238.
17 Discussions of several examples appear in Rudy, *Postcards on Parchment* (Yale University Press, 2015), pp. 287–98.
18 The version of history presented to tourists re-affirms the manuscript as Charlemagne's coronation prop, as in *The Secular and Ecclesiastical Treasuries* (Residenz Verlag, 1991), pp. 166–68.

future."[19] Because Charlemagne was the first European emperor since antiquity, commentators constructed an elevated backstory rich in detail and sprinkled with sumptuous objects. The manuscript upon which he was said to have sworn his oath is one of the most highly crafted books made around 800, with gold and silver letters on purple-dyed parchment,[20] and imagery based on that of classical antiquity, which, according to received wisdom, was designed to connect Charlemagne with the Roman emperors. Brandishing all of the trappings of an imperial production, the manuscript has been ripe for lore for nearly a millennium: even in the twelfth century, commentators claimed that this manuscript had been found in Charlemagne's tomb when Otto III had opened it in the year 1000, although this cannot be the case, since the Evangelists were used as models for illuminators in the ninth century. In the biggest fabrication of them all, this most unusual and impressive manuscript, famed according to scholarly literature to have survived from the court of Charlemagne (r. 768–814) at Aix-la-Chapelle (Aachen), may have actually been made after Charlemagne died in 814.

The Vienna Coronation Gospels were recast as a relic of Charlemage. The manuscript made the ruler more tangible, since it putatively touched the famous leader. Reciprocally, the story made the object more valuable, charged with an even brighter aura, when it was elevated from "dazzling purple manuscript" to "relic of the most important leader in European history." Both man and book were irrevocably changed through the act of touching, even fictional touching. Even though the story was fabricated, probably to support the memory and grandeur of Charlemagne at the time of his canonization in 1165, the book served as a tangible link with the emperor's coronation and helped subsequent generations to picture its sumptuousness and gravitas.

Although Charlemagne probably did not handle it in his ceremony in 800, the manuscript did function as a coronation Gospel for the Holy

---

19 Ideas in these paragraphs draw on Lawrence Nees, "Prolegomenon to a Study of the Vienna Coronation Gospels: Common Knowledge, Scholarship, Tradition, Legend, Myth," in *Rome and Religion in the Medieval World: Studies in Honor of Thomas F.X. Noble*, edited by Valerie L. Garver and Owen M. Phelan (Ashgate, 2014), Chapter 12, unpaginated.

20 Maurizio Aceto, Angelo Agostino, Gaia Fenoglio, Ambra Idone, Fabrizio Crivello, Martin Grießer, Franziska Kirchweger, Katharina Uhlir, and Patricia Roger Puyo, "Analytical Investigations on the Coronation Gospels Manuscript," *Spectrochimica acta. Part A, Molecular and Biomolecular Spectroscopy*, 171 (2017), 213–21.

Roman Emperors to take their oaths upon, possibly beginning in the twelfth century and continuing until 1792. In 1794, the manuscript was taken from Aachen and brought to Vienna, and since 1801 it has been on display in the Treasury (*Schatzkammer*) of the Hofburg Palace, Vienna. In other words, it has been kept in the context of imperial regalia rather than in a library. What is clear is that the manuscript is both a relic of Charlemagne and a Gospel book, even if its status as relic is entirely fictional. In the later Middle Ages and in the Early Modern period, the manuscript's fictional early history provided coronations with a sense of continuity that reached back to Charlemagne's own fingers.

Because instructions for imperial coronations were recorded in the Mainzer Ordo, which was written in the second half of the tenth century, we have an opportunity to understand the ceremony more fully.[21] The ordo specifies the words to be spoken aloud, as well as the "stage directions" for the multi-day ceremony. After uttering specific prayers, the archbishop asked the emperor-elect a series of questions. In response to each question, the emperor-elect would answer, "Volo" (I will), confirming his willingness to defend the church, the faith, the empire, and the office. After that, the emperor-elect would then make a touching gesture while uttering his oath:

> Rex, positis duobus digitis manus sue dextere super altare, dicat. Volo et in quantum divino fultus fuero adiutorio et precibus fidelium christianorum adiutus valuero, omnia premissa fideliter adimplebo, sic me deus adiuvet et sancti eius. [The emperor-elect, placing two fingers of his right hand on the altar, should say, "I will, and to the extent that I will be divinely supported by the help and prayers of faithful Christians, I will faithfully fulfill all the premisses, so may God help me and his saints."][22]

---

21 The text, which survives in 12 manuscripts, has been edited by Vogel Cyrille, Reinhard Elze, and Michel Andrieu, eds. 1963–1972. *Le Pontifical Romano-Germanique du Dixième Siècle*, Vols 1–3 (Biblioteca apostolica vaticana). Vol. I, No. LXXII. The Mainzer Ordo is analyzed and contextualized by Andreas Büttner in *Der Weg zur Krone: Rituale der Herrschererhebung im spätmittelalterlichen Reich* (Jan Thorbecke Verlag, 2012).

22 G. H. Pertz, ed. *Monumenta Germaniae historica: scriptorvm*, 20 vols (A. Hiersemann, 1963–1964), Leges (MGH LL 2), p. 386. https://www.dmgh.de/mgh_ll_2/index.htm#page/386/mode/1up

As this instruction makes plain, the emperor-elect did not touch a manuscript during his oath, but rather touched the altar, which would have contained relics of the saints he was imploring. The ordo of ca. 975 therefore had no provision for a Gospel manuscript as prop. Likewise, according to the Royal Frankish Annals, when Tassilo II, Duke of Bavaria (c. 741-c. 796) swore an oath close to the time of Charlemagne's coronation, he insisted that he swear upon the relics of four different saints.[23] This suggests that in this period, swearing on relics (and not Gospels) was the norm, and the account also suggests that increasing the number of saints could amplify the holiness of the event.

Like a relic, a book can be both precious and utilitarian at the same time. In particular, liturgical texts can both be hallowed objects and sites of practice. A book can have multiple uses, some of them activated by handling plus reading, some activated by handling alone. Some gospel manuscripts have signs of wear that indicate that they were touched ceremoniously. One manuscript used in this way is a Carolingian Gospel Book of St Amand, which has elaborate Evangelist portraits at each of the four major openings (Cologne, Schnütgen Museum, Hs. G 531).[24] Staring at the four openings with the author portraits with a soft focus reveals that the edges have been darkened from this type of use (Fig. 12; Fig. 13; Fig. 14; Fig. 15). They have been touched repeatedly. Whereas page-turning usually darkens the bottom corner of each folio, the traces of dirt in the lower edges of this manuscript tell a different story. One can imagine that someone swearing a statement would approach the book open on a lectern, utter some prescribed words, and lay his hand on the bottom of the page in order to seal the statement.

Dirt levels on the Cologne manuscript's four decorated openings reveal that users favored Mark, Luke, and especially John, but largely ignored Matthew, which has survived in a cleaner state than the openings of the other three Evangelists. This may be because the Gospel

---

23 Kolmer, p. 236, citing *Annales Mettenses priores*, edited by B. von Simson, *Monumenta Germaniae Historica, Scriptores rerum Germanicarum* (1905), p. 49. The purpose of the oath was to swear fealty to Pepin. It is possible, however, that the account of Tassilo's oath was written later.

24 I thank Jos Biemans for directing me to this manuscript. The manuscript dates from ca. 860–880, and measures 26 x 19.2 cm in its binding, which was made in Cologne ca. 1160–1170.

Fig. 12 Opening at the beginning of the Book of Matthew, Evangeliarium, St. Amand, c. 860–880. Cologne, Schnütgen Museum, Hs. G 531, fol. 11v-12r.

Fig. 13 Opening at the beginning of the Book of Mark. Evangeliarium, St. Amand, c. 860–880. Cologne, Schnütgen Museum, Hs. G 531, fols 62v-63r.

Fig. 14 Opening at the beginning of the Book of Luke. Evangeliarium, St. Amand, c. 860–880. Cologne, Schnütgen Museum, Hs. G 531, fols 97v-98r.

Fig. 15 Opening at the beginning of the Book of John. Evangeliarium, St. Amand, c. 860–880. Cologne, Schnütgen Museum, Hs. G 531, fols 151v-152r.

of St. Matthew actually condemns swearing.[25] In Matt. 5:33, Jesus says, "But I say unto you, swear not at all; neither by the heaven, for it is the throne of God; nor by the earth, for it is the footstool of his feet; nor by Jerusalem, for it is the city of the great King." Comparably clean pages at the incipit of Matthew appear in other Gospel manuscripts used for oath-taking. As we will see later in Chapter 5, some Christians refused to swear on Gospels for this reason.

Because the pattern of wear across Mark, Luke, and John differs significantly in the *St Amand Gospels*, one can deduce that these openings had somewhat different ritual functions. Mark has a darkened area just under the image of the Evangelist, revealing that many individuals placed a hand (or a few fingers) there. Most people touched only the lower border, but enough people reached more deeply onto the page to flake off the metallic paint of the Evangelist's footstool and pock his hem. (The smaller dark area near the bottom of the column may have resulted from the officiant grasping the book and finding the relevant opening, rather than the oath-taker touching that spot.) The pattern is different at the Luke and John openings, where there are two large areas of darkness: one under the respective Evangelist, and one in the lower corner of the facing text page.[26] This would be consistent with an oath ceremony involving two persons. One can imagine two right-handed people standing shoulder-to-shoulder at the foot of the book, and both touching its lower margin. One would touch the area under the image, and the other would reach his hand across his body to touch the lower corner of the text page. At Luke in particular, cumulative iterations of this ceremony have deposited a thick crust at the lower corner of the recto page. So penetrating is this layer of grime that it is visible on the verso (Fig. 16). Such use-wear evidence in the *St Amand Gospels* suggests that different ceremonies required different book openings. It also suggests that the cumulative handprints on the book helped to guide future users, who slotted their hands in where others' had previously touched. The older a manuscript is, the more difficult it is to pinpoint

---

25 Jacob Mann, "Oaths and Vows in the Synoptic Gospels," *The American Journal of Theology* 21.2 (1917), pp. 260–74, notes that Matthew's Gospel prohibits swearing.

26 Klaus Schreiner, "Litterae Mysticae. Symbolik und Pragmatik heiliger Buchstaben, Texte und Bücher in Kirche und Gesellschaft des Mittelalters," in *Pragmatische Dimensionen mittelalterlicher Schriftkultur*, edited by Christel Meier et al. (Wilhelm Fink, 2002), pp. 277–37, esp. pp. 315–22, discusses the Book of John as a powerful sacred text used in all manner of thaumaturgic rituals.

exactly when its grime accumulated. This is the case in the *St Amand Gospels*, but one can surmise that the book was in continual use for its first three centuries. It was written and illuminated ca. 860–80, and then ca. 1160–1170 it received its current binding. It is possible that the manuscript incurred its marks of wear shortly after it was made in the ninth century; however, it is more likely that it became an oath-swearing object only later, perhaps shortly before it was rebound. Its rebinding may have corresponded to its repurposing, 300 years after its production. As we have seen in the case of the Vienna Coronation Gospels, a manuscript's antiquity could give it more gravitas, with a historical gap that could be filled in with an awe-inspiring backstory. It is also possible that Gospel manuscripts take on an oath-swaring role in the late eleventh century, just as the missal was developed (discussed below, in Chapter 4). Whereas before this period, the Gospel manuscript had a central liturgical function, after the development of the missal, the Gospel may have adopted a more ceremonial function, such as for oath-swearing. Furthermore, this period also saw an increased theatricality exhibited around books, and the Gospel manuscript may have been swept up in this theatricality. Touching the Gospel manuscript would

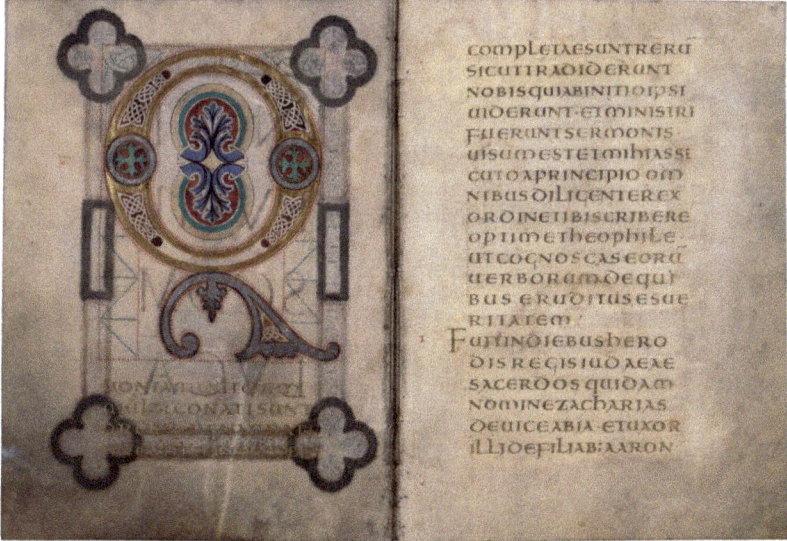

Fig. 16 Second opening in the Book of Luke. Evangeliarium, St. Amand, c. 860–880. Cologne, Schnütgen Museum, Hs. G 531, fols 98v-99r.

have appeared as a more overt gesture than merely touching the altar, with relics hidden within it.

Emperors would swear on the Gospel during their coronation, but the manuscript could also play a role in other speech acts, such as vassalage rituals. For example, when Notker, the abbot of Saint Gall, swore an oath of vassalage to Otto I in 971, the final step involved a Gospel. A record of the event survives in the *Casus S. Galli*, which details the words and gestures. The emperor uttered the words, "Now you will be mine." Then, "after receiving him by the hands, he kissed him. Soon thereafter, a gospel-book having been brought in, the abbot swore fealty."[27] In other vassalage ceremonies, such as that of Tassilo, Duke of Bavaria, who swore his fealty to Pepin the Short in 757, the duke placed his hands on relics instead of the Gospels.

The presence of the Gospel ripens the environment. The object itself is physically charged, powering its standing as a proxy for the divine. For example, Durandus describes the ceremony for consecrating a bishop, which would involve handling a Gospel manuscript:

> When a bishop is ordained, the bishops from the same ecclesiastical province must be assembled, with the metropolitan; and two bishops place and hold the codex of the Gospels over the ordinand's head and neck... the rest of the bishops who are present touch his head with their hands. The Gospel book is held over his head; first, so that the Lord will confirm the Gospel in his heart. Second, so that he will understand the labor and the burden to which he is now subjected, because whoever is preeminent in this world, that is all prelates, has more worries associated with them than the joys of being honored. Third, to note that he should not show reluctance at bearing the weight of preaching the Gospel and the things that surround it. Fourth, to admonish him and submit himself to the customary yoke and to obey the Gospel.[28]

In Western Christendom, images were not consecrated, but liturgical books were blessed. They contained images, which by extension would be blessed. Blessed images, books, holy water, and so forth, were "sacramentals" that had a charged status.[29] During the ceremony

---

27 Quoted in Le Goff, p. 243.
28 Durandus, *On the Clergy and Their Vestments: A New Translation of Books 2–3 of the Rationale divinorum officiorum*, trans. Timothy M. Thibodeau (University of Scranton Press, 2010), p. 125.
29 David Freedberg, *The Power of Images: Studies in the History and Theory of Response* (University of Chicago Press, 1989), pp. 89–91.

for consecrating a bishop, the established bishops put the Gospel manuscript above the new bishop's head to symbolize his submission to the authority of God and to demonstrate his willingness to bear the weight of scripture. He submits to the physical book.

Some Gospel manuscripts contain added texts which explicitly expand the function of the book to ritualized social bonding. The *York Gospels* (York Minster, Ms. Add. 1) were written in the scriptorium of St Augustine's monastery at Canterbury around 1000 and then brought to York by Archbishop Wulfstan around 1020. The volume contains some testaments of land ownership from the eleventh century, as well as a letter from King Cnut (r. 1016–1035), which shows that the book held an important position as a keeper of the legal record from an early date. It also contains oaths taken by the Minster's various priests in the late Middle Ages and was used by them for swearing.[30] Because the book had such an impressive origin story, it embodied sufficient gravitas to seal oaths. It is even possible that such books were made with this legal function in mind.

That seems to be the case with the *Arenberg Gospels* (New York, Morgan Library and Museum, M.869), which are contemporary with the *York Gospels*. It too was used for swearing oaths and reveals how the manner of touching books was locally specific.[31] Written in Caroline minuscule in Canterbury between 1000 and 1020, the *Arenberg Gospels* were furnished not with the normal four, but rather with five full-page images. Those images were made using colored line drawings with some areas of solid color, which are typical of Anglo-Saxon manuscripts. Shortly after it was finished, someone brought it to Cologne. Extensive dirt and inscriptions reveal how its German recipients used the exotic book. Its four full-page images of the Evangelists are relatively clean, indicating that these portraits, unlike those in the Gospels in Cologne, were not used for laying on layers of hands (Fig. 17). Instead, a full-page image near the beginning of the manuscript representing Christ Crucified bears signs of extensive user contact (Fig. 18). This Crucifixion

---

30 Matthew Collins, Matthew D. Teasdale, Sarah Fiddyment, Jiří Vnouček, Valeria Mattiangeli, Camilla Speller, Annelise Binois, Martin Carver, et al. "The York Gospels: A 1000-Year Biological Palimpsest," *Royal Society Open Science* 4.10 (2017), pp. 1–11, with further references.

31 Richard Gameson, "Manuscript Art at Christ Church, Canterbury, in the Generation after St Dunstan," in *St Dunstan: His Life, Times, and Cult*, edited by Nigel Ramsay, Margaret Sparks, and Tim Tatton-Brown (1992), pp. 190, 200–03, 208–16.

page, which is integral with the quire structure, was no doubt part of the original production.³² It prefaces the unusual historiated Canon tables.³³ Users gave it a second role—to bear witness to hundreds of oaths.

Fig. 17 Evangelist portrait of John, full-page drawing, *Arenberg Gospels*, Canterbury, ca. 1000–1020. New York, The Morgan Library & Museum, Ms. M.869, fols 126v.

---

32 The Crucifixion page, fol. 9, forms a bifolium with fol. 16.
33 Jane E. Rosenthal, *The Historiated Canon Tables of the Arenberg Gospels* (Columbia University Dissertation, 1974).

3. Swearing on Relics and Gospels 65

Fig. 18 Crucifixion page, full-page drawing with painted elements. *Arenberg Gospels*, Canterbury, ca. 1000–1020. New York, The Morgan Library & Museum, Ms. M. 869, fol. 9v.

The Crucifixion page has been heavily handled and follows the pattern of many people dry-touching the image once. Some people touched the body of Christ at the center of the image, while others merely touched the borders, with a large concentration of people touching the lower border. This left a thick layer of dark crud at the bottom of the image, a layer so thick and unsightly that someone attempted to scrape some of it away. Because of the curvature of the book and the inaccessibility of the gutter, the person scraping left a patch of dirt where his tool could not reach.

Generations of local users have exploited the blank spaces in this manuscript to copy out oaths and decrees, beginning with the decrees issued by Pope Gregory VII in 1073 and 1075 to canonize Archbishop Heribert of Cologne. A German scribe has written this onto available space he found on fol. 14. Other texts added to the blank space refer to the church of St Severin in Cologne. In fact, throughout the manuscript, scribes from the fourteenth to eighteenth centuries added oaths for officials; these are mostly concentrated on fols 1–9, 14, and 124–125v. The contrasting parchment of the first eight folios indicates that, having run out of space, the book's keepers added a quire to accommodate more oaths. Oaths on these pages appear in a generalized template, so that the person swearing the oath could fill in his name as appropriate.

Since St. Severin in Cologne was a collegiate church, each canon's benefice was linked to an altar, at which he was to say Mass. In some canonries, the canons were only paid if someone was sitting in their stall during the office, so they often employed lower-level clerics—vicars— to conduct some of their duties, including singing the office. At first these vicars were personal employees of the canons, but their positions became official.[34] In the oath for one of these vicars, on folio 4r (Fig. 19), he swears allegiance to the church of St Severin, to his canon, and to his deacon. The oath begins, "I am [fill in name], vicar of the altar of St [fill in name]." In this way, the oaths were not person-specific but role-specific, and could be used in perpetuity. Such oaths reiterate the hierarchy of the various roles and institutions within the church. All the deacons, canons, and vicars would have to proclaim this hierarchy and to reiterate their place within it, while touching the main manuscript treasure of the church of St Severin. Hundreds of these low-level vicars must have sworn this oath, or one of the others on folio 4r, because this folio is particularly worn and sullied at the lower corner, so much so that some of the text became abraded and had to be re-inscribed.

---

34 I am grateful to Berthold Kreß for this information about canons and their surrogates.

3. Swearing on Relics and Gospels   67

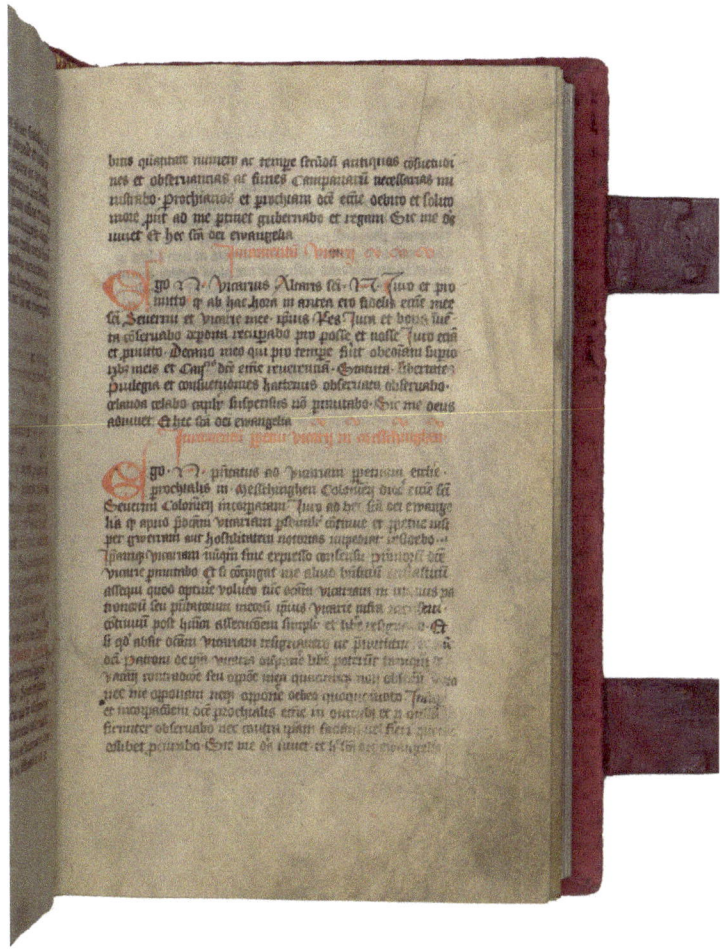

Fig. 19 Added oaths. *Arenberg Gospels*. New York, The Morgan Library & Museum, Ms. M. 869, fol. 4r.

Among the various additions to the manuscript, layered over time, someone has inscribed what appears to be an oath directly on the back of the Crucifixion miniature (Fig. 20). At some point later in its history, someone scraped the text off. It is still faintly visible. The original rubric mentions the church of St Severin, and is written in a large, formal script. It is likely that the person who inscribed it here not only took advantage of a blank surface, but also wanted to place this inscription as physically close to the depicted body of Christ as possible: on the other side of a thin, semi-transparent membrane. This would no doubt have given the oath more power.³⁵ Although this manuscript was made in England in the eleventh century, it contains many additions from later centuries, indicating that it was used continually as an oath-swearing book until the eighteenth century. The book's foreignness may have enhanced its status as an object of legal standing.

Fig. 20 Scraped inscription on the back of the Crucifixion miniature. *Arenberg Gospels*. New York, The Morgan Library & Museum, Ms. M. 869, fol. 9r.

---

35 I discuss a similar case of a testament inscribed on the back of a Crucifixion image in Rudy, *Piety in Pieces* (Open Book Publishers, 2016), pp. 70–75, https://doi.org/10.11647/OBP.0094.

II. Proffering the Book

Images that depict swearing ceremonies shed light on another set of marks imprinted on many manuscripts, revealing that they were used in such ceremonies. Whereas many codices used for swearing rituals—such as the Carolingian Gospels discussed earlier—have handprints in the margin that are consistent with the manuscript's having lain in a cradle or on a pillow during these ceremonies, others have more complex marks. Specifically, they are worn at both the upper and lower margins, in a pattern that would have resulted from their being held open for the oath-swearer, as is pictured, say, in the Coronation Book of Charles V of France (r. 1364–1380), the densely illustrated manuscript that the French king commissioned in 1365, after the coronation.[36] It contains two cycles of miniatures depicting the step-by-step sacring rituals of both his coronation and that of his queen, Jeanne of Bourbon. The king, who even wrote the colophon in his own hand, played a large role in shaping this manuscript. Its historical underpinnings are clear: the manuscript contains an abbreviated copy of the Register from ca. 1230, which describes the French sacring ritual from the time of Saint Louis. Wrapping together past, present, and future, the manuscript contains vestiges of the ritual of France's most important saint-king, a description of a recent event, a prescription for future events, and perhaps most importantly—as Carra Ferguson O'Meara demonstrates—a testament to the legitimacy of Charles's rule.[37]

One of the illuminations depicts the king putting his hand on a book, held open by the Archbishop of Reims, while both stand near an altar that frames the other regalia of kingship: most notably, a crown and sword that were used later in the ceremony (Fig. 21). Charles carefully places his hand on the bottom margin of the open book, while the bishop extends the book into the space directly above the cathedra, a charged void between the worldly and ecclesiastical realms. Charles's secular entourage stands on the left of the cathedra, while the religious

---

[36] The Coronation Book (fols 35–80) was formerly bound with a twelfth-century pontifical (fols 3–34, 81–197), but now forms a separate volume. A facsimile was made in the late nineteenth century: E. S. Dewick, ed. *The Coronation Book of Charles V of France; Cottonian Ms Tiberius B Viii* (Vol. 16) (Henry Bradshaw Society, 1899). It has also been the subject of a sustained study: Carra Ferguson O'Meara, *Monarchy and Consent: The Coronation Book of Charles V of France: British Library Ms Cotton Tiberius B.viii* (Harvey Miller, 2001).

[37] O'Meara, *Monarchy and Consent*, pp. 16–17, pp. 19–35.

officials stand on the right, with the book separating the two, as if it were the instrument for bridging the secular and the ecclesiastical. Charles's hand alone reaches across the divide, to swear the oath upon the open book, presumably a Gospel.[38]

Fig. 21 Charles V swearing an oath on an open book being held by a bishop, Paris, 1365. London, British Library, Cotton Ms. Tiberius B VIII/2, fol. 46v.

---

38 As O'Meara, *Monarchy and Consent*, p. 131 points out, the oath Charles V took was the same as that taken by Charles the Bald, with an additional phrase about the inalienability of the Crown of France. Charles V therefore swore to defend the Church, to guard the peace, to judge with equity and mercy, and to expel heretics.

Use-wear analysis attests that, although Gospel manuscripts were the type most frequently used for oath swearing from the period from ca. 900 to ca. 1300, missals were also appropriated for this function after 1300. For example, the heavy damage visible in a missal made in 1455–1474 for the Use of Clermont is consistent with its having been used for oath swearing (Fig. 22).[39] The missal's canon page has expanded to a two-page spread, with the traditional image of Christ Crucified on the left, and God in Majesty on the right. The latter image is surrounded by the Evangelists' symbols, evoking the Gospel books on which oaths had traditionally been sworn. The extensive damage in this opening follows a different pattern of wear than that of the Amand Gospels, where the marks were confined to the bottom and sides.

Fig. 22 Christ Crucified, and God in Majesty, full-page miniatures in a missal for the Use of Clermont, 1455–1474. Clermont-Ferrand, Bibliothèque municipal, Ms. 65, fols 216v-217r. Cliché: IRHT-CNRS

In the Clermont Missal, the extraordinary degradation concentrated in multiple areas of the opening requires an explanation: this book

---

39   For a description and bibliography, see http://initiale.irht.cnrs.fr/codex/1641/4894.

may have been proffered by an officiant to an oath-swearer in a set-up like the one depicted in the Coronation Book of Charles V, where the bishop holds out the book to the king. Likewise, the abrasion in the Clermont Missal seems to have been made by two people touching the book simultaneously: one who held the book open from the bottom and proffered it, and the other who reached into the open book to touch it. In this scenario, the officiant gripped the open book forcefully, so that his thumbs were tightly braced against the lower borders. Just where in the lower borders and with how much force the officiant would grasp the book would have depended on the amount of force required to counteract the torque of the book plus the pressure of the oath swearer's hands as he reached into the open book from the upper border. The officiant's bracing force could have conceivably levied sufficient heat, moisture, pressure, and lateral surface friction on the parchment book block to cause significant amounts of the decoration in the lower borders of the opening to wear off, and even to degrade the parchment substrate. These lower sections were so damaged that a modern conservator has replaced the tattered parchment with clean, modern parchment.

Here, then, is my proposed scenario of degradation: as a corollary to officiants' gestures, oath swearers have responded by reaching into the book from the top edge to touch the painted representations of Jesus and God the Father in particular. The pattern of wear across the images is diffuse. This would be consistent with multiple oath swearers each touching the figural imagery once during the ceremony, each in a slightly different place with a slightly different gesture. Each touch was a one-off, neither practiced nor routinized. Moreover, the vertical gauges in the paint in the upper registers may have been caused by oath swearers who inadvertently scraped their hands, rings, or nails across the page as they withdrew their hands. Users do not normally touch the upper borders of manuscripts in regular instances of reading and handling, nor do they damage the lower central border of folio-sized manuscripts, since page-turning normally takes place only at the lower corners. The two-person ritual I have outlined would explain the specific and extensive damage visible in the Clermont Missal.

Just as the makers of the Cologne Gospels might have anticipated the book's use for oath swearing (and therefore led to their including an image of Christ Crucified, which is anomalous for this type of book), the expansion of the missals' Canon iconography to include a two-page spread, as the Clermont Missal possesses, may have been a response to people using missals for swearing oaths. Imagery in missals changed significantly during the period from the eleventh century, when this book type emerged, until the Protestant Reformation. Whereas the earlier iconography of the Canon showed only a Crucifixion, the expanded iconography included an image of God Enthroned and surrounded by the Evangelists' attributes, which recalls the imagery in a Gospel manuscript. This expansion of the iconography in a missal may have been warranted by its extended duties, especially considering where oath swearing took place. While some oath-swearing ceremonies occurred at an altar, some were conducted beneath church portals.[40] Conducting oath rituals there resulted in public proclamations that could accommodate any number of witnesses. All of this would be framed by ecclesiastical architecture, often sculpted and featuring a carved tympanum overhead. Many Romanesque French examples depict the *Majestas Domini*, a subject that reached its peak in French architectural sculpture in the mid-twelfth century, just when the same subject began to be depicted next to the Crucifixion in French missals.[41] Missals may have absorbed the *Majestas Domini* motif from the portals under which the ceremony was taking place. The expanded iconography thereby acknowledged this non-liturgical function for the missal. The full opening of imagery would have supplied a large and palpable divine witness while also creating a bigger surface for the officiant and oath swearer to touch. Such imagery would make the ceremony more visible from a distance and possibly more theatrical.

---

40 On settings for court proceedings, see Barbara Deimling, "From Church Portal to Town Hall," in *The History of Courts and Procedure in Medieval Canon Law*, edited by Wilfried Hartmann and Kenneth Pennington (Catholic University of America Press, 2016), pp. 30–50; and Helen Gittos, *Liturgy, Architecture, and Sacred Places in Anglo-Saxon England. Medieval History and Archaeology* (Oxford University Press, 2013), pp. 272–73, who discusses legal transactions under church portals. For a thematic survey of iconography of Romanesque portals, see Marcello Angheben, *Les portails romans de Bourgogne: Thèmes et programmes* (Brepols, 2021).

41 Éliane Vergnolle, "'Maiestas Domini' Portals of the Twelfth Century," in *Romanesque Art and Thought in the Twelfth Century. Essays in Honor of Walter Cahn*, edited by Colum Hourihane (Index of Christian Art, Department of Art & Archaeology, Princeton University, in association with Penn State University Press, 2008), pp. 179–99.

It is possible that many kinds of books were repurposed for oath-taking. For example, a deluxe copy of the Bible Historiale has been marked by targeted touching on its frontispiece (HKB, Ms. 78 D 43; Fig. 23).[42] The Bible Historiale is a version of Peter Comestor's *Historia Scholastica*, translated into French by Guiard des Moulins (b. 1251, according to the prologue in his *magnum opus*). Around the central quatrefoil with the *Majestas Domini*, a user has targeted two of the evangelists' portraits: Mark and John, precisely those touched most often in oath-taking rituals. The manuscript was made in Paris in the 1370s, probably for a noble patron, given the size and luxury of the book. Whether its commissioning owner was the person who used the elaborate frontispiece to add solemnity to a series of promises is ultimately unknowable. He or she may have also touched the presentation scene, showing Petrus Comestor presenting his book to Archbishop Guillaume of Sens (Fig. 24); or touched the scenes of God creating the world in seven days. In particular, he or she touched God measuring the universe with a compass (Fig. 25), the division of the waters above and below the firmament (Fig. 26), the creation of the sun and moon (Fig. 27), and the creation of beasts of the field and Adam (Fig. 28). None of the numerous other miniatures in the manuscript has been rubbed. Putting this use-wear evidence together helps to paint a portrait of an early owner who used his or her fingers to reiterate divine authority, ecclesiastical authority, and the supernatural origins of the Gospels and of the universe itself, someone who called upon these forces when sealing an oath.

***

The book—primarily the Gospel book, but also the missal—gradually replaced relics in solemn ceremonies where parties needed God to witness their vows and promises. Just as relics were "enfleshed" in reliquaries, which made them more visually appealing and relatable, so too did the abstract words in the "Word made flesh" take on a human, relatable form through their illuminations. Those swearing oaths, witnessed by the authority of liturgical books, sought a tangible bond with divine persons in heaven—the evangelists, Christ, Mary,

---

42 For an overview of this text and author, see Rosemarie Potz McGerr, "Guyart Desmoulins, the Vernacular Master of Histories, and his Bible Historiale," *Viator*, 14 (1983), pp. 211–44.

3. *Swearing on Relics and Gospels* 75

Fig. 23 Opening folio of *Guiard des Moulins, Bible Historiale Complétée*, with God in Majesty surrounded by the evangelists' symbols. Paris, ca. 1370–1380. The Hague, Koninklijke Bibliotheek, Ms. 78 D 43, fol. 1r.

Fig. 24 Presentation scene: Petrus Comestor presenting his book to Archbishop Guillaume of Sens, in Guiard des Moulins, *Bible Historiale Complétée*. Paris, ca. 1370–1380. The Hague, Koninklijke Bibliotheek, Ms. 78 D 43, fol. 2r.

Fig. 25 God measuring the Universe with a compass, in Guiard des Moulins, *Bible Historiale Complétée*. Paris, ca. 1370–1380. The Hague, Koninklijke Bibliotheek, Ms. 78 D 43, fol. 3r, detail.

3. *Swearing on Relics and Gospels* 77

Fig. 26 Creation: division of the waters, in Guiard des Moulins, *Bible Historiale Complétée*. Paris, ca. 1370–1380. The Hague, Koninklijke Bibliotheek, Ms. 78 D 43, fol. 3v, detail

Fig. 27 Creation: sun and moon, in Guiard des Moulins, *Bible Historiale Complétée*. Paris, ca. 1370–1380. The Hague, Koninklijke Bibliotheek, Ms. 78 D 43, fol. 4r, detail

Fig. 28 Creation: beasts of the field and Adam, in Guiard des Moulins, *Bible Historiale Complétée*. Paris, ca. 1370–1380. The Hague, Koninklijke Bibliotheek, Ms. 78 D 43, fol. 5r, detail

or God—by physically touching their representations in books, rather than the words. The many people involved in these rituals, whose fingerprints have cumulatively worn the volumes, carried lessons about book-handling away with them. Lay people appear to have adopted these gestures when using their personal prayer books (as will be discussed in Volume 3).

Through their darkened parchment, manuscripts divulge how they were handled, but only when that handling was repeated and caused cumulative (and visible) damage. That damage speaks to an ephemeral, gestural language that sealed speech acts through props and gestures. These marks might be difficult or impossible to ascertain when the ceremonies involved closed volumes, but frequently the ceremonies called for an open book, where creamy parchment would record the tracks of sweaty, greasy, or dirty hands. Sometimes these marks show that one actor handled the page at a time, and other marks reveal that two people—such as an officiant and an oath swearer—handled the book simultaneously, each fulfilling a different role. This was the case with proffered volumes.

The Clermont Missal is anomalous in the extensive pawing it received on both upper and lower margins, indicating that it was used ceremoniously outside a strict liturgical context. Namely, it was proffered. In addition to these handprints, further marks on the page reveal that priests and bishops handled missals in another way that resulted in severe degradation of the paint and parchment: by kissing them. This theatrical gesture with the book will be taken up in the next chapter.

4. Kissing

From Relics to Manuscripts

In a twelfth-century *Life of St Edmund*, two tiny monks kneel in the margin to kiss the feet of the great saint (Fig. 29).[1] Protruding into the stark white margin with their groveling positions starkly silhouetted, they grasp the saint's ankles and kiss them with great deliberation and intensity, to demonstrate affection and show reverence. Their diminutive scale and powerless profile view contrast with the large saint and the immortal hands of angels that frame his fearful symmetry.[2] The place where they kiss establishes a hierarchy between the osculator and osculatee. Their gesture shows respect and externalizes a hierarchy, also made apparent by the relative sizes of the actors. Not only does kissing create a theatrical display, it demonstrates their physical bond.

Late medieval people used osculation in several rituals adapted from the pre-Christian past. In Roman times there were three types of kiss: the osculum (kiss of friendship), the basium (kiss of love), and the suavium (passionate kiss). These kisses were the medieval inheritance, where multiple kisses with different meanings persisted, all of them used for engaging in ritual while externalizing an emotion.[3] Yannick

---

1 For a discussion of this manuscript, see Cynthia Hahn, "*Peregrinatio et Natio*: The Illustrated Life of Edmund, King and Martyr," *Gesta* 30, 2 (1991), pp. 119–39, and Rebecca Pinner, *The Cult of St Edmund in Medieval East Anglia* (Boydell Press, 2015).

2 For a groundbreaking essay about the powerlessness of sitters in profile portraits, see Patricia Simons, "Women in Frames: The Gaze, the Eye, the Profile in Renaissance Portraiture," *History Workshop*, 25 (Spring 1988), pp. 4–30.

3 Yannick Carré, *Le Baiser sur la Bouche au Moyen Âge: Rites, Symboles, Mentalités, à Travers les Textes et les Images, XIe-XVe Siècles* (Le Léopard d'Or, 1992); Willem Frijhoff, "The Kiss Sacred and Profane: Reflections on a Cross-Cultural Confrontation," in *A Cultural History of Gesture: From Antiquity to the Present Day*, edited by Jan N. Bremmer and Herman Roodenburg (Polity, 1994), pp. 210–36, esp. p. 211; Kiril Petkov, *The Kiss of Peace: Ritual, Self, and Society in the High and Late Medieval West*, Cultures, Beliefs, and Traditions, Vol. 17 (Brill, 2003); Frits Scholten, "Een Nederlandse Ivoren Pax uit de Late Middeleeuwen," *Bulletin van het Rijksmuseum* 52.1 (2004), pp. 2–23, here p. 3.

Fig. 29 Monks kneeling and grasping the feet of St Edmund and kissing them, in a Miscellany on the life of St Edmund. England, Bury St Edmunds, c. 1130. New York, The Morgan Library & Museum, Ms. M.736, fol. 22v

Carré has traced the medieval gesture of kissing, which finds outlets and nuanced functions in different political, religious, and amorous spheres. In particular, medieval people adapted the osculum for people, relics, rings, the hems of garments, and manuscripts. As Carré points out, the target of one's kisses also inflects their meaning—the mouth, the hand, or the feet, the latter communicating the utmost in submission.[4]

Nobles were steeped in a culture of ritual that saw them plant not just a single kiss but a series of small kisses. When Louis the Pious (778–840), the future emperor and saint, met Pope Stephen IV (r. 816–817) near Reims, Stephen kissed Louis's hands, plus both eyes, and they grasped hands, with fingers interlaced.[5] Such actions were both intimate and public. In a courtly setting, kissing the king or lord became a ritual of displaying fealty while showing respect. One of the many illuminations of the Coronation Book of Charles V (r.1364–1380) shows part of the ceremony in which the king (central, larger, and visually heightened by his crown and scepter) receives the kiss on the mouth by a vassal. A scroll emanates from the vassal's hand, as if he were uttering ritualized speech (Fig. 30).[6] Even if the osculation gesture were performed in a stylized way, it still meant bringing the lips into intimate contact with a person, a ring, or an ankle, and publicly displaying an emotion, so that witnesses could interpret the gestures.[7]

In the late Middle Ages, the gesture of the kiss became embedded in the practice of Christianity, a religion that drew its authority from the written word. Books recorded and prescribed rituals and actions, and even purportedly held the Word of God. Rituals that took place in churches focused on the book, which stood as a material witness to the Word of God. One defining feature of Christianity is that its officials—bishops and priests assisted by deacons and subdeacons—regularly performed the liturgical celebration of Mass, a theatrical event with a script and instructions. According to Josef A. Jungmann, who wrote extensively and perceptively about the history of the liturgy, the various clerics who conducted Mass, even in the seventh century, kissed the altar

---

4   Carré, *Le Baiser sur la Bouche*, p. 15, considers kissing to have four levels: a corporal level, an affective level, an intellectual level, and a spiritual level—each with its social aspect.
5   Carré, *Le Baiser sur la Bouche*, p. 13.
6   Percy Ernst Schramm, *A History of the English Coronation* (Clarendon Press, 1937); P. L. Ward, "The Coronation Ceremony in Mediaeval England," *Speculum*, 14.2 (1939), pp. 160–78; H. G. Richardson, "The English Coronation Oath," *Speculum*, 24.1 (1949), pp. 44–75.
7   David Ganz, "Touching Books, Touching Art: Tactile Dimensions of Sacred Books in the Medieval West," *Postscripts*, 8.1–2 (2017), pp. 81–113, argues that certain manuscripts were activated through touch, and that decoration on the page structured that touching.

Fig. 30 Osculation, in the Coronation Book of Charles V, Paris, 1365. London, British Library, Cotton Ms. Tiberius B VIII/2, fol. 64r.

when they approached it and kissed the Gospel manuscript when they picked it up. Priests regularly kissed other altar furnishings, including the corporal, the altar cloth, the chalice, the paten, and closed service books such as a missal (see below) at the altar, with a combination of emotion and theater.⁸ Doing so demonstrated respect for those objects. These clerics also kissed relics, including those of saints that populated (and to medieval believers, animated) every altar in Christendom. If relics on earth provided a conduit with the eternal saints, who were said to dwell in heaven, kissing a saint's relics was tantamount to kissing the saint herself. The development I wish to underscore here is not the kissing of relics, or even of books, but rather the kissing of images, words, and decoration within books. The practice of kissing the image of Christ, for example, gained fervor in the eleventh through the fifteenth centuries. This act accompanied an increase in the size of Crucifixion images painted in missals, so that the gesture of kissing could be more visible and theatrical.

I. Kissing Missals

When late medieval priests and bishops kissed open missals while performing the Mass, specifically as part of the Canon of the Mass during the ritual of transubstantiation, those in attendance expected a miracle from every performance of this event: the transformation of the wafer into the body of Christ.⁹ From the eleventh century until the Protestant Reformation, the ritual surrounding transubstantiation became more oriented around the image of the suffering Christ, and concomitant with this shift, the gesture of kissing became more overt, possibly more emphatic, expected, and scripted. Anticipating this

---

8   Josef A. Jungmann, *The Mass of the Roman Rite: Its Origins and Development* (2 vols), trans. Francis A. Brunner (Benziger, 1951), Rev. and abridged ed. *Notre Dame: Christian Classics* (Vol. 1), [2012], pp. 68–73.

9   A comprehensive study of service books across the European Middle Ages with all their geographical and chronological variants has yet to be written, but useful regional studies exist, including Agnès Babois-Auboyneau, *l'Illustration des Sacramentaires et Missels de l'An 1000 aux Années 1150. I: Synthèse. II: Annexes et Catalogue. III: Illustrations* (3 vols) (University of Poitiers, unpublished MA thesis, 1995). V. Leroquais, *Les Sacramentaires et les Missels Manuscrits des Bibliothèques Publiques de France* (Tiip. Macon, 1924), analyzed the service books in the BnF, which are overwhelmingly from France. For Italian manuscripts, see the *Iter Liturgicum Italicum* database (https://www.irht.cnrs.fr/fr/ressources/base-de-donnees/iter-liturgicum-italicum), together with Laura Albiero and Eleonora Celora, "La base des données Iter Liturgicum Italicum: Problématiques et perspectives," in Laura Albiero and Eleonora Celora, eds. "Décrire le manuscrit liturgique: Méthodes, problématiques, perspectives," *Bibliologia* 64 (Brepols, 2021), pp. 209–18. The other items in this volume include useful tools for studying liturgical manuscripts.

gesture, illuminators designed, and redesigned, the images to be kissed. How the images appeared—their size, placement, framing, and decoration—both responded to and shaped the gestures of the clergy using them.

Although gestures were ephemeral, kisses that touched down physically left a trace, at least in their cumulative form. The repeated nature of these osculations, as well as their introducing warm, moist air to the surface of the parchment, resulted in patterns of damage to the manuscripts. A brief history of service books will reveal how the imagery within them supported their functions.

II. A Brief History of the Missal

Priests performed two main kinds of services—Masses and Offices—for which specific kinds of manuscripts were developed. Priests prayed daily offices at the canonical hours (Matins, Lauds, Prime, and so on), as directed by a service book called the breviary. Additionally, they celebrated Mass on important days during the year, either those that were included in the temporal (covering feasts such as Christmas, Easter, and Pentecost), or the sanctoral (presenting the saints in the order that they would be celebrated during the year). Masses could also be performed daily. The Canon rite—the solemn ceremony of transubstantiation—took place within the Mass at an altar.

A sacramentary was a book that contained texts, prayers, and instructions for a priest to perform High Mass. This book was supplemented by several other role-specific books: the Gospels for the deacon, an epistolary for the sub-deacon, and the gradual for the choir. Around the twelfth century, texts from these books were brought together into a single volume, the missal, which contained all the texts a priest would need to conduct the Low Mass.[10] As Low Masses became increasingly common in the later Middle Ages, the missal evolved, its production surpassing that of the sacramentary.[11]

---

10   For an analysis of High vs Low Masses, see Josef A. Jungmann, *The Mass of the Roman Rite: Its Origins and Development*, trans. Francis A. Brunner, 2 vols. (Benziger, 1951), Rev. and abridged ed. Christian Classics, [2012].

11   Useful introductions to these book types can be found in John Plummer, *Liturgical Manuscripts for the Mass and the Divine Office* (The Pierpont Morgan Library, 1964),

Because the Canon rite occurred at every Mass and was the most important part of the ceremony, its relevant texts were usually arranged so that they fell midway in the missal; when the priest was performing this part of the service, the book would be opened with half the pages on the left and half on the right. If he elevated the book at this opening it would be perfectly balanced. In broad terms, the Canon celebration always involved the priest's uttering particular words, but over time, the gestures and the props shifted. Ecclesiastical authorities developed a set of rituals that involved objects including the paten, chalice, altar, and ecclesiastical robes. Books mediated these rituals by providing instructions while at the same time serving as a prop; thus, both the contents inscribed on its pages and its recognizability as a book by the audience had ritualistic value. The theatrics around book-handling became increasingly lavish. In fact, liturgical books increasingly received highly ornamented bindings, so that they could signify their importance from a distance without even being opened.[12]

The liturgy itself changed over time—from the days of the early Church until the time of the Protestant Reformation—as well as changing regionally, with the papal city producing a Roman Rite, England celebrating according to a Sarum Rite, and the Dominicans developing their own distinctive service, to name but a few variants. Service books, which both drove and responded to changes, evolved accordingly.[13] Moreover, different kinds of liturgical celebrations (monastic, presbyteral, episcopal, and papal) each used books slightly differently. Categorizing these regional, temporal, and confessional changes is

---

     pp. 9–10; and Robert G. Calkins, *Illuminated Books of the Middle Ages* (Thames and Hudson, 1983), pp. 161–206.

12 Eyal Poleg, "The Bible as Talisman: Textus and Oath-Books," in *Approaching the Bible in Medieval England, Manchester Medieval Studies* (Manchester University Press, 2013), pp. 59–107; David Ganz, *Buch-Gewänder: Prachteinbände im Mittelalter* (Dietrich Reimer Verlag, 2015).

13 Robert G. Calkins, *Illuminated Books of the Middle Ages* (Cornell University Press, 1986), makes this point in his concise overview of the shifts in liturgical manuscripts from the early to the late Middle Ages. Gregory Dix, *The Shape of the Liturgy* (Dacre Press, 1945), pp. 546–612, discusses the many regional differences in the performance of Mass in the West (although it was more uniform in Byzantium). Jungmann (Vol. I), pp. 104ff offers the fullest analysis of the transition of the books for Mass.

beyond the scope of this study.¹⁴ Instead, the purpose of this chapter is to survey a selection of missals from the twelfth until the early sixteenth centuries to show major trends over this period in how the Canon imagery was presented and used. The other purpose of this chapter is to investigate the use-wear in these manuscripts to better understand how gestures of handling changed over time. By considering signs of wear in individual liturgical manuscripts, this chapter considers how priests physically interacted with books during religious ceremonies. More broadly, I argue that the way in which priests handled missals both reflects and shapes how medieval Europeans handled different kinds of manuscripts in other settings.

In the present context, one can note that a wave of changes occurred around the twelfth century, making the liturgy more theatrical as the Mass increasingly took on the role of holy drama. Jungmann sees evidence of these changes in the increasing number of churches using the hand gesture of the "sign of the cross," blessing objects, and kissing them. He writes:

> The Gothic principle of cumulation, the repetition of the same detail, the heaping up of ornament, had its effect on the kissing of the altar. Although up to the twelfth century, this was customary—in line with tradition—only when first approaching the altar and again when leaving, since the end of the thirteenth century it was performed every time the celebrant turned around at the altar. The kiss at High Mass when handing the celebrant an object and the kiss of greeting for the celebrant are also added at various places. The extension of the hands after the consecration became, after the thirteenth century, a vivid imitation of the outstretched arms of the Crucified. For a time, too, the ceremonial was built up further; the priest at the anamnesis, on recalling the Resurrection and Ascension of our Lord, was supposed to mimic these movements with his hands. Bowing the head at the end of the Memento of the Dead, and striking the breast while saying "Nobis quoque" in a loud voice—these actions appear to have been introduced as a vivid presentation of our Lord's death and the impression it made on the bystanders.¹⁵

---

14   For further resources, see Éric Palazzo, "Performing the Liturgy," in *Early Medieval Christianities, c. 600-c. 1100*, edited by Thomas F. X. Noble and Julia M. H. Smith (Cambridge University Press, 2008), pp. 472–88; and Éric Palazzo, "Art and Liturgy in the Middle Ages: Survey of Research (1980–2003) and Some Reflections on Method," *The Journal of English and Germanic Philology* (The State of Medieval Studies series), 105.1 (Jan. 2006), pp. 170–84.
15   Jungmann (Vol. 1), pp. 107–08.

Perhaps priests sought opportunities to enlarge gestural language because the ceremony took place while the priest faced the altar, obscuring much of the action with his body and uttering many of the words inaudibly.

The increased theatrics can be seen in at least two shifts in the missal. First, they took on more instructions in the form of rubrics, which codified various gestures.[16] These prescriptions appeared, inter alia, in the Ordo (pl. Ordines), which is a text with the rule of ordinance for a religious ceremony. The second shift concerned the decoration at the central section of the missal, namely the part that contains the Canon of the Mass (which begins *Te igitur clementissime pater*) and the words of consecration. Unlike other texts in the missal, this was central to the Mass and performed every time, and as such, this is often the most worn part of the manuscript.[17]

This theatricality was made manifest in another change: from the eleventh to the fourteenth centuries, the humanity of Christ—and with it the Eucharist—became increasingly emphasized, as Rachel Fulton has argued with painstaking erudition.[18] This accompanied an increase in affective piety, with imagery that foregrounded Christ's humanity and suffering. Believers sought tangible divinity in the form of the Eucharist. A structural response to this desire was the creation of the

---

16 In addition to Jungmann, see: Anne S. Korteweg, *Liturgische Handschriften uit de Koninklijke Bibliotheek* (Rijksmuseum Meermanno-Westreenianum, 1983); Christine Schnusenberg, *The Relationship Between the Church and the Theatre: Exemplified by Selected Writings of the Church Fathers and by Liturgical Texts Until Amalarius of Metz (775–852 A.D.)* (University Press of America, 1988). Andrew S. Hughes, *Medieval Manuscripts for Mass and Office a Guide to Their Organization and Terminology* (University of Toronto Press, 1995) analyzes the text and is not concerned with images within manuscripts nor with gestures of officiants. Nicholas Orchard, *The Leofric Missal*, Vol. 113–14 (Boydell Press for the Henry Bradshaw Society, 2002); David Ganz, "Giving to God in the Mass: The Experience of the Offertory," in *The Languages of Gift in the Early Middle Ages*, edited by Wendy Davies and Paul Fouracre (Cambridge University Press, 2010), pp. 18–32.

17 See Christopher de Hamel, *A History of Illuminated Manuscripts* (D.R. Godine, 1986), pp. 206–09.

18 Rachel Fulton, *From Judgment to Passion: Devotion to Christ and the Virgin Mary, 800–1200* (Columbia University Press, 2002), pp. 60–63, 140–46, and *passim* convincingly argues that theologians had to rewrite Christian history after the year 1000, when Christ failed to return as promised. Liturgy and devotion shifted to accommodate this disappointment. After the First Crusade (1096–1099), when Christians conquered Jerusalem, devotion and liturgy shift again, becoming more emotional, fervent, and theatrical, with more metaphors around blood and suffering.

feast of Corpus Christi, established in 1264. Around this time, the priest began elevating the Eucharist to make the small disk more visible to the gathered congregation. Late medieval devotion fixated on the Eucharist, and members of the lay public were reported traveling from one church to the next on a Sunday to see not just one, but multiple elevations of the Eucharist. Until the Reformation there was an increasing emphasis on seeing the host, and on the visibility of the suffering savior. This emphasis had several manifestations, one of them being the increasing size of the image of the Crucified Christ in the missal, which might just be visible to onlookers. To gain some sense of how late medieval lay persons experienced the Mass, we should remember that the ceremony was conducted in Latin and (for the most part) sub-audibly, so that the main experience for those in attendance was visual, not auditory.[19] As book design reveals, the target of the priest's osculation morphed from the letter T (in *Te igitur*) to an image of the savior on the cross, from the inaudible Word to the ever-larger image. Likewise, the size of the priest's gestures changed when using the missal, just as the size of the target changed from a single initial to a two-page spread. The growing size of the Canon plate—the full-page image or two-page-spread with the Crucifixion image—accompanied an increased theatricality.

In earlier service books, such as a missal for the Abbey of Saint-Desle de Lure made before 1073, the initial T was made to resemble a crucifix, and the priest would venerate this shape, with its double meaning of "crucifix" and "letter representing the Word of God" (Fig. 31). Over the twelfth century, illuminators experimented with the *Te igitur*, expanding its proportions and nuancing its features. First they defined the T as a crucifix, so that the form was both letter and object. Then they added Mary and John in the space below the cross's arms, and then moved the Crucifixion from the confines of a letter to a miniature on its own, as with a French missal of the thirteenth century (Fig. 32).[20] In other

---

19 Edouard Dumoutet, *Le Désir de voir l'hostie et les origines de la dévotion au Saint-Sacrement* (Beauchesne, 1926); Charles Caspers, "The Western Church During the Late Middle Ages: *Augenkommunion* or Popular Mysticism?" In *Bread of Heaven: Customs and Practices Surrounding Holy Communion, Essays in the History of Liturgy and Culture* (Liturgia Condenda, Vol. 3), edited by Charles Caspers, Gerard Lukken, and Gerard Rouwhorst (Kok Pharos, 1995), pp. 83–98

20 For a description of Mazarine 422 and bibliographic notices, see http://initiale.irht.cnrs.fr/codex/6497.

words, what had at first been a letter—a symbolic form representing an element of language—became an image. That the body of Jesus and his instrument of torture could be superimposed on the letter that initiated the Canon mirrored the idea that Christ was the Word made flesh.

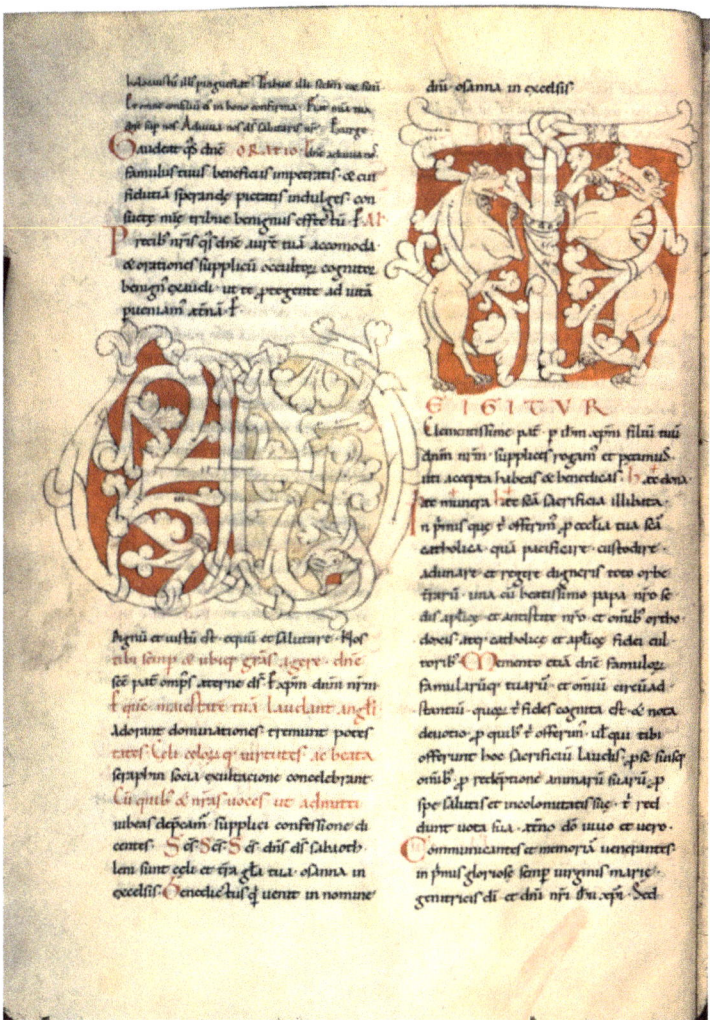

Fig. 31 *Te igitur* folio from a missal for the use of the abbey of Saint-Desle de Lure, made before 1073. Besançon, Bibliothèque municipale, Ms. 72, fol. 13v. Cliché: IRHT-CNRS

Fig. 32 Opening at the Canon from a missal, France, thirteenth century. Paris, Bibliothèque Mazarine, Ms. 422, fols 125v-126r. Cliché: IRHT-CNRS

Next, the image of the Crucifixion was enlarged, with illuminators dedicating an entire folio to the subject. For example, a twelfth-century missal from the abbey of Notre-Dame in Belval (France) presents this arrangement (Fig. 33).[21] While the manuscript would have been usable and complete without the Crucifixion miniature, those at the abbey desired such an image—apparently so that they could use it in a kissing ritual. This practice has abraded the paint and deposited stains, especially near the lower cross, the legs of Jesus, and the lower drapery of Mary and John. Some of the stains have been impressed onto the facing folio.

In her groundbreaking book *Corpus Christi: The Eucharist in Late Medieval Culture* (1991), Miri Rubin showed that standard rituals enacted at Masses across Christendom had the effect of destroying books. When Siegfried Wenzel reviewed Rubin's book, he did not believe this to be the case. Listing the book's "serious factual mistakes," he included "interpreting the crosses found in handwritten and printed editions of

---

21 For a bibliography of this manuscript, see http://initiale.irht.cnrs.fr/codex/1413.

4. Kissing: From Relics to Manuscripts   93

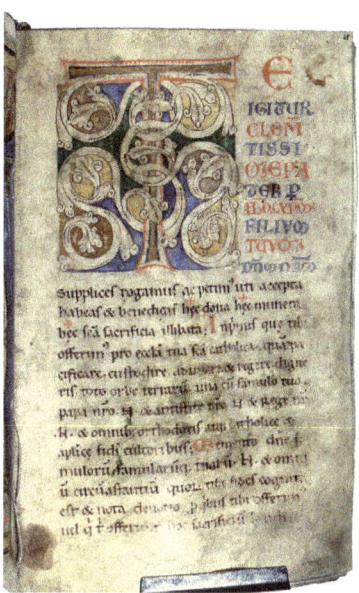

Fig. 33 Opening of a missal at the Canon, from the abbey of Notre-Dame in Belval, twelfth century. Charleville-Mézières, Bibliothèque municipale [Médiathèque Voyelles], Ms. 3, fols 44v-45r. Cliché: IRHT-CNRS

the Canon of the Mass as marks 'for the priest's kiss' (they are signals for the priest to make a manual sign of the cross)."[22] Although the line-high crosses within the texts of liturgical manuscripts indicate that the priest is to make the sign of the cross manually, other crosses, gross and unseemly as it may be, did in fact signal a physical, oral osculation, and not merely a hand gesture. The manuscripts themselves bear evidence of the physical procedures they underwent. Rubin was, of course, right.

In the missal from Notre-Dame in Belval, and the missal now in the Bibliothèque Mazarine in Paris, traces of priests' kisses appear in the form of smears, weakened parchment, and deposited facial grease, which all reveal the intimate interactions between book and user. Priests

---

22 Miri Rubin, *Corpus Christi: The Eucharist in Late Medieval Culture* (Cambridge University Press, 1991). Siegfried Wenzel, review of Miri Rubin *Corpus Christi: The Eucharist in Late Medieval Culture*, *Notes and Queries* (1992), 39 (2), pp. 212–13. Esther Meier, "Turning Toward God and Outward Actions: The Priest in the *Te Igitur* Initials of the Middle Ages," in *Iconography of Liturgical Textiles in the Middle Ages*, edited by Evelin Wetter and Michael Bangert (Abegg-Stiftung, 2010), pp. 79–88, has further explored these gestures.

treated books as if they were, in fact, the body of Christ. Even the ink used to inscribe the text could become a metaphor for Christ's blood.[23]

By the early fourteenth century, canon images increased in size again; it became de rigueur for missals to have a full illuminated opening, with Christ Crucified on one side, and God Enthroned on the other side. Such is the case with a missal made in Paris in 1317 or 1318, probably for the Use of Sainte-Chapelle, the royal chapel in Paris (LBL, Harley Ms. 2891; Fig. 34).[24] Parallel with the development toward ever-larger images of Christ, and a concomitant emphasis on images rather than divine logos, an increasingly elaborate set of ritual actions accompanied the performance of the liturgy. Manuscripts acquired more and more instructions for gestures, in the form of rubrics. The rubrics in the *Sainte-Chapelle missal* provide a sense of how a late medieval priest might have performed the liturgy. The *ordo missae* and the Canon of the Mass together require a full 11 folios (141r–152v) near the middle of the book, because extensive rubrics draw this section out. They direct the priest to undertake various actions, including to wash his hands, to don various liturgical vestments, to light candles, to kiss the altar, to open the manuscript to the image of the crucifix, to regard it with devotion and then to kiss the feet of the Crucified Christ, to bless the gospel book, to elevate the chalice and the paten with the host, to return the chalice and the paten to the altar and to cover them with a corporal, to place the offering of the people in the middle of the altar, to bow his head and body and clasp his hands together, and then to wash his hands. These actions form a ritualized performance, with the altar and various objects including the missal as protagonists on the white-draped stage.

Besides kissing, other ritual actions of the Mass could likewise sully the book. While reciting the canon, the priest would incense the book as part of a purification procedure, and he would wash his hands ritualistically in preparation for handling the Host. The signs of wear in a missal made for Knights Hospitallers in Southern Germany in 1469

---

23 Marlene Villalobos Hennessy. "The Social Life of a Manuscript Metaphor: Christ's Blood as Ink," in *The Social Life of Illumination: Manuscripts, Images, and Communities in the Late Middle Ages* (Medieval Texts and Cultures of Northern Europe), edited by Joyce Coleman, Mark Cruse and Kathryn A. Smith, pp. 17–52, (Brepols, 2013), pp. 17–52.

24 For a full bibliography, see www.bl.uk/catalogues/illuminatedmanuscripts/record.asp?MSID=6620. The entire manuscript has been digitized: www.bl.uk/manuscripts/Viewer.aspx?ref=harley_ms_2891_fs001r.

4. *Kissing: From Relics to Manuscripts* 95

Fig. 34 Opening of a missal at the Canon, Paris in 1317 or 1318. London, British Library, Harley Ms. 2891, fols 145v-146r.

reveal this aspect of its early use ('s-Heerenberg, Huis Bergh Castle, inv. no. 281, Ms. 15). The first opening of the canon, with a full-page miniature of the Crucifixion, is relatively clean (Fig. 35), although the raking light reveals creases and buckling in the parchment, especially in the lower corner of the recto side, as a result of grasping the folio there and turning it many times (Fig. 36). The edges of the opening also have dirt deposited in several locations by both the right and left hands; this opening has even more pronounced creasing and buckling, suggesting that not only has the page been turned many times, but that moisture has also been introduced. An opening deeper in the canon is the filthiest (Fig. 37). One of the rubricated instructions reads *"in ablucione digitorum"*: this prayer is to be read while the priest washes his fingers. Dark marks in the margins of the opening, plus severely buckled parchment, indicate that he did not dry them effectively. The book itself became his hand towel.

Materially, treating the book as a suffering body to be kissed resulted in the degradation of the very object of veneration. Illuminators responded by painting a small cross at the bottom of the page, so that priests would

Fig. 35 Crucifixion in a missal at the Canon. Southern Germany (Augsburg?), 1469. Ms. 15, Inv. nr. 281, fol. 70v. 's-Heerenberg, The Netherlands, Collection Dr. J. H. van Heek, Huis Bergh Foundation, Ms. 15. Image © The Huis Bergh Foundation, CC BY 4.0.

kiss this instead, thereby leaving the main miniature unscathed.[25] A pair of such osculatory targets appears in the Sainte-Chapelle missal (BL Harley 2891), below both the Crucifixion and Enthroned Christ images. Slight degradation suggests that both pages were kissed, especially the Crucifixion, where the feet of Christ and the osculatory target are darkened, plus the round boss in the frame halfway between the two.

---

25 de Hamel, *A History of Illuminated Manuscripts*, p. 210 makes this point.

4. Kissing: From Relics to Manuscripts

Fig. 36 Opening of a missal within the Canon. Southern Germany (Augsburg?), 1469. Ms. 15, Inv. nr. 281, fols 70v-71r. 's-Heerenberg, The Netherlands, Collection Dr. J. H. van Heek, Huis Bergh Foundation, Ms. 15.

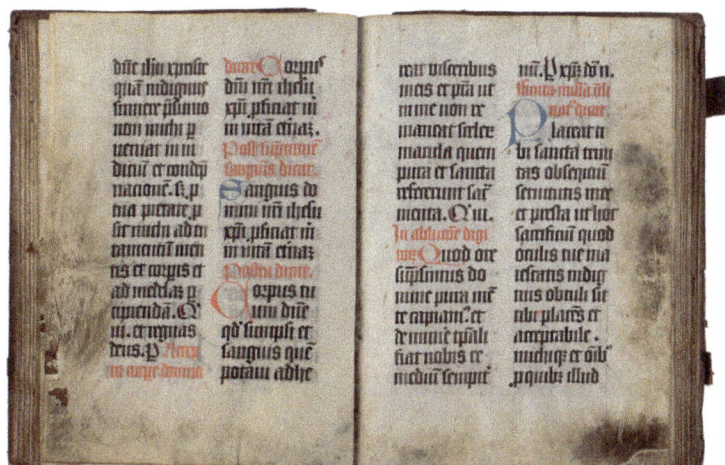

Fig. 37 Opening of a missal within the Canon. Southern Germany (Augsburg?), 1469. Ms. 15, Inv. nr. 281, fols 78v-79r. 's-Heerenberg, The Netherlands, Collection Dr. J. H. van Heek, Huis Bergh Foundation, Ms. 15. Image © The Huis Bergh Foundation, CC BY 4.0.

While this missal survives in good condition—suggesting it was used only for the most special ceremonies—many other missals reveal heavy physical use.

A missal made in Paris around 1315 contains heavily used osculatory targets (Paris, BnF, Ms. lat. 861; Fig. 38).[26] Instead of a simple cross, the target is a miniature version of the Crucifixion above, complete with the figures of Mary and John, and has thereby been offered by the illuminator as a diminutive replica of the main image. An obedient priest who followed the illuminator's graphic instructions has severely degraded the tiny image. He has also kissed Christ's feet and shins, and the blue mantel of the Virgin in the large image, suggesting that the main illustration exerted an overwhelming pull on this priest's attention.

Fig. 38 Opening of a missal at the Canon. Paris ca. 1315. Paris, Bibliothèque national de France, Ms. lat. 861, fol. 147v-148r.

Not all priests obeyed the graphic instruction of the osculatory target. An elaborate example appears in the missal written in 1482–1483 by

---

26 For a description and bibliography, see https://archivesetmanuscrits.bnf.fr/ark:/12148/cc623294; see Leroquais, *Missels et sacramentaires*, II, pp. 248–49; François Avril, *Manuscript Painting at the Court of France: The Fourteenth Century (1310–1380)* (George Braziller, 1978), pp. 42–43.

the Brethren of the Common Life of St. Gregory in Nijmegen for the bakers' guild in that city. The missal also contains a full-page miniature depicting Christ Crucified, this time painted in a style and palette typical of the German-Dutch border region, with bright sherbet-like colors and heavy gilding (Fig. 39).[27] A motif in the lower gilt border specifically refers to the bakers' guild: it shows a man putting a loaf into an oven with a long paddle. As if in response to the bread motif, the artist has created an elaborate osculatory target of gilded arabesques; kissing the shape would bring the priest's mouth into contact with the baker and his bread, in both a blessing for the guild and symbolic contact with the body of Christ. But the Nijmegen priest avoided the target, perhaps because the gilded surface felt cold and metallic. He tried to restrain himself to kissing the ground below Christ's feet, but eventually smeared Christ's midriff and groin across the distant landscape. This example suggests that priests strongly desired to kiss the main image of Christ, rather than a diminutive substitute.

Fig. 39 Opening of a missal at the Canon, missal of the Nijmegen Bakers' Guild, 1482–1483. Nijmegen, Museum Het Valkhof, Ms. CIA 2, fols 125v-126r.

27　The manuscript was recently in the collection of the Museum Commanderie van St Jan, but the collections were transferred to the Museum Het Valkhof in Nijmegen.

At the end of the fifteenth century, at least one priest from Amiens gave his missal air kisses. He gripped his missal until he had dislodged paint from the lower corners of the pages (Fig. 40). To achieve this level of wear, he must have performed the Mass hundreds or thousands of times, handling these pages at least once for each Mass. Holding the parchment at the corner has weakened its fibers, and caused the gold, blue, and white paint to flake off. However, even with this much handling and attention, the images bear no signs of oral moisture or facial grease: despite all this physical attention, the priest avoided contact, possibly so as not to ruin the pictures.

Fig. 40 Opening of a missal at the Canon, for the use of Amiens, ca. 1490–1500. Amiens, Bibliothèque Municipale, Ms. 163, fol. 155v-156r. Cliché: IRHT-CNRS

There seems to have been no single way for the priest to kiss an image. Rather, patterns of wear reveal considerable latitude in kissing targets, which suggests that priests exerted some emotional response in their choice of where on the page to kiss and with how much contact or restraint. The ritual itself demanded that priests carry out certain actions, but within that fixed ritual was the flexibility to express zeal and personal emotion. Places to kiss include the right hand of Christ, as in a thirteenth-century missal for the use of Arras (Arras, Bibliothèque

Municipale, Ms. 888; Fig. 41).[28] A priest has aimed for this spot again and again, thereby wearing a hole in the gold background and causing a pigment shift from fleshy tan to sickly gray in Christ's right forearm. Christ's midriff is also a popular target, seen in a thirteenth-century missal now in Paris (Bibliothèque Mazarine, Ms. 422; see Fig. 32). There, moisture from the priest's mouth has been applied to Christ's torso, groin, and thighs. This moisture has loosened some of the paint and caused it to adhere to the opposite page. Handling the book with dry hands has also abraded the bottom margin, inadvertently erasing the inscription below the miniature.

Fig. 41 Opening of a missal, with a Crucifixion, thirteenth century, use of Arras. Arras, Bibliothèque Municipale, Ms. 888, fol. 175v-176r. Cliché: IRHT-CNRS

An early fifteenth-century Parisian priest aimed repeatedly for the charged area between the depicted cleric and the feet of Christ Crucified (Fig. 42). Water-based saliva has liquefied the paint, and then abrasion has redistributed it. The effects of these repeated actions are more visible in a photograph shot with backlighting (Fig. 43). Against the cleric's distinct, opaque lead-white robe, the re-liquefied brown paint of Christ's cross and feet have been smeared over the top. On the facing

---

28 For a description and bibliography, see http://initiale.irht.cnrs.fr/codex/297?contenuMaterielId=1427.

folio the priest has duplicated the kissing gesture at the feet of God the Father: it is the presence of the second image in this context, rather than a long-standing tradition of kissing the feet of God, that has prompted the duplicate gesture. Photographs of the back of both leaves confirm that facial oils have seeped through the parchment, which indicates that the priest's face did indeed come in contact with the parchment (Fig. 44 and Fig. 45). Whereas saliva is water-based and reconstitutes the tempera paint, facial oils are hydrophobic and do not reconstitute water-based paint; oils seep into the parchment, both darkening it and decreasing its opacity. (For this reason, fatty parchment often looks yellow-brown, but letters on the other side of the membrane are visible through the semi-transparent oily parchment.)

Fig. 42 Opening of a missal at the Canon, early fifteenth century, made for Paris. Paris, Bibliothèque Sainte-Geneviève, Ms. 97, fols 136v–137r. Cliché: IRHT-CNRS

In this context, I would like to revisit the missal presented to Jean Michel in Angers, discussed earlier (Angers, Archives départementales de Maine-et-Loire, J(001) 4138; see Figs 1 and 3). The fugitive detail of the front of the Crucifixion miniature indexes its thorough handling. The back of the Crucifixion miniature reveals that grease—which I am

Fig. 43 Canon page shot with backlighting, made for Paris, early fifteenth century. Paris, Bibliothèque Sainte-Geneviève, Ms. 97, fols 136v. Photograph: author

interpreting here as facial oils—only appears in one area of the page: at the center of the lower border. If this is correct, it follows that the priest, perhaps Jean Michel, only kissed the osculatory target painted at the lower border, and that his nose or forehead touched down repeatedly in the middle of the marginal decoration. This would imply that the damage to the rest of the image—especially the removal of surface detail from the face and body of Christ, and the faces of Mary and John—has been caused by a different action. I suggest that this action was wet-touching with a finger, which would transport moisture but not oil to

Fig. 44 Back of the folio with the Crucifixion, made for Paris, early fifteenth century. Paris, Bibliothèque Sainte-Geneviève, Ms. 97, fol. 136r. Cliché: IRHT-CNRS

the surface. In this model, the scenario would operate like this: having kissed the osculatory target, the priest apparently regarded the image, and then kissed his finger and carefully alighted on meaningful details, with Christ's face and torso taking the brunt of his fawning attention.

4. Kissing: From Relics to Manuscripts

Fig. 45 Back of the folio with God the Father, made for Paris, early fifteenth century. Paris, Bibliothèque Sainte-Geneviève, Ms. 97, fol. 137v. Cliché: IRHT-CNRS

The wet-touching action would also explain why the blue sky and the Virgin's blue mantle look pock-marked, as spots of paint in these areas have been liquefied, loosened, and lifted. These actions formed part of his habit and practice.

As with the fifteenth-century Parisian missal just discussed, this example from Angers also offered the priest a two-page spread, and the Angers priest, possibly Jean Michel, has likewise addressed the figure of God the Father with physical handling (see Fig. 1). A view of the back of this miniature reveals that the priest has once again kissed the lower margin and deposited his facial oils in the border decoration (Fig. 46). I suspect that the folio once had an osculatory target, which was excised when the corner was repaired, and the priest heeded the cross's tacit instruction to plant a kiss on the page. He also touched the painted area with careful aim. Specifically, he touched the hem of God's tawny garment, and he also let his wet finger touch down repeatedly on the four evangelists' symbols in the corners of the frame. It is as if he were acknowledging the sacrality of each Gospel through his action.

Fig. 46 Opening of a missal within the Canon, Use of Angers, 1439? Angers, Archives départementales de Maine-et-Loire, J(001) 4138, fol. 196v (quarter) – 196r (quinquies). Cliché: IRHT-CNRS

That priests wet-touched figures in missals, presumably while they had the book open in front of them at the altar, is made plain in a Dutch example (Fig. 47). Bistre at the foot of the cross indicates grease from facial contact. Kissing with the lips, however, does not explain the paint losses on Mary's and John's robes. These round forms were more likely caused by a very wet finger, which, when pressed down, squashed the moisture to the edges of the contact zone. That moisture then liquefied and lifted the pigment from the parchment. It would appear, therefore, that in addition to the practice of kissing the osculatory target or the foot of the cross, priests were also in the habit of wet-touching the figurative imagery.

Fig. 47 Crucifixion (Delft, ca. 1460–1480) mounted in a missal (South Holland, ca. 1440–1450). The Hague, Koninklijke Bibliotheek, Ms. B 76 E 2, fol. 101v

Clearly, those who conducted Masses had a menu of different techniques for making physical contact with the painted and inscribed page. A missal now in Oxford (OBL, Canon Liturg. 344) shows heavy use and reveals stains of crispy brown dirt in the lower corners at the Canon (Fig. 48). This book had no figurative illuminations. In the absence of an image of the Crucifixion, the priest touched the T initial (of *Te igitur*) with a wet finger. His fingerprint is visible on the right frame of the T, where the moistened black ink has been redistributed into radiating whorls (Fig. 49). It appears he used the T as a proxy for the Cross, a practice evident in Canon pages in twelfth-century missals. Moreover, he has used the decoration around the page as a "body," and so has smeared areas of the long, thin gold decoration, called a "baguette," that separates the text columns. In other words, he has treated the text page as a kissable, touchable body, and has allowed the abstract designs to guide his finger. This priest selectively touched other initials and decoration, such as the six-line A at the beginning of the manuscript that marks the incipit for Advent, and the four-line initial P for the Nativity. Priests selectively kissing initials in this way did not form part of the script, as kissing the Canon page did. This instead provides an example of the kisser taking the codified behavior and applying it to a different situation.

III. Transformations of the Book

A missal originally made in Augsburg in the twelfth century (OBL, Ms. Canon. Liturg. 354) reveals another aspect of handling that was transmitted to future audiences: simply treating the book as a tool over several centuries could degrade it significantly.[29] Like many other missals, this one has a full-page image of Christ Crucified, which has been heavily damaged by hands and lips (Fig. 50). The Crucifixion has been kissed consistently in the region of Christ's midriff. In addition to the wear from facial contact, hand dirt, grease, sweat, and saliva from many priests have been layered on and ground into the parchment, causing the

---

29 Otto Pächt and J. J. G. Alexander, *Illuminated Manuscripts in the Bodleian Library Oxford*, edited by J. J. G. Alexander (Clarendon Press, 1966–1973), Vol. I, p. 102, XII; and Friedrich Simader, "Das so genannte 'Reiner Musterbuch'—Notizen zum Forschungsstand," in *Zisterziensisches Schreiben im Mittelalter—Das Skriptorium der Reiner Mönche: Beiträge der Internationalen Tagung im Zisterzienserstift Rein, Mai 2003*, edited by Anton Schwob and Karin Kranich-Hofbauer, *Jahrbuch für Internationale Germanistik, Reihe A: Kongressberichte* (Peter Lang, 2005), pp. 141–50, p. 148.

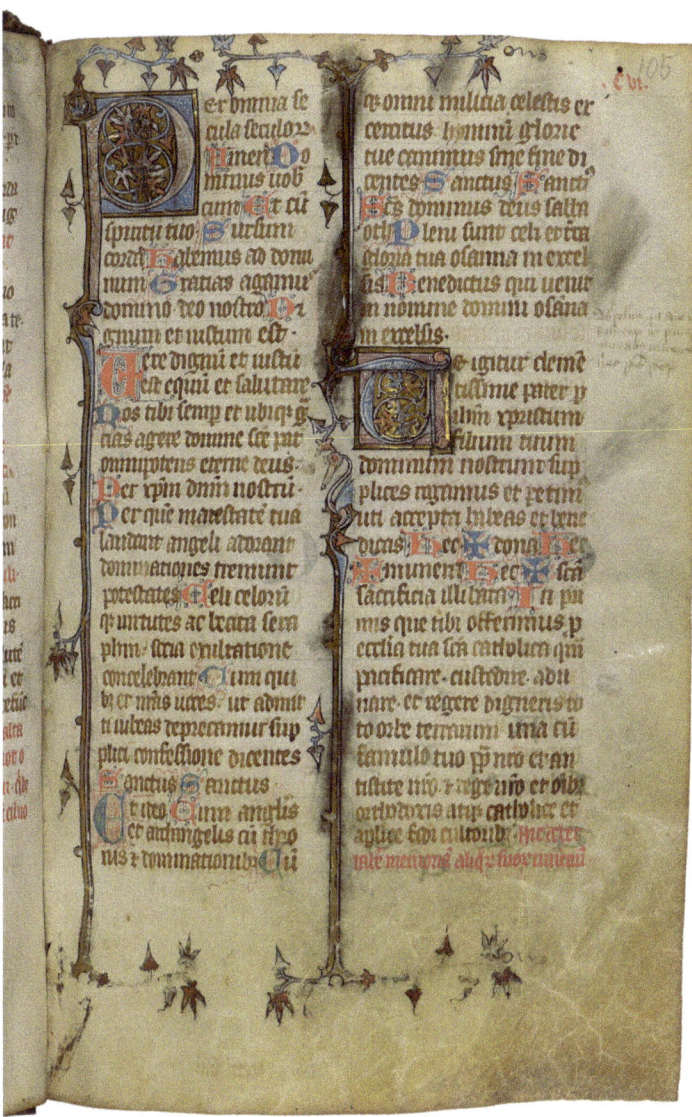

Fig. 48 *Te igitur* page from a missal, fourteenth century, Use of Chartres. Oxford, Bodleian Library, Canon Liturg. 344, fol. 105r (*cvi* in the original foliation).

lower corner to become fully discolored. Priests have kissed the image of Christ, especially his head, torso, and knees, as well as the faces of Mary and John. Mary's lower garment was painted with a type of bright green pigment that falls off easily. Many whiskers have challenged its

Fig. 49 Detail from previous image: fingerprint and wet-touched baguette. Oxford, Bodleian Library, Ms. Canon Liturg. 344, detail of 105r.

adherence. This folio bears witness to another form of touch: at the outer margin are two rectangular patches of wear circumscribed by stitching holes, where leather tabs were once sewn in, so that the priest could find this page by feel. After repeated fingering loosened the first tab, someone replaced it in a different position rather than sewing it onto already compromised parchment. But the second one, too, has fallen off. When priests used this book in public, they demonstrated not only emotional intimacy by kissing the images, but also book-manipulating technology that fell within the grasp of those with a needle and thread to apply to their own books.

Fig. 50 Crucifixion in a missal at the Canon, twelfth century with later additions, Augsburg. Oxford, Bodleian Library, Ms. Canon. Liturg. 354 fol. 67r (which is fol. Lxfij in the original foliation).

The users of Ms. Canon. Liturg. 354 found other ways of handling the manuscript that involved touching and re-touching it: they used every blank space to inscribe more texts, even writing on the back of the Crucifixion page (Fig. 51). And then they proceeded to read this urgent text so often and handle it so vigorously that they rubbed the lower corner of the text right off. The standard professional photographs I commissioned in 2018 (reproduced in the two previous images) are competent, well-lighted, and flat. From these it is difficult to imagine how early users handled the book. I therefore ordered fresh photographs that would reveal these folios in their bookish contexts (Fig. 52 and Fig. 53).

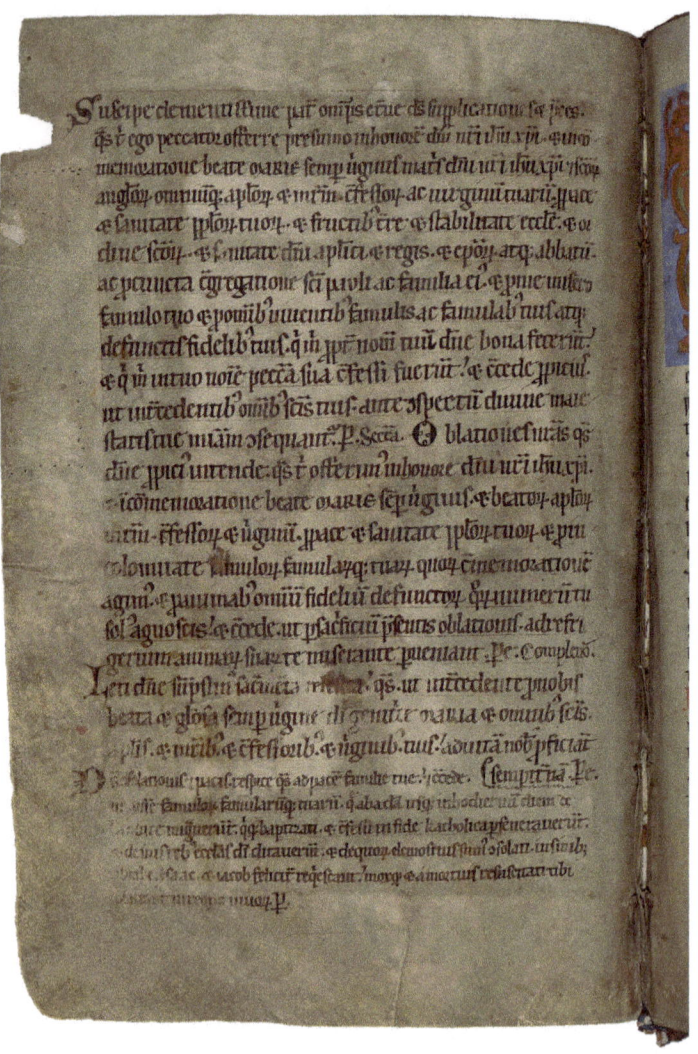

Fig. 51 Back of the Canon page (which faces the *Te igitur*) in a missal, twelfth century with later additions, Augsburg. Oxford, Bodleian Library, Ms. Canon. Liturg. 354, fol. 67v

Fig. 52 Crucifixion in a missal at the Canon, twelfth century with later additions, Augsburg. Oxford, Bodleian Library, Ms. Canon. Liturg. 354 fol. 67r (which is fol. Lxfij in the original foliation). Photographed in its material context

The liturgy bore so many additions that the owners found it expedient to foliate their creation-in-progress in the fifteenth century. They even repurposed some of the folios to make more room for the ever-expanding liturgy. For example, fols Lvij–lxij (verso) form a quire that was destined to be a calendar, but only January dates remain, as well as "KL" at the top of every folio. Someone has scraped these down and repurposed them. One of the texts written over the calendric palimpsest on fol. Lviij (verso) is the office of Corpus Christi, added in a fourteenth– or

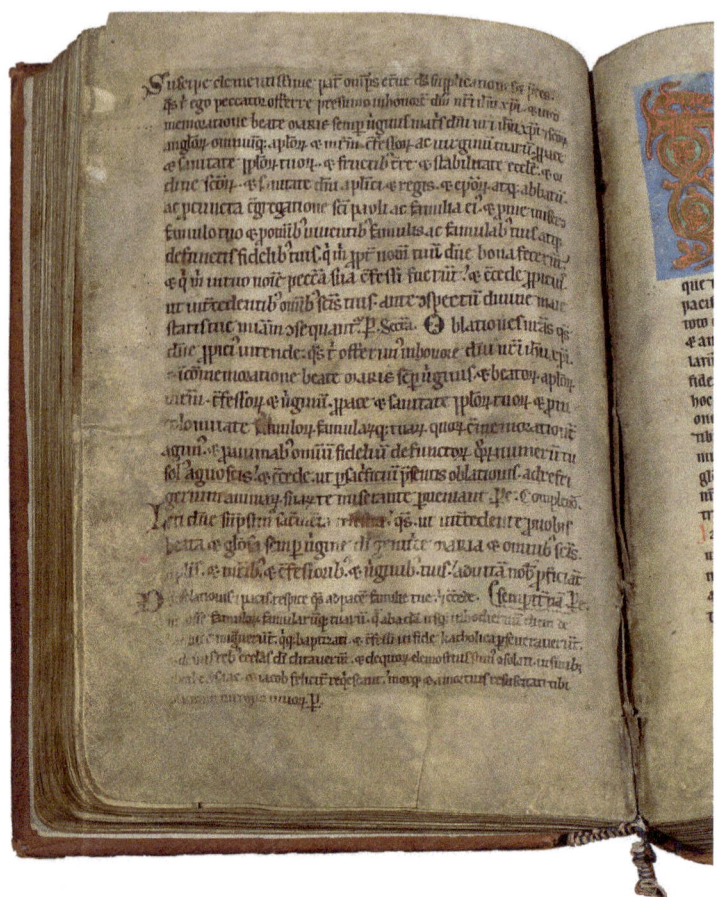

Fig. 53 Back of the Canon page (which faces the *Te igitur*) in a missal, twelfth century with later additions, Augsburg. Oxford, Bodleian Library, Ms. Canon. Liturg. 354, fol. 67v. Photographed in its material context

fifteenth-century script; another, at fol. Lxij (recto) is the office of the Crown of Thorns (Fig. 54). In this way, the calendar was repurposed as a place to insert the new offices that had emerged since the book's original production. This manuscript reveals how generations of priests added material to blank areas of the book.

Because a priest used the Canon at every Mass, this part of the book fell in tatters first. The differential usage of a missal demanded a particular approach to conservation, as is apparent in a missal written

Fig. 54 Added office of the crown of thorns in a twelfth-century missal, Augsburg. Oxford, Bodleian Library, Ms. Canon. Liturg. 354, fols 61v-62r.

and illuminated in the first decade of the fifteenth century, possibly in Guelders (Fig. 55). It must have been partly ruined by the end of the century—partly because a priest would use the book unevenly during the course of a year. Because the margins of this page are largely unpainted, it is easy to see that they are somewhat discolored from wear. For example, fol. 7v, near the beginning, has the text to be read "for the first Sunday in Advent" (*Dominica prima in adventu*). Its illuminated initial at the top, as well as the painted and gilt decoration around the border, help the reader to find this passage for the first Sunday of the liturgical year. The priest would have turned to this folio once a year, and the book was probably in use for about a century, beginning shortly after 1400. In comparison, the Canon is significantly more beaten up from wear (Fig. 56). Its left-hand side has a full-page image of Christ Crucified, flanked by Mary and John, with an osculatory target at the bottom. The priest has not obeyed the target, but has kissed the foot of the cross, the feet of Jesus, the torso of Jesus, and the top of the cross. In other words, he has kissed all along the central vertical axis of the image. In so doing, he has had to hold the book open with his hands, which have left dirt and signs of abrasion at the bottom of the image, in the margin. This dirt and abrasion is mirrored on the right-hand side of the opening, the text page, beginning *Te igitur*, as the priest would have had to pick it up with both hands to kiss it, and the moisture he has deposited on the image has also loosened the ink and paint on the text page.

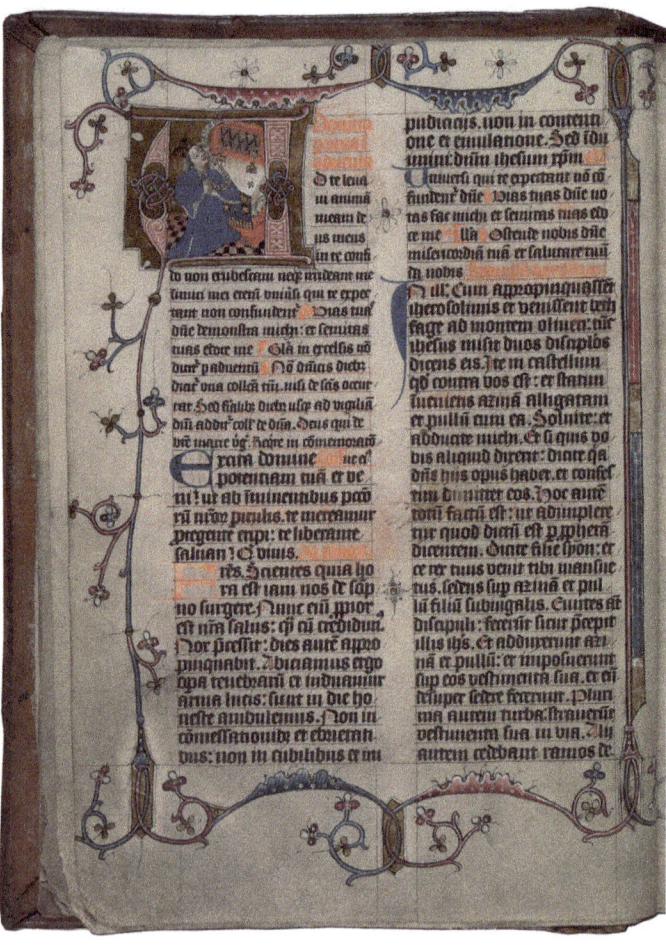

Fig. 55 Folio from a missal for the Use of Utrecht, with a historiated initial depicting David at prayer for the first Sunday of Advent in the Temporal, ca. 1400–1410 with added sections, Northern Netherlands. The Hague, Koninklijke Bibliotheek, Ms. 128 D 29, fol. 7v.

4. Kissing: From Relics to Manuscripts 117

Fig. 56 Opening of a missal at the Canon, Use of Utrecht, ca. 1400–1410 with added sections, Northern Netherlands. The Hague, Koninklijke Bibliotheek, Ms. 128 D 29, fols 128v-129r.

Whereas the other sections of the manuscript contain penwork and painted decoration typical of Guelders around 1400–1410, the quire at the Canon in the very center of the book (fols 129–34) has been added or, more accurately, replaced. This quire has decoration typical of South Holland around 1490–1500. One can imagine the following scenario: a missal made in Guelders around 1400–1410 had a Canon that was used daily. By about 1490, severe wear rendered it no longer usable. The priest or churchwardens had the manuscript repaired in South Holland, which meant discarding the tattered Canon and replacing it with a new one. That new one, with decoration typical of South Holland, was heavily used for several decades until the book was put away or retired during the Reformation. In other words, the Canon would wear out many times faster than any other part of the book, but scribes collaborating with illuminators could easily replace the worn section with a substitution.

Substituting the canon was more straightforward than trying to clean it. Clergy took the cleanliness of the items on the altar seriously. Durandus even specifies the ceremony around washing textiles:

> When the palls, that is, the corporals [*corporalia*], and the veils, that is, the ornaments of the altar, or the coverings hanging on the altar become dirty, the deacons along with the lower orders of ministers will wash

them in the sacristy, and not outside of it. And for washing the veils that service the cult of the altar, they will use a new basin; the palls, that is, the corporals, will be washed in another basin; the veils of the doorways, that is, the curtains that hang in church on feast days and during Lent are washed in another basin. Hence it was decreed by the Council of Lérida, that there be proper vessels for no other use than washing the corporal and the altar coverings, in which nothing else ought to be washed. But according to the same Clement, if the palls, that is, the vestments of the altar, or the chair covered with sacred vestments in which the priest sits, or the candelabrum, or the veil, that is, altar cloth [pannus], or the curtains hanging over the altar are consumed by old age, they shall be burned, and their ashes shall be cast in the baptistery, or into the walls, or into the cracks of the pavement where no one will pass. And note that the ecclesiastical ornaments are blessed, as discussed under the heading On consecrations and unctions.[30]

Durandus does not discuss how to clean manuscripts, nor how to refurbish them if they become tattered, but clearly the items on the altar had to be clean and, when they became sullied, had to be ritually washed. It is intriguing to think about the ashes of ornate missals, or at least of their most worn folios, scattered inside the walls of medieval churches. The moral charge to keep altar goods clean sheds light on the *Arenberg Gospels*, whose margins have been carefully scraped of their crud (see Fig. 19).

IV. Printed Canon Pages

Since Canon pages in missals required more cleaning and even replacement, they can be considered to have separate careers from the books into which they were mounted. This idea that the Crucifixion miniature could be made separately and inserted into a missal took on new significance in the era of print. One missal, printed on paper, contains just one folio of parchment, the Crucifixion page (OBL, Auct. 6 Q 1.15; Fig. 57).[31] Areas of the image that have been kissed are the left

---

30 Durand, Book 1 (2007), p. 48.
31 The print is 164 x 246 mm. The entire missal could also be printed on parchment, to match the status of the material to the gravitas of the ritual, and to allow the missal to be more richly painted. For an example, see Ursula Rautenberg, "Medienkonkurrenz und Medienmischung: Zur Gleichzeitigkeit von Handschrift und Druck im ersten Viertel des 16. Jahrhunderts in Köln," in *Die Gleichzeitigkeit von Handschrift und*

and right ends of the cross, the top of the cross, the bottom of Mary's and John the Evangelist's robes, and John's halo. The wetness introduced to these parts has caused paint to transfer to the opposite page. The image itself was printed from a woodblock and has been hand-painted in a manner typical of German prints, with a streaky blue sky and extra red blood that did not form part of the matrix. Onto the printed page, which begins with a fancy printed T (for the Te igitur), someone has written a carat, with an addition in the margin: Primo osculetur altare (First kiss the altar). The written prompt signals ritual action, although the smears to the image also serve as prompts for further osculations. Other clues in this book signal the degree to which its use was predicated upon touch: the book has leather tabs pasted in, and these have been redone, meaning that the tabs were useful enough to be replaced when they wore out (or gave way). Their thick heartiness stands at odds with the flimsiness of the paper, and in many cases the paper has torn around the tabs from the stress. The friable paper contrasts with the much tougher parchment, which also has a different sound, surface quality, and temperature. It is no wonder that bookmakers printed this page alone on parchment. Only parchment would hold up to the rituals subjected onto the Word made Flesh.

In the print era, when manuscripts were being cut up to be used as binding material, one binder saved a double-page Canon image and bound the folios as pages, rather than packing them into the binding. That book is Eusebius's *Ecclesiastical History* (OBL, Auct. 7 Q 2.13). Although the black letters are printed, a craftsperson has gone through the text, stroking some of the letters in yellow, adding red rubrication symbols, and illuminating the initials. These aspects of the production still point to the hand-applied, pre-printed world. To face the first printed text page, the prologue of the text, he or she has placed the image of the blessing God, flanked by the symbols of ecclesia and synagoga and surrounded by the four Evangelists' symbols (Fig. 58). Deeper in the manuscript, to preface Book Two (the Lives of the Saints after the Ascension of Christ), he or she has inserted the Crucifixion page (Fig. 59). Not surprisingly, the patterns of wear on these two colorful images reveal that they once faced each other. In their old situation, the

---

Buchdruck, edited by Gerd Dicke and Klaus Grubmüller. Wolfenbütteler Mittelalter-Studien (Harrassowitz, 2003), pp. 167–202.

Fig. 57 Opening of a missal at the Canon in a printed missal, Switzerland or Germany (Basel?), c.1487. Oxford, Bodleian Library, Auct. 6 Q 1.15, unf.

priest regularly kissed the area of the cross below Christ's feet, and the moisture has caused the blue paint from the facing page to adhere to the painted wood in blobs. The priest also regularly kissed the blessing right hand of the Father on the other page, and the dirt and oils from his face has darkened the hand, while his saliva caused a similar transfer of blue paint onto the opposite surface.

This holds true for the entire Canon (a text often written on two quires placed in the center of the manuscript), and for the "canon plate," which was, with few exceptions, the only illumination in missals made in Northern Europe (those from Southern Europe often have a full program of illumination). Manuscript catalogues rarely provide descriptions of added material, and unless they have a high level of detail, they will not indicate "thirteenth-century missal with fifteenth-century canon," for example.[32] It became a common enough operation

---

32 A systematic study of replaced canons in missals would be a welcome topic for a PhD thesis.

Fig. 58 Folio from a manuscript missal depicting God in Majesty (Paris, 1370–1380) bound into *Eusebius Historia Ecclestica*, printed by Nicholas Ketelaert and Gerardus Leempt of Nijmegen in 1473 with hand-flourished initials. Oxford, Bodleian Library, Auct. 7 Q 2.13.

Fig. 59 Folio from a manuscript missal depicting Christ Crucified (Paris, 1370–1380) bound into *Eusebius Historia Ecclestica*, printed by Nicholas Ketelaert and Gerardus Leempt of Nijmegen in 1473 with hand-flourished initials. Oxford, Bodleian Library, Auct. 7 Q 2.13.

that some workshops must have specialized in replacing canons, and some illuminators apparently specialized in making Canon miniatures depicting the Crucifixion.[33]

---

33 I make this point in Rudy, *Piety in Pieces*, pp. 154–55, https://doi.org/10.11647/OBP.0094, with a discussion of Canon pages produced by the Masters of Otto van Moerdrecht as replacements. See also Hanns Peter Neuheuser, "Die Kanonblätter aus der Schule des Moerdrecht-Meisters *Wallraf-Richartz-Jahrbuch*, 64 (2003), pp. 187–214, who emphasizes the ways in which the Moerdrecht Masters streamlined production rather than how they created replacement folios when old Canon pages wore out.

5. Swearing

From Gospels to Legal Manuscripts

Recording laws and swearing oaths helped to uphold promises and to minimize future uncertainty. Legal agreements between rulers and the oaths that bound them had, by the later Middle Ages, passed into all manner of interpersonal connections—rituals involving words, gestures, and props operated to assert oaths and guarantee promises. As discussed in the previous chapter, a new trend emerged, which saw Gospel manuscripts replace relics as the props used in oath-swearing. This chapter reveals a further trend: an expansion of oath-swearing that relied upon new legal books and new books of privileges and statutes to serve the administrative needs of an ever-broader array of civic organizations. Where oath-swearing on books might once have been the purview of emperors and kings alone, by the late Middle Ages the literate public had also adopted the practice. These new legal books began to include excerpts from the Gospels so that oaths could be sworn on the legal manuscripts themselves, as if people were making a binding gesture not just with the Gospels, but also with the new forms of stabilizing civic law.

Medieval cities in Northern Europe that had a Jewish population kept a separate oath for them, because it would make no sense for Jews to swear on the Gospels.[1] Instead, Jews were compelled to swear on the Hebrew Bible while reading a vivid statement about the punishments that would befall them should they lie under oath. Sometimes they had to endure the added humiliation of touching the judge's staff or standing

---

[1] For Jews and oath-taking, see Mann, "Oaths and Vows in the Synoptic Gospels," pp. 260–74; and Guido Kisch, "A Fourteenth-Century Jewry Oath of South Germany," *Speculum*, 15.3 (1940), pp. 331–37.

[Des dich dute sculdegit des bistut vnschuldic. So dir got helfe. Der got der himel vnde erdin gescuf. loub, blumen vnde gras, des da uore nine was. Vnde ob du unrechte swerist, daz dich di erde urslinde, di datan vnde abiron urslant. Vnde ob du unrechte swerist, daz dich di muselsucht bitze, di naaman nen liz vnde iezi bestunt. Vnde ob du unrechte swerist, daz dich di e urtilige di got moisy gab, in dem berge sinay, di got selbe screib, mit sinen uingeren ander steinin tabelen. Vnde ob du unrechte swerist, daz dich uellin alle di scrift di gescriben sint an den uunf buchen moisy. Dit ist der uiden heit den di biscof cuntrat durre stat gegebin hat.]

Fig. 60 Erfurt Jewish Oath, parchment and a wax seal, ca. 1200, Erfut. Erfurt, Old Synagogue. Photo kindly supplied by the Municipal Archive Erfurt, 2006

on the skin of a freshly killed animal. The earliest surviving example, the Erfurt Oath, made around 1200, is a short text on a small piece of parchment inscribed with gold initials and with its wax seal attached, to give the document official authority. Its text comprises a statement for Jews to read ceremonially before making statements in court (Fig. 60). Medieval oaths for Jews typically invoke the name of God, recall miraculous events that testify to God's omnipotence, and curse perjury.[2] Of course the Erfurt Oath has no signs of repeated wear, for it was not touched ritualistically; only an accompanying Pentateuch would have been touched. This treatment underscored how Christians alone were permitted—and indeed required—to touch the most powerful symbols in the dominant culture: images of Jesus and Mary, which found their way into a new class of manuscripts for civic law.

I. Last Judgment Imagery for Reinforcing Obligation

In the early thirteenth century, Eike von Repgow compiled customary law in the Holy Roman Empire. He translated his sources from Latin into German and gathered it into the *Sachsenspiegel*, or "Saxon mirror," which began circulating by 1235. Those in certain Germanic-speaking lands, from the Netherlands to Ukraine, translated it into local vernaculars and adopted it as the main written legal code.[3] Considered the fountainhead of German jurisprudence, the *Sachsenspiegel* operated in some places until the nineteenth century. The text, which survives in some 400 manuscript copies, was instrumental in codifying property law, inheritance, and neighborly relations, as it offered rules for preventing conflict and resolving disputes by addressing potentially frictive items, such as the

---

2   Christine Magin, "So dir Gott helfe: Der Erfurter Judeneid im historischen Kontext," *Erfurter Schriften zur Jüdischen Geschichte* 4 (2017), pp. 14–28; J. E. Scherer, *Die Rechtsverhältnisse der Juden in den Deutsch-Österreichischen Ländern. Mit einer Einleitung über die Principien der Judengesetzgebung in Europa während des Mittelalters* (Duncker & Humblot, 1901); Jacob Rader Marcus, *The Jew in the Medieval World: A Source Book*, (Cincinnati: Hebrew Union College Press, 1990, originally published in 1938), pp. 49f; Otto Stobbe, *Die Juden in Deutschland während des Mittelalters* (L. Lamm, 1923), pp. 7, 153–9, 262–5. See also www.jewishvirtuallibrary.org/jsource/judaica/ejud_0002_0015_0_14995.html.

3   For a translation of the text, see Dobozy, Maria and Karras, Ruth Mazo, *The Saxon Mirror: A "Sachsenspiegel" of the Fourteenth Century* (University of Pennsylvania Press, 2014). They use the manuscript in Wolfenbüttel. For a comprehensive study about how the *Sachsenspiegel* operated during the land settlements of the thirteenth century, see Klápste, Jan, *The Czech Lands in Medieval Transformation* (East Central and Eastern Europe in the Middle Ages, 450–1450), trans. Sean Mark Miller and Katerina Millerová (Brill, 2012).

quality of fences, where to build ovens and toilets, how to prevent water run-off, and how to position windows to preserve neighbors' privacy. For Eike von Repgow, good fences made good neighbors. Eike's book promoted rituals around making oaths and keeping promises, but how those promises were sealed shifted over time.

Of the roughly 400 surviving manuscript copies of the *Sachsenspiegel*, only four extant copies, all German, contain fulsome illustrations.[4] These take the form of marginal drawings which are keyed by capital letters to the texts they accompany. In the copy now in Oldenburg, dated 1336, for example, the book opens with images showing the divine origins of law that are described in the rhyming prologue: the Holy Spirit brings the law (represented as a dove clumsily delivering a tome); Christ wields the sword of justice while seated on a rainbow; and God creates Adam, to show that he is the origin of all things on heaven and earth, including law (Fig. 61).[5]

Other illustrations in the early *Sachsenspiegel* manuscripts usefully show the gestures and objects of jurisprudence, including court benches and reliquaries, which are rarely mentioned in the text. Swearing is an essential act for sealing oaths and proving innocence, as the terminology indicates. The term "Unschult" is used in the book to mean "the act of proving one's innocence by means of an oath sworn on a reliquary."[6] Both women and men could take oaths. For example, a woman could take an oath to claim her morning gift (given by the husband to his new bride the morning after their wedding) when she was widowed. The Oldenburg manuscript describes this in the text. Another episode dealing with women and property shows, in the marginal imagery, the widow of a knight returning the military equipment he used until he died. As the text puts it, the equipment comprised "her husband's sword, his best charger or riding horse with saddle, his best coat of mail and tent, and also the field gear, which consists of an army cot, a pillow, linen sheet, tablecloth, two washbasins, and a towel" (Fig. 62).[7] The text

---

4   The four illuminated copies are in Heidelberg (https://digi.ub.uni-heidelberg.de/diglit/cpg164/), Oldenburg (dated 1336, https://digital.lb-oldenburg.de/ssp/nav/classification/137692), Dresden (https://www.loc.gov/item/2021667916), and Wolfenbüttel (https://www.sachsenspiegel-online.de/cms/).

5   Guido Kisch outlines ways in which Eike von Repgow draws upon the Bible in *Sachsenspiegel and Bible* (Publications in Mediaeval Studies, Vol. 5) (The University of Notre Dame Press, 1941).

6   Dobozy, p. 183.

7   I am relying on the translation in Dobozy, p. 77, no. 22.

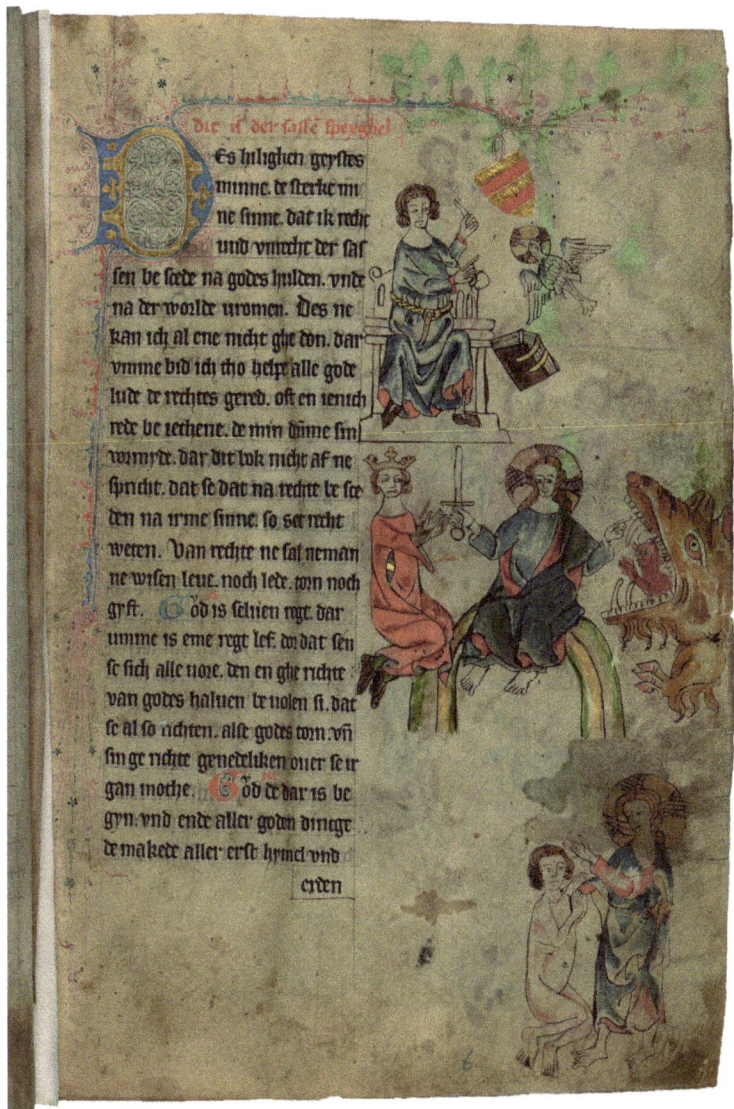

Fig. 61 Opening folio of the *Sachsenspiegel* by Eike von Repgow, copied in 1336, Rastede (Lower Saxony). Oldenburg, Landesbibliothek, Ms. CIM I 410, fol. 6r

goes on to explain that "The wife need not supply the articles she does not have as long as she dares to swear that she does not possess them. This is to be done separately for each and every such item. However, if it can be proven, no man or woman can cleanse himself with an oath."

The thinking in this text is that a widow would not perjure herself for a pillow. The image shows the widow taking this oath by placing her hand on a reliquary, although the reliquary is not mentioned in the text. The illuminator either copied the reliquary from his exemplar or added it because this was the conventional way of swearing oaths at the time.

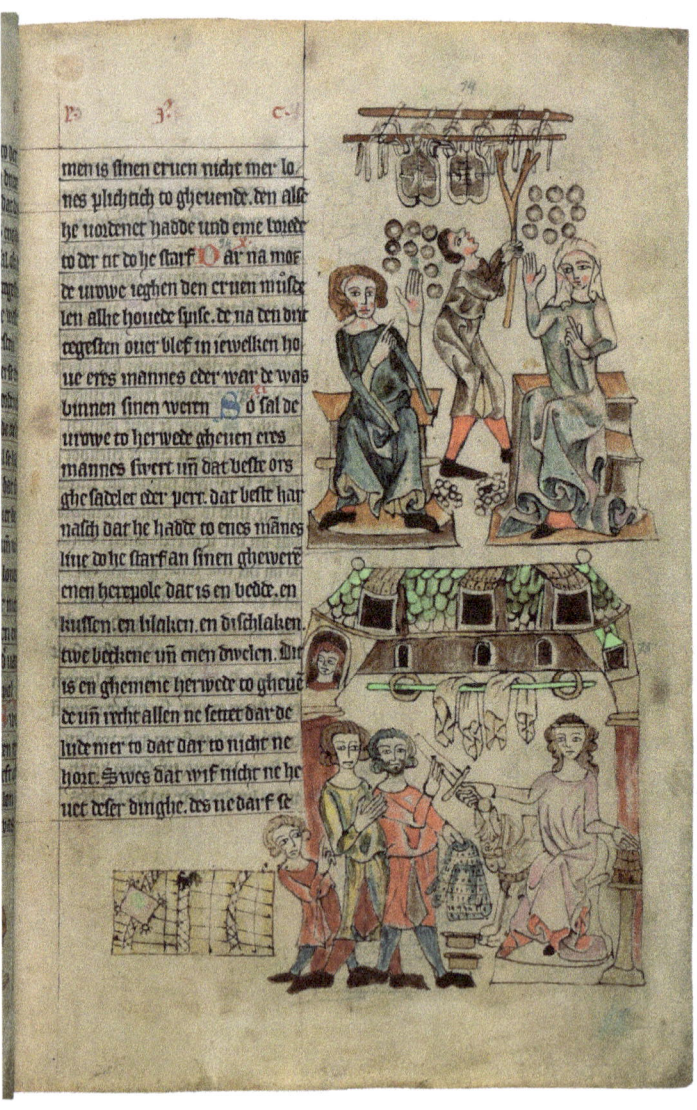

Fig. 62 Folio from the *Sachsenspiegel* by Eike von Repgow, copied in 1336, Rastede (Lower Saxony). Oldenburg, Landesbibliothek, Ms. CIM I 410, fol. 18r.

At least in the idealized world of the images accompanying the four fully illuminated early copies of the *Sachsenspiegel*, figures with oversized hands make elaborate oath-swearing gestures by extending two long fingers toward a golden reliquary. The *Heidelberger Sachsenspiegel* (Heidelberg, University Library, Cod. Pal. Germ. 164), contains numerous scenes showing people gesturing in this way. On fol. 15r, for example, figures in the first, second, and third registers are depicted placing two fingers on a reliquary situated on a pedestal (Fig. 63).[8] This gesture, made with the appropriate prop and uttered with the correct words, means that their respective testimonies will carry weight. These images help to instruct the users of the new legal code on how to put it into practice.

Around 1400, Duke Albert of Bavaria brought the *Sachsenspiegel* with him to his new throne in The Hague, from which he ruled Holland. In a copy still in The Hague, a rhyming prologue explains that this book was translated into Middle Dutch, or dietsch (HKB, Ms. 75 G 47).[9] Scribes in Utrecht, the main center for manuscript production in the Northern Netherlands at that time, copied the text. In this copy, the marginal imagery disappeared, except for two images. The first of these depicts a Last Judgment, the ultimate legal event (Fig. 64). This image appears in the initial at the start of the rhyming prologue, wherein the image of Christ as judge summarizes a judicial system within a Christian context.

The image of the Last Judgment in the Dutch manuscript is severely damaged. Imagining the manuscript in use is easier with my amateur photograph where my fingers provide a human scale (Fig. 65). It has been used ritually and touched with what may be two different gestures. First, the image appears to have been touched with a wet finger, especially around Christ's knee, where the blue paint defining his cloak as been liquefied and rubbed off. Court officials may have touched

---

8   Peter Bell, Joseph Schlecht, and Björn Ommer use machine learning to identify and quantify the instances of oath-swearing on relics within the images in the *Heidelberg Sachsenspiegel* (University Library, MS Cod. Pal. Germ. 164), in "Nonverbal Communication in Medieval Illustrations Revisited by Computer Vision and Art History," *Visual Resources*, 29.1–2 (2013), pp. 26–37.

9   The Hague, KB, 75 G 47: Eike von Repgow, *Saksenspiegel*, made ca. 1405 in Utrecht. 119 folios, parchment, 209x150 (145x96) mm, 2 columns, 28 lines, littera textualis. Henri L.M. Defoer, Anne S. Korteweg, and Wilhelmina C.M. Wüstefeld, *The Golden Age of Dutch Manuscript Painting*. Exh. cat. (The Pierpont Morgan Library, 1989), no. 6.

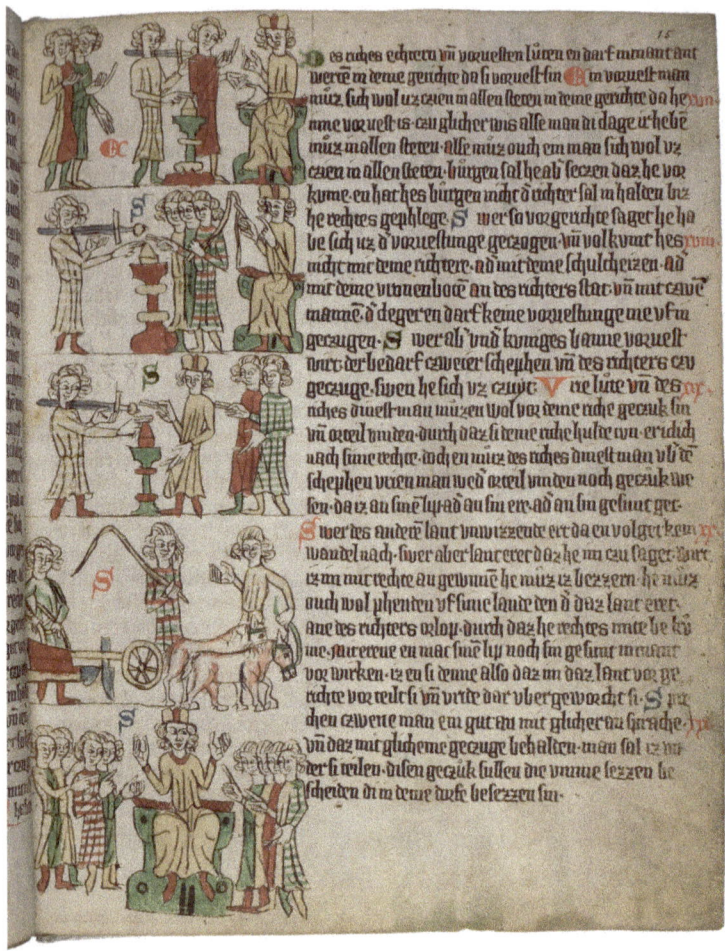

Fig. 63 Folio from the *Sachsenspiegel* by Eike von Repgow, early fourteenth century, central-eastern Germany. Heidelberg, University Library, Cod. Pal. germ. 164, fol. 15r. Reproduced under a CC-BY-SA 4.0 license

this initial when they read the prologue out loud, possibly as a gesture to set the tone in a legal hearing. As with other instances of prolectors touching initials, this oath-swearing gesture may also have attested to the accuracy of the pronouncement of the written words, functioning as a seal of authentication for oral delivery. Such a gesture could also draw the audience's attention to the authority of the book from which the court official was reading.

Fig. 64 Folio from the prologue of the *Sachsenspiegel* by Eike von Repgow, translated into Middle Dutch, with a miniature depicting the Last Judgment, copied ca. 1405, Utrecht. The Hague, Koninklijke Bibliotheek, Ms. 75 G 47, fol. 6r

This explanation also makes sense in the context of the manuscript, since the prologue is written in rhyme, and rhyming texts as a rule are designed to be voiced. In other words, given the rhyming nature of the prologue, it is highly likely that it would have been read aloud in public. One can imagine that a legal official read this aloud before a court

Fig. 65 Amateur photograph showing the opening of the *Sachsenspiegel* by Eike von Repgow, translated into Middle Dutch, with a miniature depicting the Last Judgment, copied ca. 1405, Utrecht. The Hague, Koninklijke Bibliotheek, Ms. 75 G 47, fols 5v-6r.

procedure to prime the audience's acceptance of the law as God-given. Considering the way in which several areas of the image seem to have been wet-touched (three panels of the decorative frame, the orb that symbolizes his rule, and the hem of his blue robe), the official may have made the sign of the cross on the image, tapping it in four places with his finger, while uttering the words "Father, Son, Holy Spirit, Amen." I caution that this interpretation is speculative but note that a more plausible hypothesis is not forthcoming.

A second, more diffuse kind of touching is oriented toward the top of the page. A considerable amount of the pigment from the page—both paint and the ink framing the gold—have been pulled upward into the margin. This pattern of wear is consistent with a scenario in which an official proffered the book to people who reached in to touch the image, perhaps to swear an oath, and then pulled the hand out of the book, dragging some of the pigment with it. This exchange meant that the person touching the image would encounter the page upside-down, without reading the text. It is possible that when the *Sachsenspiegel* was copied and lost most of its images, the gestures around touching relics were also lost. Although the gesture appears numerous times in the imagery of the four manuscripts mentioned above, swearing on reliquaries does not figure much in the text. It is possible that in Holland, plaintiffs and those trying to prove their innocence swore on books—including this very legal manuscript—rather than on reliquaries. The use-wear evidence in the later copy made in The Netherlands suggests a shift from using relics as oath-swearing props to using the book itself for that purpose.

Other legal manuscripts similarly borrowed Last Judgment iconography, such as a *Promptuarium iuris* ("Repository of Law") now in Graz (Fig. 66).[10] The manuscript was written in two volumes, probably in Seckau. Its singular image, at the beginning of the first volume, shows Christ as *Salvator Mundi* seated atop a double rainbow with swords emanating from his mouth, symbolizing the justice he metes out. Christ overshadows two groups of men, the representatives of the spiritual realm under his right hand (the pope and three cardinals) and representatives of the worldly realm under his left (the emperor and magistrates). Ulrich IV von Albeck (d. 1431) was Bishop of Seckau from 1417 until his death. He both authored and commissioned the volumes.[11] In the image he kneels directly under Christ, offering the book to the pope. Pope Eugenius IV had wanted to appoint Ulrich cardinal, but Ulricht died on 12 December 1431 on his way to Rome. His intestines were buried in the cathedral in Padua, and the rest of his body was returned to the cathedral in Seckau.

As an aspirant to the spiritual administration, Ulrich IV not only wrote this book, but apparently used it, as well. Ulrich IV began composing the book in 1408 when he was working in the church at Mainz. The book consists of a summary of legal concepts from writers such as Gratian, organized by lemmata in alphabetical order. Ulrich's signature copy does not survive, and it only survives in the fair copy

---

10 For a description, bibliography, and images, see https://unipub.uni-graz.at/obvugrscript/content/titleinfo/5951855.

11 It has been studied by Ivo Pfaff, "Das *Promptuarium juris* des Reichskanzlers und Bischofs Ulrich von Albeck," *Zeitschrift der Savigny-Stiftung fur Rechtsgeschichte. Romanistische Abteilung* (1921), 42, pp. 158–75.

Fig. 66 Opening and dedicatory image of Ulrich IV von Albeck's *Promptuarium iuris*, copied and illuminated in 1429. Graz, University Library, Ms 23, vol. 1, fol. 1r

now in two volumes in Graz. The first volume was copied by Marci Kaiichstain Pruteni de Osterrad from Pomerania and finised on 20 April 1429, and the second volume by Georius Salsator of Glatz and finished on 30 August 1429. Ulrich apparently split his book into two volumes and had two scribes work on it so that it would be finished faster. As Ivo Pfaff has pointed out, Ulricht apparently added several entries to the margins of the manuscript after the volumes were completed. Ulrich may have also touched the frontispiece in specific ways. The abrasion is faint, however, because he was only alive for a year and a half after the volumes were complete. The open book that Ulrich offers the pope in the image is darkened, and the figure of Ulrich has been smudged. The pope's chest, too, seems slightly abraded. Is it possible that Ulrich enacted the dedication of his book to the pope over and over during the months before his trip to Rome to become a cardinal?

Other kinds of official books borrowed Last Judgment iconography to reinforce a sense of duty and obligation. For example, the testament of ecclesiastical stewards (register of dismeesters) for the Church of St Salvator in Bruges opens with an image of Christ in Judgment, surrounded by the four evangelists' symbols (Fig. 67).[12] The incipit announces: "The following is the schedule of who is responsible to fulfill the role of steward, to clothe and serve in the Church of St Salvator in Bruges, beginning with the Mass of St Jan in the summer, and finishing at year's end." Written in 1457, the text is furnished with headings for each day of the half-year, which the Master Steward would fill in. Having one's name inscribed into one of the spaces, underneath the eye of Christ the Judge and the Evangelists, would impress the severity of one's obligation to ensure that the Mass would be properly resourced on one's chosen day, annually from 1457 onward. This manuscript is the inverse of a necrology, which also consists of an empty calendar designed to be filled in with the names of the dead on their death dates. For a necrology, the church is responsible for serving the congregants annually on their death dates; for the register of dismeesters, the congregants are responsible for serving the church annually on their appointed day. The

---

12   Bruges, Kathedraal Sint-Salvator, no signature, fol. 1r: Dit daervolghende es de ordonnancie hoemen de disschen sculdich es te cleedene ende te stellene in sinte Salvatoors kerke in Brugghe. Beghinnende telken Sinte Iansmesse middle somers. Ende de lasten vanden jaerghetiden. Ende voort alle andre lasten. Daer inne dat de voorseiden disch verbonden state. Te wat daghen datmense sculdich es van doene. Ende was desen bouc gheordoneert ende ghemaect bij Janne [..]erke. Jan de Fevere ende Jan de bliec[?] als dischmeesters vanden dische voorseit. Ende Jan de [Ra?]m Lauwereins zone, als [?]nttan[?]ghere vanden zelven dissche. Int jaer onse herren als ic screef dusentich viere hondert zeven ende vichtich upten twintschsten dach van laumaendt (my transcription).

image is slightly damaged, as if some of the volunteers had sealed their obligations by touching it with a wet finger.

Fig. 67 Opening folio of the register for the *dismeesters* (stewards) of the Cathedral of Sint-Salvator, Bruges, 1457, Bruges. © KIK-IRPA, Brussels (Belgium), cliché z011761

II. Local Government: Customary Law Books

A smoothly running civic and ecclesiastical order relied on parties swearing to binding terms by sealing them with rituals. However, in an era when church constantly seeped into state, oaths for earthly rulers and for more run-of-the mill testimonies borrowed elements from religious rituals. Books of civic rituals often contain Gospel passages and images closely related to those designed for missals, because Mass formed the central ritual of the culture, from which other rituals drew upon and adapted. Such images seem to have been implicated in overt, public bodily gestures that, like the ritual of the Canon of the Mass, depended on making physical contact with the image, even at the cost of destroying the image piecemeal.

In the fourteenth century, cities increasingly adopted separate, secularized legal codes, but the ceremonies nonetheless borrowed from older gestural traditions and therefore included images on which to swear. Separate legal codes also corresponded to the formation of new types of building—court houses and city halls—in which acts of jurisprudence took place, instead of being practiced in churches or under church portals. The books and the corresponding architecture marked the beginning of secular law distinctive from ecclesiastic or canon law, although it is not helpful to distinguish too sharply between sacred and secular. In Germanic lands, the new books were largely versions of the *Sachsenspiegel*, and in French-speaking lands, versions of coutumes or coutumiers (custom books). Written in the vernacular, they contained laws and legal examples, organized by theme.[13] They became the basis of legal rights and obligations, and marked a turn away from despotism and toward universal justice. Whereas previously, justice had been meted out in churches, sometimes under an image depicting Christ's Last Judgment, in the late Middle Ages, justice increasingly came to be practiced in separate courthouses, although these, too, sometimes brandished images of the Last Judgment or scenes of judgment drawn from antiquity.[14] Their architectural settings, either a town hall or a church

---

13 A regional example from the northern Netherlands is discussed in Remi van Schaïk, with assistance from Jildou Bijlstra, "Het Groninger Stadboek gebonden en verlucht," *Historisch Jaarboek Groningen* (2017) pp. 6–27.

14 Hans J. van Miegroet, "Gerard David's 'Justice of Cambyses': Exemplum Iustitiae or Political Allegory?," *Simiolus: Netherlands Quarterly for the History of Art*, 18.3

portal, imply a public audience for the book-centered ceremonies. The size of the space provides a clue as to the size of the audience, but in any setting, the gestures involving quite large books would have the effect of amplifying the gestures and their visibility to the gathered audience.

Coutumiers

In the thirteenth century, French towns began to collect their legal codes and write them into coutumiers.[15] These included prescriptive laws and oaths to swear. Several of these books survive and one early example, which dates from the thirteenth or early fourteenth century (Agen, Archives départementales de Lot-et-Garonne, Ms. 42), contains the customary laws practiced in the southern French town of Agen, with frequent references to how to use this very book. Although several close copies of the manuscript survive, only the Agen exemplar is illustrated, with historiated initials that mostly depict occupations, and with column-wide miniatures of men and women undergoing judicial procedures and legal ceremonies.[16] These differ altogether from the images in the *Sachsenspiegel*. For example, one miniature introducing a text about adultery shows the punishment of an adulterous couple: they are tied together and led through the streets behind a parade of trumpeters (Fol. 39v). Ron Akehurst has discussed the Agen manuscript and analyzed its imagery from the perspective of a social historian, offering a basic

---

(1988), 116–33. https://doi.org/10.2307/3780674; Hugo van der Velden, "Cambyses for Example: The Origins and Function of an Exemplum Iustitiae in Netherlandish Art of the Fifteenth, Sixteenth and Seventeenth Centuries, *Simiolus: Netherlands Quarterly for the History of Art*, 23.1 (1995), 5–62. https://doi.org/10.2307/3780781.

15   Agen, Archives Départementales de Lot-et-Garonne, Ms. 42. See Alison Stones and François Avril, *Gothic Manuscripts, 1260–1320: Part Two*, 2 vols. (Harvey Miller Publishers, 2014), Vol. 1, pp. 261–75 for a full description and bibliography; pp. 191, 243–46, 254–56 for comparanda. Maïté Billoré and Esther Dehoux, "The Judge and the Martyr: Images of Power and Justice in Religious Manuscripts from the Twelfth to the Fifteenth Centuries," in *Textual and Visual Representations of Power and Justice in Medieval France: Manuscripts and Early Printed Books*, edited by Rosalind Brown-Grant, Anne D. Hedeman, and Bernard Ribémont (Ashgate, 2015), pp. 171–90 analyze images of judgment in *coutumiers*. See also Esther Cohen, *The Crossroads of Justice: Law and Culture in Late Medieval France* (E.J. Brill, 1993).

16   The text has been edited: Amédée Moullié, "Coutumes Priviléges et Franchises de la Ville d'Agen," *Recueil des travaux de la société d'agriculture, sciences et arts d'Agen* (1850), 5, pp. 237–343. The source text for this edition was a manuscript in roll form, which has been lost or destroyed.

description of the vignettes and remarking on issues of class, gender, and clothing, but not on the physical use of the book.[17]

Four of the miniatures in the Agen coutumier show people taking oaths on a book. The first of these intra-textual miniatures depicts a swearing ceremony, at which a lord, seated before a standing crowd, places his hands on a book (Fig. 68). According to the text, first the lord swears on the Gospels to the citizens, then the citizens swear to the lord. Such oaths of allegiance, which draw upon lord-vassal oaths discussed earlier, formed part of the social glue in late medieval France.

One of the other miniatures in Agen Ms. 42 depicts someone swearing on a book in the presence of council members (Fol. 40v). This relates to the next miniature, which shows a lawsuit taking place before the council, therefore suggesting that swearing such an oath was a prerequisite to giving testimony. A chapter dedicated to the subject of newcomers reiterates the iconography of touching the book: it shows a recent arrival swearing his allegiance to Agen (fol. 53v; Fig. 69). These figures are therefore demonstrating a physical context for a coutumier, or at least for one containing the Gospels. Although it is dangerous to treat medieval miniatures—which are stylized, selective, based on models, and designed in part to enhance the texts they accompany—as documentary evidence for medieval reality, in this case other evidence confirms that judicial books were indeed used in ceremonies such as those pictured. The entire book is designed to demonstrate, through words and images, how justice should be practiced.

Patterns of wear near the beginning of the manuscript reveal that many people used the Agen manuscript to swear oaths. First, it contains the incipits of the four books of the Gospels, each introduced by a historiated initial (Fig. 70). These clearly refer to the Gospel books discussed earlier, which were an essential element in oath-swearing in the early Middle Ages. Old conventions, such as including evangelists'

---

17 F.R.P. Akehurst, "Illustration and Decoration in Agen Archives Départementales de Lot-et-Garonne 42," in *"Li Premerains Vers": Essays in Honor of Keith Busby* (Faux Titre), edited by Catherine M. Jones and Logan E. Whalen (Rodopi, 2011), pp. 1–11. Images of all folios of this manuscript are available online: http://www.cg47.org/archives/coups-de-coeur/Tresors/tresors-archives.htm. It has been refoliated since Akehurst's article and also since the photos were taken. The new foliation in pencil is rational and supersedes the various foliations in Roman and Arabic numerals. Akehurst's foliation = the current pencil foliation + 3. Therefore, the adulterous couple appear on what is now fol. 39v, which corresponds to Akehurst's fol. 42v.

Fig. 68 Swearing ceremony, with a lord seated before standing crowd. From the *Livre des statuts et coutumes de la ville d'Agen*, ca. 1300. Agen Archives départementales de Lot-et-Garonne, Ms. 42, fol. 14v.

portraits and texts from the Gospels, lent authority to the legal book and created a bond with tradition. Although their presence may have helped to give credence to the new vernacular legal code in the body

5. Swearing: From Gospels to Legal Manuscripts 141

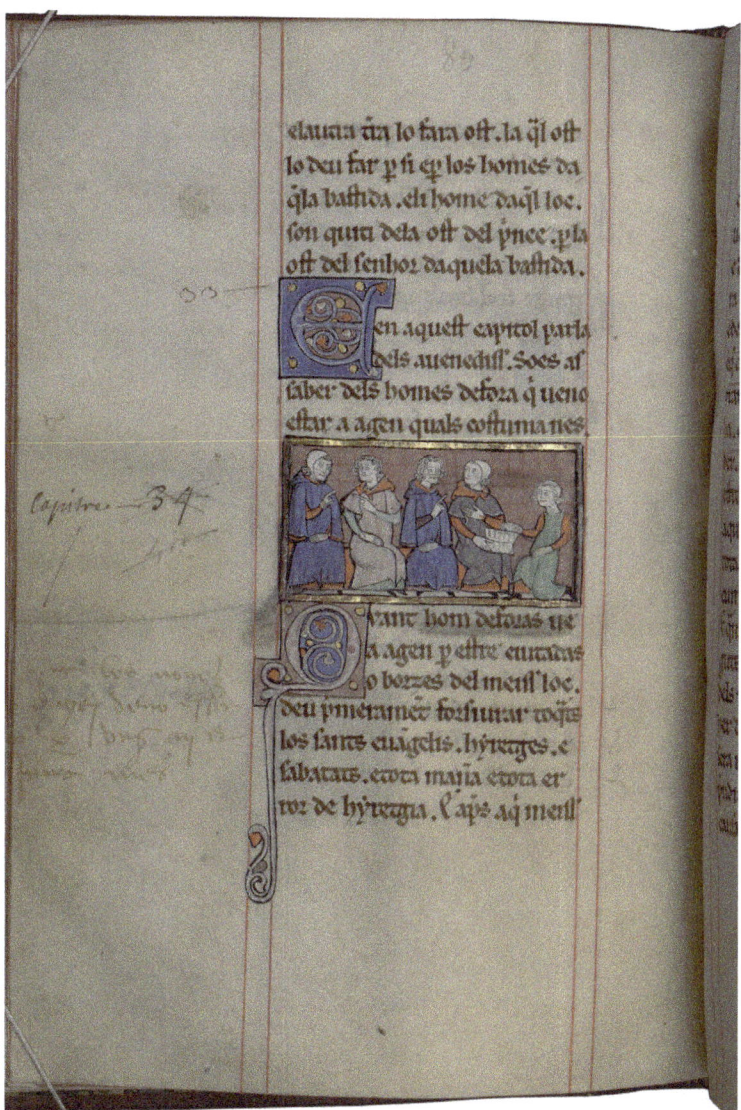

Fig. 69 Newcomer swearing on a book. From the *Livre des statuts et coutumes de la ville d'Agen*, ca. 1300. Agen Archives départementales de Lot-et-Garonne, Ms. 42, fol. 53v.

of the book, the Evangelists' pages were clearly not used extensively, as their still-clean state attests.

142 Touching Parchment

Fig. 70 Incipit of the Gospel of John. From the *Livre des statuts et coutumes de la ville d'Agen*, ca. 1300. Agen Archives départementales de Lot-et-Garonne, Ms. 42, fol. 10r.

Users of this coutumier swore their oaths not on the Evangelist portraits but on a much larger target—an enormous two-page spread which prefaces the Gospel readings (Fig. 71). The full-page images were painted on a separate bifolium. These images are now so thoroughly worn that they are difficult to make out, but scrutiny reveals, on the left side of the gutter, an image of the Throne of Mercy in a mandorla, flanked by Mary, John, and angels, with the Evangelists' symbols in the corners. On the right side, the Virgin in blue, her crowned head in front of a mandorla, holds the Christ Child, flanked by two angels. She appears between two narrow towers, possibly suggesting that she is the Portal of Paradise, one of her guises.

Fig. 71 Opening bifolio, with the Throne of Mercy in a Mandorla with the Evangelists' Symbols, and the Virgin and Child Flanked by Angels, full-page miniatures in the *Livre des statuts et coutumes de la ville d'Agen*, ca. 1300. Agen Archives départementales de Lot-et-Garonne, Ms. 42, fols 7v-8r.

Vigorous wear affirms how the book was used ceremonially: the officials who controlled the book obviously used these full-page images for swearing oaths rather than the smaller Evangelist portraits elsewhere in the manuscript. One explanation is that the two-page spread includes the imagery of the Evangelists (their symbols in the corners of the verso), of God in Majesty, of the Passion (with the Christ Crucified that God holds), of the Queen of Heaven, and the mystery of the Incarnation (on the recto). These images therefore united the most powerful symbols of love and nurturing alongside those of suffering and judgment.

Many clues on the bifolium (fols 7–8) reveal ways in which it was handled. It has been glued onto another piece of parchment for reinforcement. This was undoubtedly necessary because of the frequent hard wear that the bifolium received, akin to that in the Clermont Missal, discussed above, whose oath-swearing folios had fallen into tatters. So abused was it that dirt and wear have caused the sheets to crack. Both the top and the bottom of the page are worn and shiny, as an effect of offering the book toward the oath-swearer. Either the officiant held the top, so that the image would be oriented toward the recipient, or he held the bottom, so that the recipient touched the image upside down. The grasping pattern is therefore like that in the Clermont Missal. Oath-swearers then deliberately touched the face of God, or the body of Christ, or the face of the Virgin or any of the angels around them, both recto and verso. The Child and the area to his right have been rubbed down to the parchment. Most of the gilding on his halo, and on the decoration in the tree, has worn off. The diffuse but frequent way in which this image was touched is consistent with many people touching it once with a dry hand. Given this use-wear, it appears that the judge held out the book to be touched: in fact, several of the ceremonies depicted in the manuscript, as discussed earlier, confirm that it was handled in this way.

Rood Privilegeboek

After ca. 1300 many cities wrote customs books, not only in France but throughout Europe. Only a few of these survive, perhaps because they were housed in civic buildings rather than libraries, and therefore did not follow the established routes for groups of manuscripts that were later swept into national libraries for preservation. The customs book in 's-Hertogenbosch is still in the place for which it was written.[18] Written

---

18 As of 2004, the red book of 's-Hertogenbosch is on long-term loan from the city archives to Het Noordbrabants Museum. A digital facsimile is availble: https://zoeken.erfgoedshertogenbosch.nl/detail.php?id=748605440. The city has notable local pride and maintains a website, *Bossche Encyclopedie*, that collects information about the city's history, written by amateur and professional historians. For the item under discussion, see Valentijn Paquay, "Het Rood Privilegeboek (1): Kroonjuweel van de stad," and "Het Rood Privilegeboek (2): Kroonjuweel van de stad," *Bossche Bladen* (n.p. [2009]), pp. 84–89 and 117–22, reproduced in *Bossche Encyclopedie*, edited by A.F.A.M. (Ton) Wetzer, https://www.bossche-encyclopedie.nl/. See also Hanno Wijsman, "Een eed zweren op een miniatuur," *Handschriften*

in various campaigns from ca. 1430 until the late sixteenth century, the manuscript received its current red binding stamped with the date 1580 (Fig. 72). At the center of the front cover, a medallion brandishes the arms of Philip II, King of Hapsburg Spain (r. 1556–1598), below a titular label behind protective horn, which indicates "Dit privilegieboeck genoemt het roode previlegieboeck, inder cameren der Heren Scepenen van Tshertogenbossche berusten" (This privilege book called the "Red Privilege Book" is kept in the chambers of the Lord Aldermen of 's-Hertogenbosch).[19] Ceremonies that involved this manuscript were conducted in that room. A chain connected the book to a lectern there, as a hole at the top of the binding testifies. Metal settings in the front cover, now empty, once held jewels that would have made the book's ceremonial gravitas visible even from a distance, like that of a ceremonial Gospel manuscript in a jeweled binding.

The manuscript contains copies of charters and other texts, plus some images, discussed below. Charters are formally recognized legal acts and privileges. Those for 's-Hertogenbosch were granted by successive dukes of Brabant, beginning in 1191 with the foundation of the city. Fols 1–99 were written in one hand on parchment and were copied to consolidate all the various charters pertaining to 's-Hertogenbosch through 1427. These texts were probably copied shortly after 1430, when Philip of Saint-Pol, the last Duke of Brabant, died. The Burgundian dukes who replaced him, beginning with Philip the Good, ruled from Brussels and tried to impose new regulations and taxes. The citizens of 's-Hertogenbosch reacted by copying their founding documents and charters to try to revert to the agreements made by the previous, less oppressive government.

Fols 100–21, also on parchment, were added in the fifteenth century by a different hand, and fols 122–204, on smaller paper quires, were added piecemeal until ca. 1560. Of the privileges copied into the manuscript, 84 of them appear in their original versions elsewhere in the archive, and 63 survive only as copies in the Rood Privilegeboek. The privileges

---

voor het hertogdom. De mooiste verluchte manuscripten van Brabantse hertogen, edellieden, kloosterlingen en stedelingen (Veerhuis, 2006), pp. 146–51 nr. 20.

19 Other cities' analogous books were likewise bound in red and called "red books," for example, the Rotes Stadtbuch Hamburg from 1301–1306 (Staatsarchiv der Freien und Hansestadt Hamburg, Senat CI VII Lit. LaNr. 2 Vol. 1b), whose images appear online at https://drw-www.adw.uni-heidelberg.de/hdhs/objekte/2268k.htm#2334.

Fig. 72 Front cover dated 1580, Roodt Privilegieboeck. 's-Hertogenbosch, Stadsarchief, oudarchief inv. nr A 525.

range in scale from the local (an agreement in 1485 by Simon van Gheel, the owner of watermills outside Rosmalen, to maintain the bridge by the watermills, fol. 208v) to the inter-regional (a peace agreement in 1390 between William, Duke of Gelderland and Johanna, Duchess of Luxembourg, fol. 73v).[20] Technically, the manuscript is a cartulary,

---

20 The charters and privileges in Den Bosch are summarized in order of date by the former archivist of 's-Hertogenbosch, J.N.G. Sassen, in *Charters en privilegiebrieven, berustende in het archief der gemeente 's Hertogenbosch* (Stadsarchief 's-Hertogenbosch,

since it contains transcriptions of privileges and laws, but its function is broader than most cartularies because the volume itself represented legal authority and served as a prop in ceremonies.

The Rood Privilegeboek draws upon structures for establishing authority from both the missal and the Gospel. It opens with the "In Principio" text, which may have been added as an afterthought onto the otherwise blank page prefacing the colorful opening (Fig. 73). Perhaps its placement at the beginning of the manuscript helps to authenticate the rest of the contents of the book. Like the Agen and other related manuscripts, it has one large miniature for swearing, in this case, a full-page crucifixion (Fig. 74).[21] The image, with its diaper background, resembles in style and execution a Canon plate in a missal made ca. 1425–1450 in Utrecht (Fig. 75).[22] The Crucifixion in the Rood Privilegeboek likewise dates to this period and was probably inserted into the manuscript in the 1430s when the first group of charters was copied. In other words, it forms part of the apparatus for establishing the authority of the city's pre-1430 laws and privileges.

Two questions about the Crucifixion page need to be addressed: What was its original placement, given that the book was put together over several centuries, and what does the pattern of damage say about how the book functioned? The leaf with the Crucifixion is a singleton that was not expressly made for this manuscript: it is too large, and it had to be trimmed slightly to fit the book block. Was this sheet taken out of another manuscript, a missal, and swept up in the rebinding of 1580? No. The pattern of wear it has incurred differs significantly from that of a missal, such as those discussed in the previous chapter. Specifically, there is no sign of facial oil or saliva within the severely damaged leaf.

1862); he discusses the Rood Privilegeboek and keys its contents to the original charters on pp. 173–83. The full text appears online https://catalog.hathitrust.org/Record/011557104. The manuscript itself is digitized: https://zoeken.erfgoedshertogenbosch.nl/detail.php?id=748605440. I thank Lianne van Beek, Senior archivist, Erfgoed 's-Hertogenbosch, and Marlisa den Hartog, curator at Het Noordbrabants Museum, for assistance with this item.

21 I have nuanced my ideas about this manuscript since I first published it in Rudy, *Postcards on Parchment*, pp. 288–90; Jos Koldeweij, "Gezworen op het kruis of op relieken," in *Representatie. Kunsthistorische bijdragen over vorst, staatsmacht en beeldende kunst, opgedragen aan Robert W. Scheller*, edited by Johann-Christian Klamt and Kees Veelenturf (Valkhof Pers, 2004), pp. 158–79.

22 The Utrecht Missal is now in the treasury of the Sint-Salvatorskathedraal in Bruges and may have been commissioned for that church. For a description of this manuscript, bibliography, and images, see http://balat.kikirpa.be/object/144774

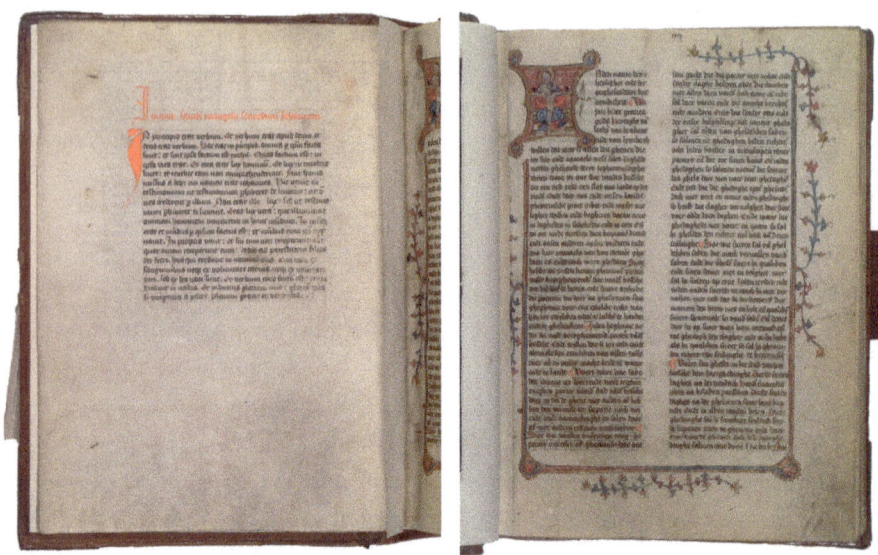

Fig. 73 Opening in the Roodt Privilegieboeck, with the beginning of the Book of John, and the beginning of the charter. 's-Hertogenbosch, Stadsarchief, oudarchief inv. nr A 525, fols iii (verso) – iiii (recto).

Fig. 74 Full-page miniature depicting Christ crucified between Mary and John bound into the book of civic statutes for the city of 's-Hertogenbosch, called the Roodt Privilegieboeck, ca. 1430. 's-Hertogenbosch, Stadsarchief, oudarchief inv. nr A 525, fols 55v-56r

5. Swearing: From Gospels to Legal Manuscripts 149

Fig. 75 Opening of a missal at the Canon, made in Utrecht and exported to Bruges. Bruges, Sint-Salvatorkathedraal, treasury. © KIK-IRPA, Brussels (Belgium), cliché Z011681

Given the parchment size difference, and the fact that it was obviously made in a different campaign of work, can one say that the Crucifixion folio was added later? Studying the previous opening provides the answer (Fig. 76). The leaf with the Crucifixion forms part of the original material, which was present when the manuscript was first inscribed. This is apparent because the back of the Crucifixion leaf is inscribed in the original hand. This means that the Crucifixion was planned, from the manuscript's inception, in its current location.

Nevertheless, I suggest that the aldermen who made the Rood Privilegeboek instead purchased a ready-made parchment sheet with the Crucifixion, of the sort made to be inserted into missals. Since the Crucifixion was usually the only image in a missal, they were typically made separately elsewhere and integrated into the book block at the time of binding. These loose Crucifixion sheets found other homes and purposes, and one was purchased, possibly from a painter in Utrecht, to form part of the Rood Privilegeboek.

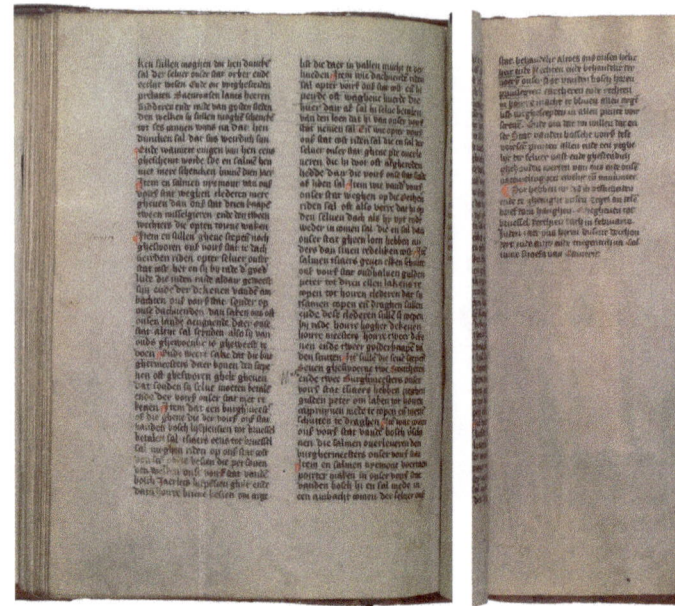

Fig. 76 Roodt Privilegieboeck,'s-Hertogenbosch, Stadsarchief, oudarchief inv. nr A 525, fols LX verso– LX bis recto

The Crucifixion image and its parchment substrate have undergone severe abrasion resulting from a particular pattern of dry-handling. The image has been touched vigorously and by many people, who each reached for a slightly different place on the image. Valentijn Paquay has shown that the members of the city government of 's-Hertogenbosch used this manuscript to swear their oaths of office, doing so from its location chained to a lectern in the town hall. The seven aldermen each served only a one-year term, and therefore the entire college of aldermen changed annually. This event took place on 1 October. As they took their respective oaths, they placed their hands on the Canon plate in the manuscript.

Jos Koldeweij suggests that the little cross at the bottom of the folio in the Rood Privilegeboek "was intended to spare the miniature: the user of the manuscript must lay his hand on it and not on the costly ... image of the Crucifixion."[23] This may be the case (and an analogous example

---

23 Koldeweij, "Gezworen op het kruis," p. 161.

containing statutes and regulations of the Chapter of St Servatius in Maastricht, discussed in Volume 2, likewise has a cruciform touching target). However, there is another possible explanation: as suggested earlier, illuminators manufactured such images on spec for missals. With that destination in mind, the illuminators included such crosses as osculation targets. When this folio was purchased for the Rood Privilegeboek rather than for a missal, the function of the little cross fell away. In other words, the scribe of the Rood Privilegeboek selected the Crucifixion image because it was clearly recognizable as one that activated the most dramatic moment of the Mass, but in the Rood Privilegeboek and the ceremonies in which it was used, the supernatural presence and gravitas of transubstantiation were re-deployed in a new setting. The new rituals, however, did not involve kissing.

Building on these observations, I note that the left margin is severely discolored because pigment has been pulled from the center of the image into the left boundary. This pattern suggests a scenario: when used for oath-swearing rituals, the manuscript lay open, while both an officiant and the alderman swearing the oath stood around the open book. Each alderman stood to the left of the manuscript and placed his hand on the image. The official stood at the bottom of the book, so that the text was oriented toward him. After the oath was recited, the alderman retracted his hand, leaving a leftward smear in its wake.

In addition to its role for swearing in aldermen, the manuscript may have also played a part in another ritual, involving the dukes and duchesses who ruled Brabant. Johanna of Brabant and her husband Wenceslaus of Luxembourg ratified the land charter of Brabant in 1356, and this formed the basis for law until 1792 for the Southern Netherlands. Johanna executed this during her "Blijde Inkomste" (or joyous entry) into the city in 1356, and successive rulers swore an oath to uphold this document during their respective joyous entries into the four major cities of Brabant: Antwerp, Brussels, Leuven, and 's-Hertogenbosch. (Leuven still has a street in the middle of town called Blijde-Inkomstestraat along which the rulers would have paraded into town.) In addition to Johanna, rulers who staged joyous entries into Brabantine cities include: Jan IV (in 1415), Philip of Saint-Pol (in 1427), Philip the Good (in 1430), Charles the Bold (in 1467), Mary of Burgundy (in 1477), Philip the Handsome (in 1482), and Charles V (in 1506). Scholars, however, disagree whether they all conducted joyous entries into 's-Hertogenbosch, but according to Jos Koldeweij, they did so, and for those entries that took place after 1430, the respective rulers swore their oaths on the Rood Privilegeboek.[24] Many of the added pages in the manuscript even contain notes and details about the joyous entries, which further place the manuscript in the ambit of these formal events.

As Valentijn Paquay points out, however, the *ordo* indicates that rulers should swear on a Gospel manuscript, not on the Rood Privilegeboek.[25] I would point out, however, the scribe has copied the incipit of the Book of John, *In principio erat verbum*, perhaps so that the volume could take on the role of a Gospel manuscript in oath-taking ceremonies. The Crucifixion image faces fol. 56r, which contains the incipit of the Book of John. This biblical text accompanies numerous oaths and oath-swearing plates, including the one from Agen discussed above. The text that immediately follows the beginning of John is also telling. It is a copy of the very land charter issued by Johanna in 1383, which includes a section about the rights of people who move into one of the cities of Brabant. In other words, the small amount of text from John transforms the manuscript into a "Gospel," at least for this ceremonial purpose, while the presence of the land charter further lends the manuscript and its attendant ceremonies legitimacy.

In short, the Rood Privilegeboek strategically incorporates elements from the Gospel (John), the missal (Crucifixion), and civic law (foundational document). In fact, the manuscript has a second copy of John's Gospel text near the beginning of the manuscript on fol. 3r. Although it is unusual to include the same text twice, it is in fact common to see John's Gospel copied into all kinds of manuscripts that serve as witnesses. In short, the Crucifixion image fulfils a role like the full-page images in the Agen manuscript, which also prefaces a Gospel text before the legal texts begin. In the Rood Privilegeboek, this initial Gospel text and Crucifixion miniature draw on the power of Gospel manuscripts and missals, respectively, to witness the laws in what is ostensibly a civic, non-liturgical book.

---

24 Jos Koldeweij, "'Vanden eedt op het heylige evangelie'. Het 'Roode Previlegie-boek' en de Blijde Inkomste," *Bossche Bladen*, 6 (2004), pp. 16–22. Valentijn Paquay, "Het Rood Privilegeboek," (2009) states that several of the joyous entries did not take place, but he does not cite his evidence.

25 Valentijn Paquay, "Het Rood Privilegeboek," (2009).

Given the streaky pattern of wear on the outer margin of the Crucifixion, I propose that the oath-swearer enclosed his hand in the book while the relevant texts, copied elsewhere in the book, were being pronounced aloud by an official. If this hypothesis is correct, then the hand position may refer to another symbolic aspect of vassalage: the vassal signaled his willingness to be subject to a lord by having his hands enclosed within the lord's hands. This gesture is intimate, in that it involves touching, and it also reiterates a symbolic hierarchy, in which the lord's hands on the outside signal his protection of the vassal, and the vassal, with his hands on the inside of the clasp, signals his submission. In the case of the Rood Privilegeboek, the book represents authority, while the swearer demonstrates his acquiescence. The book closes onto the "vassal's" hand, as if the book itself were the hands of the overlord.

Other medieval cities likewise produced and used books of privileges which combined aspects of the cartulary—that is, a recopied summa of all charters, laws, and privileges for a given place. To recopy the loose sheets and assemble them into one codex would give them a heft and authority appropriate to their new ceremonial role. Many of the resulting volumes are bound in red and referred to as "red books." For example, the Rotes Stadtbuch of Hamburg from 1301 is in a bright red leather binding that not only clasps shut but has a tiny keyhole to prevent malfeasance.[26] Before the table of contents, this manuscript brandishes a full-page miniature depicting Christ the Judge, standing on a rainbow, prevailing over men from different social stations. An angel unlocks the portal to paradise for the virtuous, while devils pull sinners into the maw of hell. The image seems like an intermedial translation of a church portal, wherein the carved Last Judgment presided over public terrestrial judgement below. This image, however, has not been repeatedly and systematically touched. As with all of the examples discussed in this chapter and the next one, local tradition dictated how ceremonial books would function.

---

26 Hamburg, Staatsarchiv, 111–1 Senat CI. VII Lit. La Nr. 2 Vol. 1b. Images and a description appear at https://diglib.hab.de/wdb.php?dir=mss/ed000059&distype=thumbs.

The city of Cologne likewise produced a book of oaths in 1398 (an Eidbuch).[27] Like the Rood Privilegeboek of 's-Hertogenbosch, this one also has a full-page Crucifixion of the sort normally made for missals. This Canon plate is encircled by the symbols of the four evangelists, and two coats of arms. The image is not damaged, however, demonstrating that the ritual surrounding the manuscript did not involve laying hands on this image.

Use-wear analysis suggests that the ceremonial use of such legal and privilege books must have been highly localized, with specific rituals building around individual volumes. Each has a different pattern. For example, the Rotes Privilegienbuch der Stadt Regensburg contains the privileges granted to the city of Regensburg from the twelfth century until the time of copying in the fifteenth.[28] Like other privilege books, this one is bound in red leather, hence its title. This manuscript is embellished with portraits of the rulers who had granted the privileges, with each portrait heading up a section of the book, performing the function of something between an author portrait and an official bust that confers value on a coin. Despite the presence of images throughout the manuscript, including a full-page Crucifixion overshadowing the kneeling pope and emperor, there is no abrasion to suggest its ceremonial use for oath swearing. How such manuscripts were handled, it would seem, depended on local tradition.

III. The University: Old Proctors' Book

The Old Proctors' Book of Cambridge (*Statuta universitatis Cantabrigiensis*) was made after 16 June 1381, when an angry mob burned the archives of Cambridge in a bonfire (Cambridge, University Archives, Collect. Admin. 3).[29] As Nicholas Rogers has astutely pointed out, this event

---

27 The *Eidbuch* of Cologne is described in *In Name der Freiheit 1288–1988*, Keulen 1988, 344, cat.nr 3.11.

28 Munich, Bayerisches Hauptstaatsarchiv, BayHStA, Reichsstadt Regensburg Amtsbücher und Akten 6. The manuscript is described and fully digitized at https://bavarikon.de/object/bav:GDA-OBJ-00000BAV80043782.

29 For a description, see Paul Binski, P. N. R. Zutshi, and Stella Panayotova, *Western Illuminated Manuscripts: A Catalogue of the Collection in Cambridge University Library* (Cambridge University Press, 2011), Cat. 185, pp. 175–76, which is superseded by the online record provided by Jacqueline Cox, Keeper of the University Archives, where the manuscript is digitized: http://cudl.lib.cam.ac.uk/view/

catalyzed the production of new copies of the burned books, including this book of statutes. A patent letter of Richard II dated 12 December 1384 in the original hand provides an approximate date for the manuscript's genesis. This early date, which indicates that the proctors lost no time in commissioning the replacement volume, attests to the central role of this manuscript for running the university.[30] The volume also contains a university calendar, incipits of the four Gospels, the oaths sworn by university officials, as well as oaths for civic officials who publicly acknowledged the power of the university over the borough at a ceremony called the "Magna Congregatio." Its tattered state and its many additional oaths, penned by several scribes in different campaigns of work, reveal the manuscript's regular use by the university proctors, the chancellor's executive officers.

An image of St Christopher forms the first folio of a quire containing oaths to be read at the "Magna Congregatio," which was to take place annually "when the magistri return to teaching after the feast of the Division of the Apostles [15 July]," according to the rubric on the verso of the very sheet with the saint's image (Figs 77 and 78).[31] A second image in the manuscript depicts the Virgin and Child enthroned, produced in a different campaign of work, which prefaces a separate series of oaths (Fig. 79). The leaf with the Virgin is bifoliate with a missing leaf that may have contained another image, perhaps a Crucifixion. While images of Jesus and Mary appear in other manuscripts for oath swearing, as discussed earlier, and their presence here is not surprising, the inclusion of St Christopher is unusual in this context. It may relate to his role in preventing false oaths. As Rogers points out, the Beaufort Hours contains a prayer to St Christopher in which the saint is invoked against "malas perversas machinaciones fraudulentas conspiraciones mendacia falsa testimonia occulta sive aparta consilia." Invoking him

---

MS-UA-COLLECT-ADMIN-00003/1. The first full treatment of the manuscript was provided by M. B. Hackett, *The Original Statutes of Cambridge University* (Cambridge, 1970), pp. 260–85, 345.

30 Nicholas Rogers, "The Old Proctor's Book: A Cambridge Manuscript of c. 1390," in *England in the Fourteenth Century: Proceedings of the 1985 Harlaxton Symposium*, edited by W.M. Ormrod (Boydell, 1986), pp. 213–23; and "From Alan the Illuminator to John Scott the Younger: Evidence for Illumination in Cambridge," in *The Cambridge Illuminations: The Conference Papers*, edited by Stella Panayotova (2007), pp. 287–99, esp. pp. 290, 297, fig. 4a.

31 Rogers, "The Old Proctor's Book," (1986), p. 213, n. 2 provides a collation.

through his image may have also helped to guard against bad and perverse machinations, fraudulent conspiracies, lies, false testimonies, and hidden or covert plans.

Rogers refers to the St Christopher and Mary miniatures as "solemnizing images," which "underline the solemnity of the oaths sworn at the '*Magna Congregatio*.'" He states that the oaths themselves were sworn on the Gospel sequences—texts that, as we have seen, are ubiquitous in oath-swearing manuscripts.[32] These are inscribed in the same hand as the oaths, beginning on fol. 9v. The problem with his assertion, however, is that the folios of the Gospel texts are not worn very significantly, and they bear no witness to having been used for swearing. I think that Rogers has inverted the purposes of the texts and images: evidence from signs of wear suggest that the Gospel sequences form a "solemnizing" component to the volume, while the images were the targets for officials' oaths. This is the inverse of Rogers's proposal.

The patterns of wear on the images testify to their having been touched. The luminous parchment of the St Christopher leaf, with its slightly waxy finish, has a surface to which water-based paint barely adheres. Curiously, only the bottom of the image is degraded from repeated acts of handling. In particular, the stream in the foreground has been rubbed so severely that the flaked paint reveals raw parchment. Equally curiously, the numerous people who caused this cumulative wear did not touch the saint's face. Likewise, the image of the Virgin has also been abraded at the lower third. There the parchment has buckled, as if the moisture from hands had caused the material to distort, and those distortions were pressed between the pages into permanent creases.

How did users handle this manuscript to cause this pattern of wear? That the bottom third of the image of the Virgin has been degraded indicates that those who swore their oaths stood at the bottom of the book. That the book's users were members of the university implies that they were literate: unlike the users of the 's-Hertogenbosch customs book, they did not need to have the oath read to them. Why did they not touch the faces of the figures? This question requires some haptic imagination. First, it is important to remember that many folios of the manuscript are now missing, and the folios may not be in their original order. It

---

32 Rogers (1986), *passim*.

5. *Swearing: From Gospels to Legal Manuscripts* 157

Fig. 77 Folio in the Old Proctors' Book of Cambridge with an image depicting St. Christopher. Cambridge, University Archives, Collect. Admin. 3, fol. 6r. Reproduced by kind permission of the Syndics of Cambridge University Library.

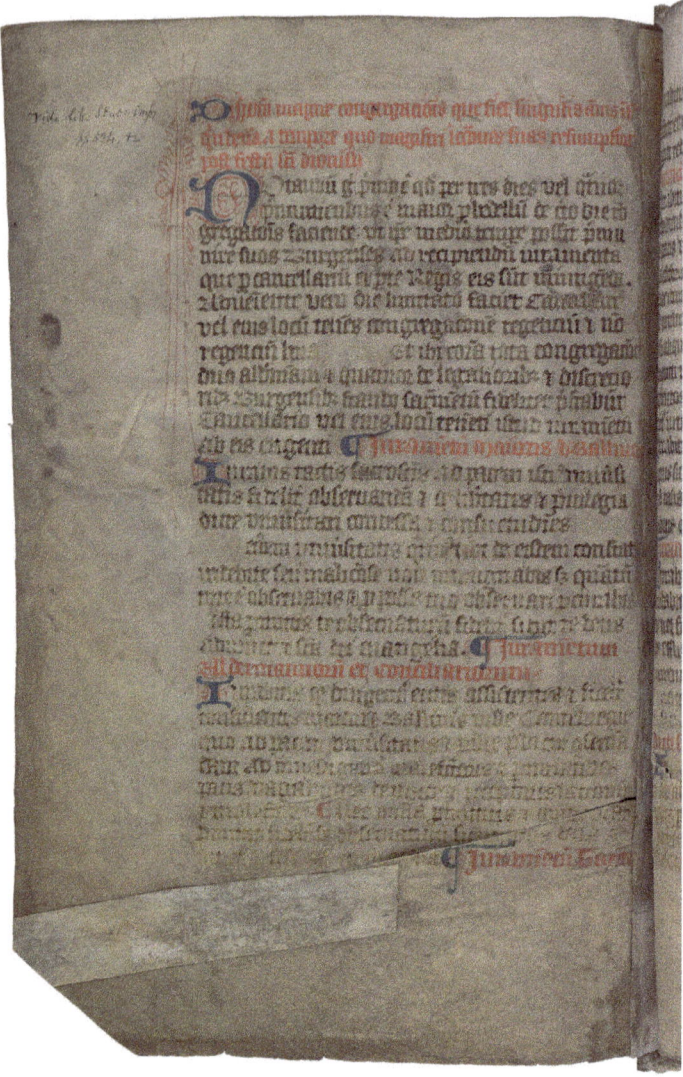

Fig. 78 Folio in the Old Proctors' Book of Cambridge with the beginning of a series of oaths. Cambridge, University Archives, Collect. Admin. 3, fol. 6v. Reproduced by kind permission of the Syndics of Cambridge University Library.

is unclear what these images originally faced. After they turned to the page containing the relevant oath and read it aloud, they did not turn back to the image page and touch it. Rather, the pattern of wear suggests

5. Swearing: From Gospels to Legal Manuscripts 159

Fig. 79 Folio in the Old Proctors' Book of Cambridge with an image depicting Virgin and Child in an architectural niche. Cambridge, University Archives, Collect. Admin. 3, fol. 8r. Reproduced by kind permission of the Syndics of Cambridge University Library.

that they held their hand on the image page the entire time they were reading the oath aloud, thereby touching the image and reading the text at the same time. In other words, the swearer had his hand stuck in the closed book and was touching an image that he was not actually looking at. This pattern of wear—abrasion at the bottom without targeting the face—fits that scenario: touching the image while reading the oath on a different page.

In particular, abrasion only along the bottom edge indicates that it was touched while the oath swearer was reading from a different page. Such a configuration would illuminate a fact about this codex and the mechanics of its handling: that one can interact with more than one page at a time, and that touching does not imply seeing, but rather can take the place of seeing. Touchers or readers must have done this because touching the image was essential to sealing the oath, but not every folio could be illuminated. In fact, they were taking advantage of one of the structural benefits of the codex: that one can have fingers or even entire hands in different openings at the same time. By acting in this way, they demonstrated that an image does not have to be visible to be in service of an outcome.

IV. The Inquisition: Inquisitor's Manual

The Waldensians, a group active in ca. 1380–1410 (especially in Germany), refused to swear oaths. These Christians were followers of Peter Waldo, a rich man who gave away his possessions around 1173 and then advocated for a simple apostolic life. Waldensians took seriously the injunction in the Book of Matthew not to swear oaths. Additionally, Waldensians did not give credence to the saints, to relics, or to the Virgin Mary, and as such, they neither invoked saints nor believed in saintly intervention. They did not believe in the consecration or dedication of churches or altars, nor did they believe in the sacrality of priests' garments, salt, holy water, or ashes. They would not use images in their devotions. Their scruples, based on close reading of scripture, vexed the Church, because the Waldensians threatened its values, beliefs, objects, and rituals. They were forerunners of the Cathars, and the Church labelled both groups heretics.

As Reima Välimäki has eloquently shown, inquisitors used manuals to root out Waldensians by questioning them about their faith and then forcing them to recant their objectionable beliefs and confirm their orthodoxy.³³ Several inquisitors' manuals survive, including one compiled in the fourteenth century in Bohemia (Linz, Oberösterreichische Landesbibliothek, Cod. 177).³⁴ This manuscript was rebound in the early fifteenth century in a red leather binding that recalls those of the oath books of 's-Hertogenbosch and the various German cities (Fig. 80). It contains some 40 different texts related to heresy, including lists of heresies, excerpts from canon law on excommunication and absolution, relevant papal bulls, texts for interrogating Waldensians, definitions of legal terms and concepts, and a formula for them to recite in which they renounced their questionable beliefs (or asserted their orthodoxy).³⁵

According to Välimäki, the Linz manual was owned by the inquisitor Petrus Zwicker. Signs of wear in the volume show that an inquisitor, possibly Zwicker, used the manuscript not only for its textual contents, but also as a physical prop in rituals in which those accused of heresy would abjure their heretical beliefs. These signs of wear occur in the first quire, which comprises the first ten folios of the manuscript. This section includes a table of contents (fols 1v-3v) to fols 11r-51r, which by virtue of its descriptive nature must have been made after the folios it describes. The person who compiled the table of contents overestimated how much parchment that job would require and added a full quire of 10 folios when four would have sufficed. Paleographical analysis indicates that various hands also added the other items within a few decades after the main body of the manuscript was written, as early users continually identified texts that would enhance the book's function. Important additions in the present context are excerpts from the beginnings of the four Gospels (at the bottom of fol. 1r; Fig. 81), questionnaires to determine whether someone was a heretic (fols 4r-5r, 6r-7r), and an

---

33   Reima Välimäki, *The Awakener of Sleeping Men: Inquisitor Petrus Zwicker, the Waldenses, and the Retheologisation of Heresy in Late Medieval Germany* (PhD thesis, University of Turku, 2016). Those considering the stakes of extracting oaths can consult R. I. Moore, *The Formation of a Persecuting Society: Authority and Deviance in Western Europe, 950–1250* (2nd ed.) (Blackwell, 2007); and more recently but with a narrower scope, Derek Hill, *Inquisition in the Fourteenth Century: The Manuals of Bernard Gui and Nicholas Eymerich, Heresy and Inquisition in the Middle Ages* (York Medieval Press, 2019).

34   Linz, Oberösterreichische Landesbibliothek (OÖLB), Cod. 177, is fully digitized https://digi.landesbibliothek.at/viewer/fullscreen/177/23/.

35   For a list of the contents, see Välimäki, *The Awakener of Sleeping Men*, 2016, pp. 382–85.

Fig. 80 Front cover of a compilation of texts about inquisition and heresy, fourteenth century. Linz, Oberösterreichische Landesbibliothek (OÖLB), Cod. 177. [to cite this according to the library's standards: Linz, AT-OOeLB, Hs.-177 (Sammelhandschrift zu Themen von Inquisition und Umgang mit Häresie, Saec. XIV). 1300.]

image depicting Christ crucified (fol. 10r, Fig. 82).[36] The simple image is drawn in ink with pen and washes, highlighted in yellow watercolor,

---

36 Välimäki, *The Awakener of Sleeping Men* (2016), describes the contents fully on pp. 382–85.

and then embellished with rubricator's red ink to emphasize Christ's tripartite halo and to make the blood leap from his body. This image, together with the added texts, contributes to the book's function.

More added texts top and tail the page: above are the incipits of the Books of John and Matthew, and below the incipits of all four Gospels. Wielding the rubricator's red ink, the scribe has framed these texts in red boxes. The same brown and red inks appear in the lower texts, their frames, and in the drawing of Christ, suggesting that the image was made by the scribe and is an extension of the texts. With the addition of these texts and images in the otherwise blank areas of the front matter, the book's early user (or users) has turned this book from one that functioned in theory—with papal bulls, canon law, and descriptions of heresy—into one that was of immediate and urgent use in practice—with questionnaires and formulas for absolution—to a use as a prop. As one can see from the way in which fols 1r and 10r are abraded, the book itself became a tool in the inquisitor's kit. One explanation for these features stands out.

Early in the book's career, an inquisitor copied the Gospel incipits onto the bottom of the first folio and required accused heretics to touch the text while swearing to their orthodoxy. The added texts would have functioned as an abbreviated Gospel manuscript and would have meant that the inquisitor would have only had to carry his work-a-day manual, and not a separate oath-swearing Gospel manuscript. Shortly thereafter, he or another inquisitor sought to expand the oath-taking apparatus in the manual by filling a blank folio with an image of the Crucifixion. There was extra space in the first quire, for the reasons discussed earlier. The expander did not add a gilded Crucifixion image like those in oath-swearing books (Eidbücher, discussed above), for several reasons. Such a small manual (only 200 x 135–140 mm) would not have accommodated the kind of Canon plate designed for missals and which were available as loose sheets. Given the less exulted context of an inquisition to try a heretic, the book would not have needed a costly gilded image anyway: the scribe's drawing would have sufficed. Recopying the Gospel incipits onto the page would have brought the abbreviated Gospel onto the active surface that the accused touched. The abraded areas on fol. 10r stretch from Christ's torso and legs where people reached in confidently and touched the image, to the entire area of the framed Gospel texts,

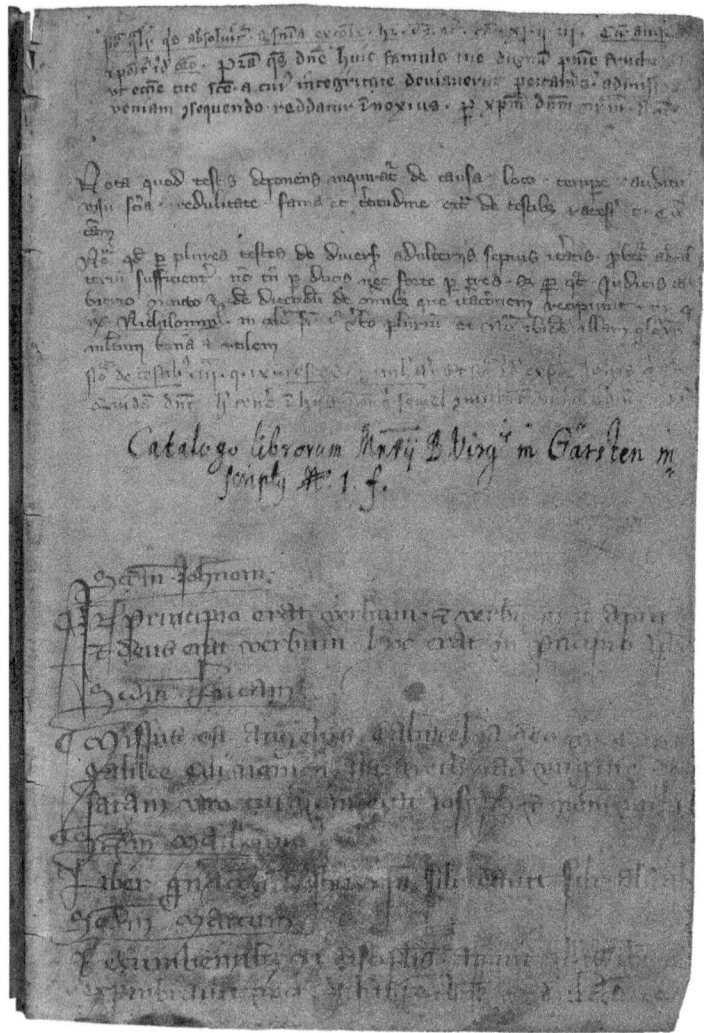

Fig. 81 Folio from a compilation of texts about inquisition and heresy, with incipits of the four Gospels. Linz, Oberösterreichische Landesbibliothek (OÖLB), Cod. 177, fol. 1r.

including the very lower border, where people have only ventured a finger or two onto the parchment.

By compelling Waldensian heretics to recant their heretical beliefs while placing their hand on the image, the heretics ipso facto demonstrated their embrace of multiple mainstream, anti-Waldensian

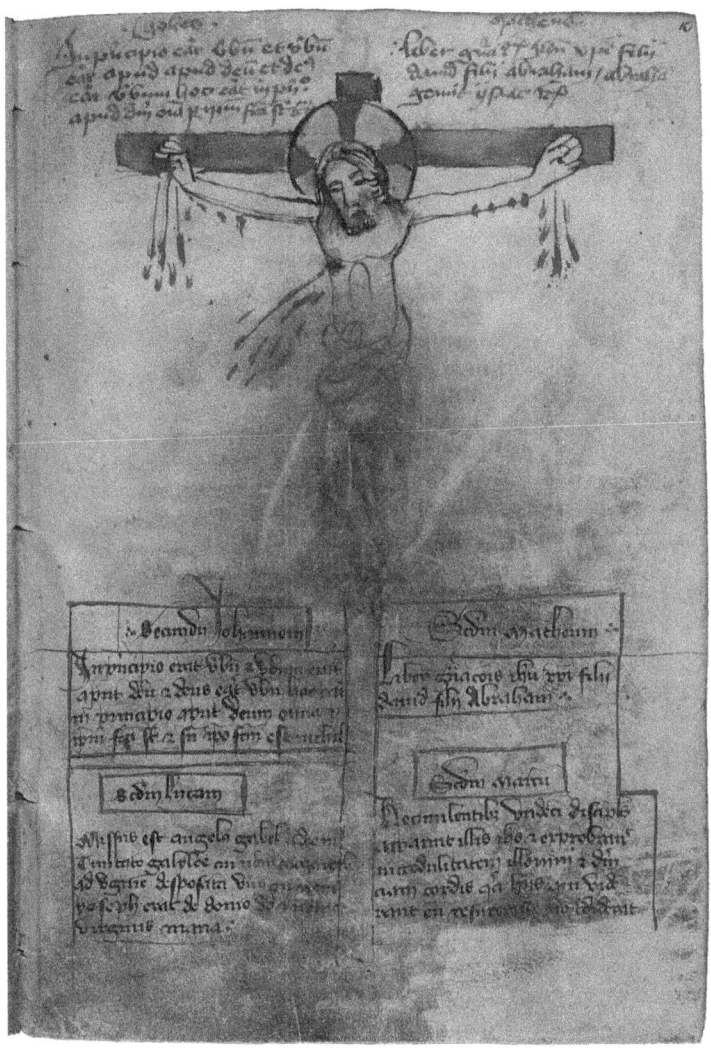

Fig. 82 Folio from a compilation of texts about inquisition and heresy, with a drawing of Christ Crucified. Linz, Oberösterreichische Landesbibliothek (OÖLB), Cod. 177, fol. 10r.

beliefs: swearing oaths, doing so on the Gospels, acknowledging the power of the Gospels, and of images, including that of Christ Crucified, and even swearing on a page with the incipit from the Book of Matthew, which as every Waldensian would have known, proscribes swearing.

That the inquisitor specifically recopied the incipit from Matthew above the Crucifixion drawing reinforces the subjugation of the accused Waldensian. Through their small, possibly coerced, ritual words and actions, the accused refuted heresy with both his mouth and his body, while the inquisitor drew upon both the texts in the little manual and the physical book itself. Gestures for acceding to the civic legal agreements were adjusted for a related purpose: to demonstrate one's membership to a group.

6. Performances Within the Church

In addition to Gospels and missals, other types of manuscripts were written for use by church officials to conduct ceremonies. Masses required music, some of which a priest himself intoned. The grander the Mass, the more actors it required, and each of those actors needed a particular book type that contained the script for his part. Masses with a choral component required the largest manuscripts in Christendom, their format scaled up to enable numerous choristers to read simultaneously from the page. These actors may have considered their chanting unexceptional, merely their quotidian routines. The books they used in order to effect their performances were anything but.

Various performances that took place in and around churches served the basic tenet of Christianity: that it was a religion that promised bodily resurrection and everlasting life. Because of this, Christians and their ceremonies were preoccupied by death. The living prayed for the dead and paid professionals—priests, nuns, and monks—to pray for lay people after they died. To have large choral Masses sung for the dead would mitigate the chances of their souls spending eternity in Purgatory. This chapter considers books used and gestures practiced in the service of liturgical singing and memorializing the dead. Normal liturgical actions, together with exceptional props, combined to commemorate death and formed an everyday part of worshippers' lives. Signs of wear in the books record how clerics used them for these practices.

I. Choral Manuscripts

The choir psalter OBL, Ms. Canon. Liturg. 395, used in the Cathedral of St Lawrence in Trogir (Trau, Dalmatia), ca. 1450–1475, is in terrible condition. Alongside two other saints, the Blessed John Orsini, patron of the town, whose feast days are 26 June and 14 November, appears on the first text folio (Fig. 83). The dedication of St Lawrence Cathedral has been added to the calendar on 12 August. This book may be in its original binding, for the paste-down on the front cover comes from a fourteenth-century Italian missal. Dalmatia belonged to the Venetian domain after 1420, so books would certainly have been exchanged across the Adriatic in this period. Measuring 385 x 270 millimeters, this large manuscript could be used for liturgical performances by the choir, who would chant from it daily during the office. Its notes are large enough to be legible from some distance. I estimate that a group of six to eight people could sing from it simultaneously. Degradation of the parchment reveals the heavy use it has incurred. The noted text implies that it was designed to be sung. As with all service books which were read or sung over, this one has been attacked by damp breath. Cascading exhalations, expelling invisible droplets, have resulted in the oft-turned pages suffering from moisture and exposure, so that the lower corners of most folios have been damaged and repaired later with paper.

As part of his ritual of using this book, the choirmaster in charge of turning the folios must have touched the initials before singing the corresponding sections. With this large manuscript at arm's length, he reached down in a dramatic gesture with his hand and touched the book so that his gesture would be visible to the whole choir. Imagining this is easier with my amateur photograph than the professional one provided by the library; I took the photo so that my hand is hovering above (not touching!) the initial, to provide a sense of scale and enactment (Fig. 84). When the choirmaster reached his hand in, he touched the area vigorously. This has left the first historiated initial P illegible and dislodged much of the tempera paint so that the subject is no longer discernible. Some of the sections of this psalter are more heavily used than others. A begrimed section begins on folio 190v, with a historiated initial C (Cantate domino canticum novum), where the initial has also been rubbed to oblivion (Fig. 85). The professional photograph, which captures the book as a three-dimensional object and not just a flat surface, as well as an amateur photograph that captures the entire opening show the context of use more effectively (Fig. 86). Perhaps the choirmaster habitually touched the initials in order to signal that reading

6. Performances Within the Church 169

Fig. 83 Folio in a noted ferial choir Psalter, possibly for St Lawrence's, Trau (Dalmatia), ca. 1450–1475. Oxford, Bodleian Library, Ms. Canon. Liturg. 395, fol. vii recto

or singing should begin. These gestures formed part of a performance that was as public as the Mass, but for an audience of choristers. His actions validated touching initials as an honorable way to add gravitas to the sacred words of the text. All of the members of the choir would by necessity have watched this action and normalized it. Did this literate group of spectators, as well as anyone witnessing the Mass with a view of the choir, adopt and absorb this lesson in book handling and subsequently apply it to their own books?

A significant number of large music manuscripts used across Europe have apparently been touched in a similar way. For example, in an

Fig. 84 Opening in a noted ferial choir Psalter, possibly for St Lawrence's, Trau (Dalmatia), ca. 1450–1475. Oxford, Bodleian Library, Ms. Canon. Liturg. 395, fol. vi verso – vii recto. Amateur photograph

antiphonary—a book of plainsong for the Divine Office—made for the use of the Benedictine Abbey of Marchiennes in northern France, a user has repeatedly touched the large opening initial (Fig. 87 and Fig. 88). The manuscript opens with music for the feast of St Nicholas, and the accompanying initial depicts the enthroned Virgin and Child presented by the feted saint. On either side of the throne are two Fig.res in religious garb, who may be the founders of the abbey. On the left, Adalbert I of Ostrevent (d. ca. 652), a Frankish nobleman who was recognized as a saint and whose relics are in Douai. The woman on the other side of the throne may be his wife, Rictrude of Marchiennes (ca. 614–688), who converted the all-male house into a double abbey and became its first abbess. (In the thirteenth century, it reverted to a male-only house.) The figures in the image have been carefully targeted, especially the Virgin and Child, and the two local founders. It is as if the monk leading the plainchant touched the image with each recital, partly to ensure that all eyes were on the starting point of the numed text, and also to touch,

6. *Performances Within the Church* 171

Fig. 85 Folio in a noted ferial choir Psalter, possibly for St Lawrence's, Trau (Dalmatia), ca. 1450–1475. Oxford, Bodleian Library, Ms. Canon. Liturg. 395, fol. 190v.

Fig. 86 Opening in a noted ferial choir Psalter, possibly for St Lawrence's, Trau (Dalmatia), ca. 1450–1475. Oxford, Bodleian Library, Ms. Canon. Liturg. 395, fol. 190v-191r. Amateur photograph

literally, the operative characters in the founding narrative of their abbey. I will leave it to music historians to discuss how this touching gesture might relate to hand signals used by liturgical singers to coordinate the voices.

Fig. 87 First folio of an antiphonary, with a small miniautre depicting the Virgin and Child flanked by founders, Abbey of Marchiennes, ca. 1450–1475. Douai, Bibliothèque municipale, Ms. 117, fol. 1r. Cliché: IRHT-CNRS

Fig. 88 Detail of previous figure. Douai, Bibliothèque municipale, Ms. 117, fol. 1r.
Cliché: IRHT-CNRS

Choirmasters across Southern Europe adopted a similar practice in handling antiphonaries. As with the Dalmatian manuscript discussed earlier, a brightly illuminated Venetian antiphonary has large colorful images that mark the beginnings of sung passages (OBL, Ms. Douce A 1).[1] A later collector cut out about a dozen of these initials; some have been taped back into their original positions, and some are mounted at the end of the manuscript into a small "album" of fragments. Signs of wear attest to their having been handled as a matter of practice. For example, an initial B with the Trinity has been wet-touched, where the user has targeted specific areas of the image: the thighs of Christ crucified, and the area of the blue sky on either side of God's face (Fig. 89). It is almost as if the user were consciously trying to touch in the vicinity of the important elements, without marring the paint on those important details.

In the same manuscript, an image of St Augustine initiates a Mass to be sung in his honor (Fig. 90 and Fig. 91). One can imagine the choirmaster touching the image of the saint, both to venerate him and

---

1   For a description and bibliography of the Venetian Antiphonary, Oxford, Bodleian Library MS. Douce a. 1, see https://medieval.bodleian.ox.ac.uk/catalog/manuscript_4758

Fig. 89 Trinity, Historiated initial cut from a Venetian antiphonary, mounted at the end of the manuscript. Oxford, Bodleian, Ms. Douce a. 1, fol. 155, item d

also to move all eyes to the beginning of the song, "Invenit se Augustinus longe esse a deo in regione dissimilitudinis tamquam audiret vocem..."[2] This time, however, the user has had no qualms about touching the face of the saint. Is it possible that a different choirmaster wrought these two habits of practice?

---

2 For other witnesses of this chant, see the excellent website Cantus: A Database for Latin Ecclesiastical Chant, https://cantus.uwaterloo.ca/chant/204516.

Fig. 90 Opening in an antiphonary, with a historiated initial depicting St Augustine, fifteenth century, Venice. Oxford, Bodleian, Ms. Douce a. 1, fols 70v-71r

A third fragment preserved in the manuscript (which may in fact have been cut from a different antiphonary) testifies to another type of precision-targeted touching (Fig. 92). The image shows St Gregory as a pope in a tripartite tiara performing his miraculous Mass. This time, the user (the choirmaster?) has touched the figure's hands. That area of the image is now heavily abraded, but with difficulty one can see that Gregory is holding aloft the host. The user has repeatedly touched this miracle-inducing wafer.

There are no instructions telling singers or choirmasters to touch initials. They could have learned to do so by putting their hands where others' hands had obviously been, or from following the lived models that their own choirmasters had set for them. An antiphonary is one of the few book types that is presented open and facing its primary audience, a group of singers gathered round it. Those who commissioned and painted them may have illuminated them in order to glorify God, while those who used them put the decoration to use. They instrumentalized the painted and gilt initials to foster group cohesion. Regarding the numed text together was something they did with their fingers.

Fig. 91 St Augustine, fifteenth century, Venice. Oxford, Bodleian, Ms. Douce a. 1, fol. 70v.

II. Books and Holy Water

Whereas antiphonaries contain no instructions for handling the physical book, pontificals are full of such instructions. Pontificals prescribed rituals such as blessing holy water, blessing the baptismal font, performing baptisms and marriages, purifying a woman, sending

Fig. 92 Cutting fron an antiphonary made in Venice, mounted at the end of the manuscript. Oxford, Bodleian, Ms. Douce a. 1, fol. 148r

off pilgrims, performing extreme unction, and burying the dead. These books contain the instructions for a clergyman—most often a bishop—to perform these tasks. Some are noted. Most are rubricated, with the instructions for the priest or bishop in red and the words he had to utter in black. As such, pontificals mandate several ceremonies that involve the pontifical itself, or other books exuding religious authority as actors in those ceremonies.

One pontifical, made for the Chapter of St Mary in Utrecht around 1450, which includes extraordinary illuminations attributed to the Master of Catherine of Cleves, depicts many of the ceremonies for which it also provides instruction, and as such reveals the central role books play in these ceremonies (Utrecht, Universiteitsbibliotheek, Ms. 400).[3] On one folio, the painter has shown a disembodied hand that extends from the text block holding aloft a book, thereby putting on display the object featured in the ceremony (Fig. 93). The accompanying text tells the celebrant to kiss the Gospel book while saying "Pax tibi" (Peace be with you). Likewise, on another folio, in the ceremony for blessing liturgical garments, the image depicts a bishop clutching a book—again, probably a Gospel book—which gives him the authority from God, channeled through the Evangelists, to make the sign of blessing over the chasubles (Fig. 94 and Fig. 95). An acolyte further ceremonializes this process by sprinkling holy water. Depictions of such rituals show that the power of the book functions as an attribute of authority even when the book is closed. Evidence from the pages of other manuscripts reveals that books might remain open during rituals such as baptisms and last rites.

Pontificals were not the only books used for performing rituals. There is a type of book simply called a ritual. Some service books contain instructions for the use of holy water, and during some enactments, holy water splashed the service books themselves. A rubricated noted ritual, made in England in the third quarter of the fifteenth century for Sarum Use, has been splashed (OBL, Ms. Laud Misc. 267).[4] In the short space of its 92 folios it has been repeatedly wetted with an aspergillum, a brush designed for sprinkling holy water. This manuscript even begins with a blessing of holy water (fol. 2) and contains instructions for blessing and performing baptism (fol. 4v). The pages near the end of the baptism section are awash with smeared ink (rather, red pigment with binder) from water damage from a dripping wet baby that has liquefied some of the rubrics, which were far more soluble than the black ink texts to

---

[3] A description of the manuscript, along with digitized images of all its folios, may be read online: http://objects.library.uu.nl/. See also Rob Dückers and Ruud Priem, *The Hours of Catherine of Cleves: Devotion, Demons and Daily Life in the Fifteenth Century* (Ludion, 2009), pp. 204–05, Cat. 32.

[4] Oxford, Bodleian, Ms. Laud misc. 267. I am indebted to S. J. P. van Dijk's typescript description of the manuscript (*Rituals and Directories*, Latin Liturgical Manuscripts in the Bodleian Library, Oxford, Vol. 3 [1957], p. 55), and to Martin Kauffmann for showing me this resource in 2016.

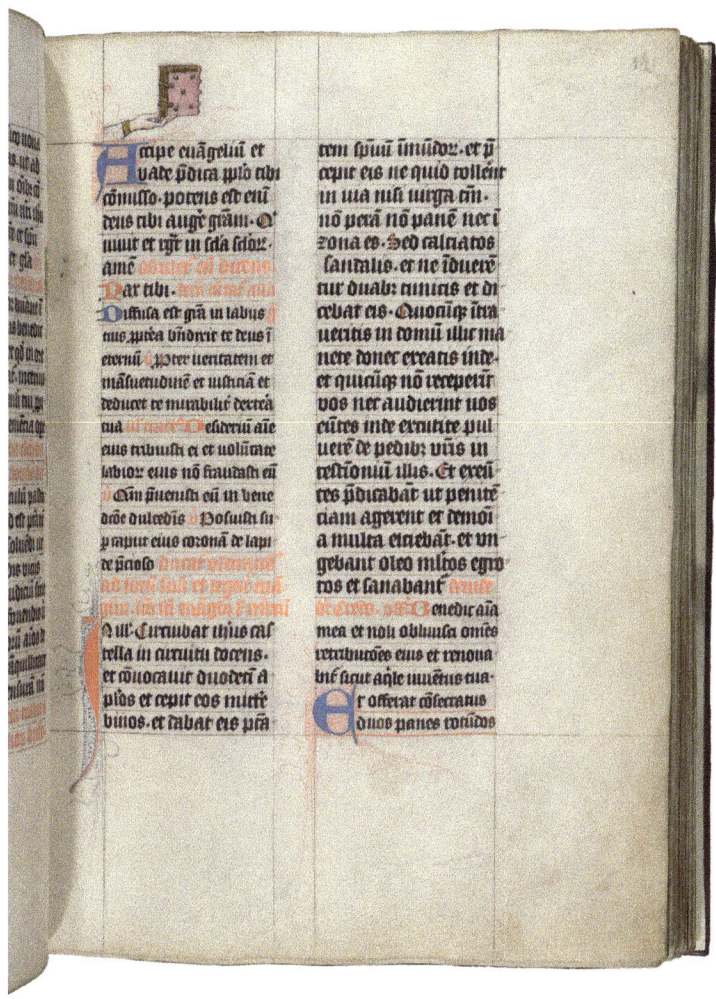

Fig. 93 Master of Catherine of Cleves, Hand of God holding book into the margin, Pontifical, ca. 1450, Chapter of St. Mary in Utrecht. Utrecht, Universiteitsbibliotheek Ms. 400, fol. 34r

be pronounced aloud. This opening—used in conjunction with a ritual performed on infants—is the only one in the book bearing such a colorful array of stains (fols 13v–14r; Fig. 96). A laboratory sample might well indicate that the substance on these pages contains regurgitated milk and baby feces. Further aspergillum use, and therefore water damage, occurred at the folios for performing a marriage (fol. 15v), for the

Fig. 94 Folio in a Pontifical Master of Catherine of Cleves, the blessing of the vestements. Utrecht, Universiteitsbibliotheek Ms. 400, fol. 99r

purification of a woman (fol. 26v), and for the blessing of a pilgrim (fol. 26v). An officiant has also used the aspergillum extensively during rituals relating to death—extreme unction (fol. 34r) and a burial service, which includes the office (fol. 49r) and Mass for the Dead (fol. 75r). There has been so much holy water sprinkled from fols 84 to 92 (the end of the book) that these pages are wrinkled and only faintly legible.

It is as if the officiant had used the book in the manner depicted in a panel depicting the Death of the Virgin, made for Clarissan nuns in Bohemia around 1400 (Fig. 97 and Fig. 98). This painting once joined

6. Performances Within the Church   181

Fig. 95 Detail of previous image. Utrecht, Universiteitsbibliotheek Ms. 400, fol. 99r

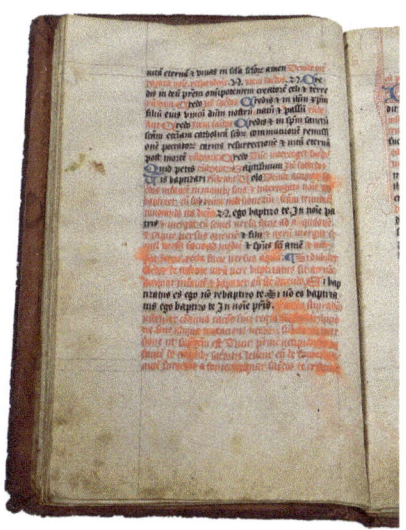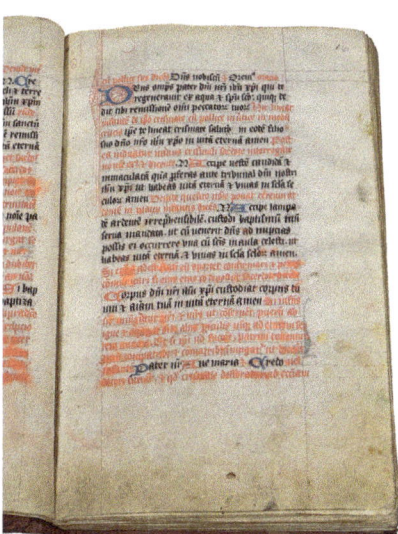

Fig. 96 Instructions for performing a Baptism, in a rubricated noted ritual, England, fifteenth century. Oxford, Bodleian Library, Ms. Laud. Misc. 267, fols 13v–14r

a pendant representing the Death of St Clare.[5] Together they may have formed the backdrop for funerary rites in the convent. A dejected apostle holds the open book, and the priest looks into the pallid Virgin's lifeless eyes while flicking holy water over book and body. In the noted ritual, a rubric on folio 85v telling the official to use an aspergillum has been so effective that the user has nearly washed those very instructions away (Fig. 99).

Fig. 97 Master of Heiligenkruz (Bohemian?), Death of the Virgin, ca. 1400–1401. Tempera and oil with gold on panel. Gift of the Friends of the Cleveland Museum of Art in memory of John Long Severance 1936.496

---

5   National Gallery of Art, Samuel H. Kress Collection, *The Death of St Clare*, attributed to the Master of Heiligenkreuz, https://www.nga.gov/collection/art-object-page.41698.html

Fig. 98 detail of previous image

Holy water can also be transported outdoors in an appropriately ceremonious vessel. Outdoor spaces marked by wayside crosses, city gates, churches, chapels, gallows, and structures that prompted Christian memory and signified justice were also sites where books and aspergilla were used. A miniature in a book of hours shows a priest leading a burial procession, his acolyte with holy water behind, followed by black-cloaked mourners, while a workman lowers the slim coffin into the ground (Fig. 100). In the image, and according to official procedure, only the cleric would carry a book to the grave. Signs of wear in their books suggest that laypeople copied clerics and subjected

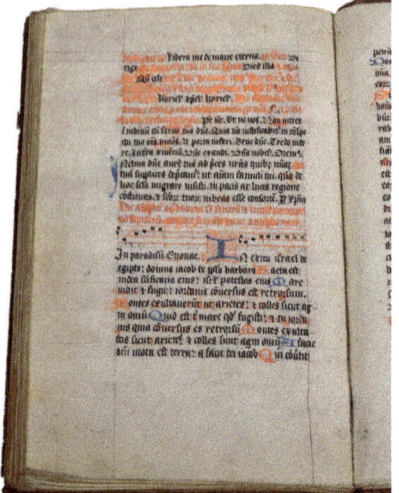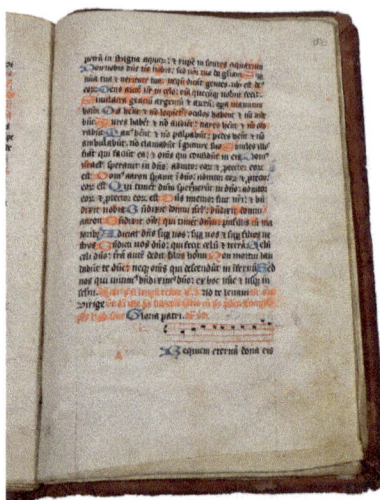

Fig. 99 Instructions for performing last rites, in a rubricated noted ritual, England, fifteenth century. Oxford, Bodleian Library, Ms. Laud. Misc. 267, fols 85v-86r

their private prayerbooks to rituals that mirrored those they witnessed clerics conducting.

A similar transmission occurred around rituals of other processions: priests (including bishops) holding manuscripts would lead people from the church to perform an outdoor ritual, and it appears that their books became damaged in the process. Analogous signs of use appear in the fifteenth-century processional cart of Gertrude of Nijvel (Nivelles), which has recesses for 21 panel paintings chronicling the life of the saint; these have been severely damaged by water, since the paintings were actually taken out on the cart once a year to circumambulate the town (Fig. 101).[6] Her relics rode at the top of the cart, where they would be scintillatingly visible from a great distance, heralded by trumpet-blaring angels at the corners of the cart. (St Gertrude's reliquary was lost and then reconstructed in the nineteenth century.) The panel paintings fit

---

6   Christina Ceulemans and Robert Didier, "Les Processions et le Char de la Châsse de Sainte Gertrude," in *Un Trésor Gothique, La Chasse de Nivelles.* Exhibition Catalogue. Cologne, Schnütgen-Museum, 24 Novembre 1995–11 Février 1996, Paris, Musée National du Moyen Age-Thermes de Cluny, 12 Mars-10 Juin 1996 (Réunion des Musées Nationaux, 1996), pp. 104–06, with further references.

6. *Performances Within the Church* 185

Fig. 100 Burial of the Dead, full-page miniature in a book of hours made in the Southern Netherlands. Chicago, University Library, Ms. 347, fol. 98v

into the lower part of the cart, thus at eye level. Sometimes it rained during these outings, and as a result, the subjects of some of the paintings have become muddled and inscrutable. Damage from rain and from holy water provides clues as to how people used books out of doors, and how clerics might have used books in spaces other than at the altar.

Fig. 101 Processional cart for the relics of Gertrude of Nijvel, ca. 1500. The cart is 412 cm long. Kept in the Church of St Gertrude in Nijvel

III. Grand Obituary of Notre-Dame in Paris

Priests kissed and touched other service books related to the activities that they performed. For example, they commemorated deceased members of their congregation who had left money specifically for Masses to be said. These were to be performed daily, weekly, or annually on the anniversary of the donor's death, for a certain number of years after their donors' deaths. Churches maintained perpetual calendars to record members' deaths and the Masses they had sponsored. Remembering the dead was the central obligation for the managers of a religion that promised to overcome death.

Most obituary manuscripts are not illuminated but take the form of a perpetual calendar ruled with large blank spaces for each day of the year to receive the names of future donors, together with a short list of their deeds. (Their form resembles that of the dismeesters of Bruges, discussed earlier in Chapter 5, with obligations to be recorded in a perpetual calendar.) Such entries typically situate the deceased person socially, and then list the donations he or she made to the church. These could be monetary or in the form of books, building works, metalwork (such as chalices), vestments, or other goods that had to be upgraded or replaced from time to time. That way, each day a priest could read elegies of those who had died on that day, recognize their gifts, and pray annually for their souls. More elaborate configurations existed, such as an illuminated example made to commemorate the dead in the cathedral of Paris—the Grand Obituary of Notre-Dame (BnF, Ms. lat. 5185 CC). As Charlotte Stanford argues, the unique images in this manuscript provide a glimpse of late-medieval death culture, which also involved laying out the body in state, performing Masses, soliciting prayers for the dead, and visiting tombs.[7] What neither she nor other commentators have discussed are the elaborate marks of wear in the book, which provide clues as to how the volume was handled in—I argue—a social context.

First inscribed around 1240–1270, the *Grand Obituary* records earlier deaths copied from other sources. Thus, its scribe recopied an older obituary manuscript (or possibly collated obituaries from loose sheets) to make a neat, new book. Scribes wrote subsequent obituaries onto the blank spaces expressly left for that purpose, and they created other, more elaborate obituaries (including illuminated ones) on separate leaves, bifolios, or more substantial quires, and then inserted them into the binding. These additions date from the fourteenth and fifteenth centuries, with the most recent ones added in the 1490s. They must have been inserted into the manuscript periodically and the book rebound. Its current nineteenth-century binding is so tight that the book opens only with difficulty, and the collation structure has been impossible to determine. Because of the tight binding, the library denied requests for professional photography.

The first part of the Grand Obituary contains a perpetual calendar (fols 1r-6v), a guide for calculating the date in terms of kalens and ides (fols 7v-43v), short readings for each day of the year (fols 44r-72r), a martyrology arranged according to the calendar (fols 72v-129v), and a

---

7 Charlotte A. Stanford, "The Body at the Funeral: Imagery and Commemoration at Notre-Dame, Paris, About 1304–1318," *The Art Bulletin*, 89.4 (2007), pp. 657–73. For the purposes of her project, Stanford does not discuss the later additions or the marks of use. For the context of this manuscript within the book production of Nôtre-Dame, see Cédric Giraud, ed. *Notre-Dame de Paris, 1163–2013: Actes du Colloque Scientifique Tenu au Collège des Bernardins, à Paris, du 12 au 15 Décembre 2012 / Actes Réunis par Cédric Giraud* (Brepols, 2013). Paris, BnF, Ms. lat. 5185 CC has been foliated twice; I use the foliation in ink at the upper recto, in which the 5s look like 9s.

noted requiem Mass (fols 130r-137v). The bulk of the manuscript contains the obituaries, which are also arranged according to the calendar (fols 138r–358v). The final section of the obituaries, fols 328–58, comprises sundry added folios, many of which contain testimonies by the living promising donations to the church in the future. In other words, the function of the various parts of the manuscript are to figure out the date, to laud the appropriate saints and appreciate the benefactors on their annual date, to perform sung requiems for the benefactors, and to recognize and appreciate past and future donations. This manuscript of 358 leaves therefore comprehends original material copied in the thirteenth century, partly from older sources, with deliberate spaces left to fill in later; texts added to those spaces over the next several centuries; added folios and quires, made in the thirteenth to fifteenth centuries, which have been bound into the book as close to the relevant date as possible; and later folios and quires added to the end of the manuscript in the fifteenth century, when it became impractical to insert them close to the date where they belonged. The manuscript marks a particular kind of time—commemorative time—a layered, circular time that demands certain actions.

These temporal layers make sense of the differential wear that the folios have incurred, which correspond to various actions. Specifically, different levels of wear reflect the age of the folio, the frequency with which it was read, and the way it was touched ritualistically. The most worn are the original, thirteenth-century parts of the manuscript, which were used daily, presumably until around 1500 (when the addenda cease). The sung part of the Mass for the Dead, copied in the original campaign of work, has been thoroughly degraded (Fig. 102). Filth emanates from the pores of the parchment in the lower third of the page, where generations of priests must have grasped the book when turning the folios. The corners fell into such tatters that medieval conservators repaired them, onto which the missing text and notes were copied. This was a common form of medieval conservation.[8] Those repaired corners continued to be used and read, as evidenced by the thick fingerprints on the corners of the newer material. In fact, these replacements have become so worn that their parchment has become floppy. That this once-crisp

---

8   See, for example, the discussion of OBL, Ms. Lat. liturg. d. 7 above.

6. Performances Within the Church

material has changed texture marks a haptic and sonorous change that is difficult to document. Normal photography of this manuscript fails to capture some of the information about the manuscript's history of use that is immediately apparent to someone handling the manuscript now; however, backlighted photography reveals the dirt ground into the crevices, the shoreline between the original and replaced material, and the degree to which the fibers have been damaged through use (Fig. 103). Daily handling gave the pages a real beating.

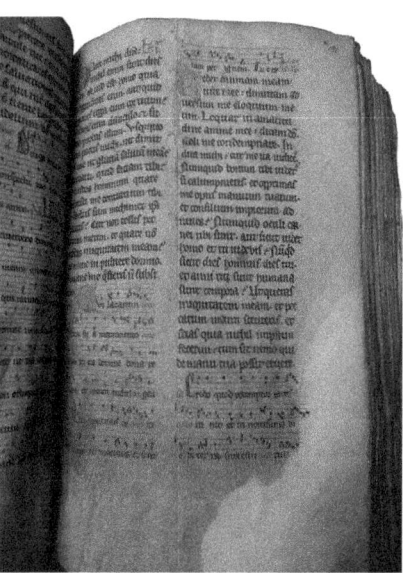

Fig. 102 Noted Mass for the dead, in the Grand Obituary of Notre-Dame. Paris, BnF, Ms lat. 5185 CC, fols 130v-131r

The next most used parts are the original obituaries, those copied in 1240–1270, which were read once annually until approximately 1500— thus, for about 250 years. Someone who had been dead for 250 years would have had 250 annual Requiem Masses said for them, with priests turning to that folio in the book at least 250 times before the volume was retired. For example, fol. 311 forms part of the original material copied in the mid-thirteenth century, with an obituary for the first of December. Backlighting shows that the lower third, especially the corner, is replete with broken parchment fibers that transmit scant light and reveal heavy wear (Fig. 104). Hundreds of creases show up as dark lines that

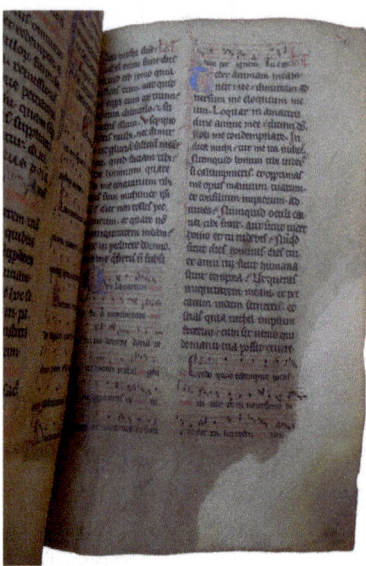

Fig. 103 Noted Mass for the dead, in the Grand Obituary of Notre-Dame. Paris, BnF, Ms lat. 5185 CC, fols 130v-131r, photographed with backlighting

correspond to events of handling those folios. Some of the parchment has been worn so thin that it is nearly transparent. The wear on this and other folios from the original parts of the manuscript suggest that later priests took their duties to read perpetual Masses seriously.

More recent deaths would not have had time to accumulate so many commemorations, and consequently, obituaries added on extra leaves in the fifteenth century received significantly less wear. For example, fols 233–35 form part of an obituary for Lodovicus de Bellomonte, who died in 1492. Assuming this section was added shortly after his death, then it could have been in use for only about a decade, which is why the fibers of the parchment, photographed with backlighting, only reveal minimal damage (Fig. 105). The difference in the parchment creasing between this and the earlier leaves, in use for 200 years longer than this one, is literally palpable.[9]

---

9   A systematic analysis of all the folios in the manuscript photographed under backlighting would certainly have revealed even more nuanced patterns of use. However, such a study was cost-prohibitive for this project.

6. Performances Within the Church   191

Fig. 104 Obituary from the original production of the Grand Obituary of Notre-Dame. Paris, BnF, Ms lat. 5185 CC, fol. 311r, photographed with backlighting

Fig. 105 Folio added after 1492 to the Grand Obituary of Notre-Dame, Paris, BnF, Ms lat. 5185 CC, fol. 235r, photographed with backlighting

Whereas the original parts of the manuscript appear in calendric order, as do the early additions (inscribed into spaces left for them), the later additions, which tend to be written on separate sheets or quires of parchment, were inserted only approximately where they belonged. A defined order for these pieces eroded in the fifteenth century, so that the final additions were simply slipped in at the end of the manuscript, without respect to the date of death. In other words, the last 31 folios (328–58) contain bits and bobs, written in dozens of hands over the course of the fifteenth century. Within this cumulative arrangement of folios and deaths, what is striking is the degree of physicality with which the priest—rather, series of priests spanning 250 years—interacted with the pages. They considered the book a site of continuous evolution.

The opening at fols 242v–243r provides a sense of the interactive nature of the Grand Obituary, which in turn reveals one aspect of how the book was used (Fig. 106). On the left side of the opening is part of the original material, containing segments organized around the calendar. In this case, the heading reads "xvii kalens Augusti," which someone in a nineteenth-century hand has helpfully translated as "16 July." That date marks the death of "Petrus de Kala vicarius sancti victoris in ecclesia parisiensi." Notice of another death was added to the empty margin. The facing page (243r) contains the obituary of the former chancellor of the University of Paris Simon de Guiberville (d. 1320), inscribed on parchment added to the book shortly after his death. Thus, this opening alone contains original material inscribed around 1240–1270; texts inscribed later on original material; and added parchment in the form of single leaves, bifolios, and quires.

Eight of the parchment supplements, added in the fourteenth and fifteenth centuries, contain illuminations of, for the most part, portraits of the deceased, such as the one for Simon de Guiberville (Fig. 107). These make the absent one present, as does any portrait or icon; furthermore, the added images in this manuscript became targets for the physical attention of priests performing ceremonies involving the remembrance of the dead. These eight added illuminated obituaries span two centuries and show an evolution of imagery associated with Requiem Masses to honor the deceased. All of the images have been deliberately touched, as if their purpose were to supply another set of activities to the Requiem Mass, a multi-sensory component involving

Fig. 106 Opening with original and added material, including the added obituary of Simon de Guiberville (d. 1320). Paris, BnF, Ms lat. 5185 CC, fols. 242v–243r

touching. Perhaps making physical contact with the remembered one was not dissimilar from touching relics, which not only honored the saint, but also reciprocally brought a tangible form of sanctity to the living person doing the touching. And perhaps the bookmakers even designed these portraits to be touched.

Simon Matifas de Bucy, bishop of Paris (d. 1304), appears in the earliest of these portraits (Fig. 108).[10] In the image, Simon de Bucy lies in state, wearing the regalia of his episcopal office. At the head of the bier, a bishop conducts a Mass with the aid of a book—either a missal or a representation of this very obituary manuscript. A group of altar boys who carry the incense and holy water integral to the ritual accompany

---

10 Mailan S. Doquang, "Status and the Soul: Commemoration and Intercession in the Rayonnant Chapels of Northern France in the Thirteenth and Fourteenth Centuries," in *Memory and Commemoration in Medieval Culture*, edited by Elma Brenner, Mary Franklin-Brown, and Meredith Cohen (Ashgate, 2013), pp. 93–118, pp. 106–09, discusses Bucy's commemorative statue in Notre-Dame, which would have contributed to the spectacle around his funerary masses.

Fig. 107 Simon de Guiberville preaching to an audience. Paris, BnF, Ms lat. 5185 CC, fol. 243r (detail)

him. On one side the bier candles burn, while on the other mourners seated in melancholic poses read from their books, which are the size of portable psalters or personal prayer books. In other words, books direct the activity depicted in two areas of the image. While the represented official stands at a lectern and only touches the bottom margins of the book (which is, in fact, how the sung components of the Mass in this manuscript were held, as my earlier analysis demonstrates), the marks on the miniature reveal another way in which mourners touched it. These marks show that someone deliberately touched the image in three places: on the depicted processional cross and on the decoration immediately above it; and at the image of the mourner wearing blue in the corner. In the case of the first, the image of the cross often attracted book users, especially, one can imagine, priests who were trained to take an action at the sign of the cross in their books, or to kiss them, as prompted by this shape. The wrinkles and wear at the bottom of the folio suggests that on many occasions a priest gripped the book open to this folio (Fig. 109). One can imagine that he turned the book to show the image to participants so that they might touch an image of a mourner, or that he might proffer the book so that the mourners in the audience could self-identify by touching the represented mourner. These are two plausible explanations for the heavy wear on this blue figure. Some of the paint has migrated to the facing folio, which suggests that a mourner wet-touched the melancholy figure.

Fig. 108 Funeral of Bishop Simon Matifas de Bucy, on an added folio in the Grand Obituary, entry for June 22, 1304. Bibliothèque Nationale de France, Paris, MS lat. 5185 CC, fol. 224r (detail)

Fig. 109 Added folio with the obituary of Bishop Simon Matifas de Bucy, in the Grand Obituary, entry for June 22, 1304. Bibliothèque Nationale de France, Paris, MS lat. 5185 CC, fol. 224r

While the image of Simon de Bucy may be the earliest example of this portrait type, the depiction of Cardinal Michel du Bec (d. 1318), copies it loosely (Fig. 110).[11] Again, the body laid out in state fills the middle of

---

11 Max Prinet, "L'illustration du Grand Obituaire de Notre-Dame de Paris," *Mémoires de la Société des Antiquaires de France*, 77 (1924–1927), pp. 109–24; Stanford, "The Body at the Funeral," pp. 657–73. Doquang, "Status and the Soul," esp. pp. 101–02,

the image. This time, the mourners in the foreground have been reduced to three. The candle-bearers have been relegated to the lower corner, and the officiating bishops have now multiplied to two and occupy the upper right corner. However, the most spectacular difference lies in how the image has been used. Rather extraordinarily, the large miniature has been touched repeatedly, smearing the pigment throughout the frame and beyond. In particular, vertical smears emanate into the upper margin, suggesting that the reader proffered the book to someone who then reached into it from the top edge to make contact with the image of the dead cardinal. Others have pulled the paint downward, as if someone oriented toward the book's script had also reached in to touch it and then drew his hand back toward himself. The timid have touched the frame and the golden leaves in the margins. Within the frame, the image has been touched in multiple places over a series of ceremonial events. Celebrants have repeatedly touched the dead bishop's face and scrubbed away the red pigment from the cloth of gold on which he lies. Pigment does not stick well to gold, so only moderate handling would send it to its fugitive state. More striking still is the level of grime on the bishop's face itself. Others have touched both the miter on his head and what appears to be a red cardinal's hat near his pillow, both kinds of headgear symbolizing his ecclesiastical office. Officials—possibly several of them layered over time—have also touched the image of the two bishops conducting, at the upper right. Did the officials identify with these figures and therefore touch them? Most surprisingly, the mourners in the foreground, especially the one in blue, have also been touched, and in fact, the entire checkered background has been touched, so that all of the gold is finger-burnished in the center of the image, and the linear pattern of the checkerboard has become blobby and misshapen.

---

discusses the large donation Michel du Bec made. The text of the manuscript is partially transcribed in Auguste Molinier, *Obituaires de la Province de Sens, Première Partie*, Vol. I (Imprimerie Nationale, 1902), pp. 93–214, under the heading "Obituaire du XIIIe Siècle." A transcription was also published byBenjamin Edme Charles Guérard, *Cartulaire de l'Eglise Notre Dame de Paris*, Collection de Documents Inédits sur l'Histoire de France. Sér. 1. Collection des Cartulaires de France. Tom. 4–7 (Imprimerie de Crapelet 1850), Vol. 4, pp. 3–212. Fol. 265 forms an added singleton.

Fig. 110 Funeral of Cardinal Michel du Bec, on an added folio in the Grand Obituary, entry for August 22, 1318. Bibliothèque Nationale de France, Paris, MS lat. 5185 CC, fol. 265r

In sum, there are several areas of targeted touching, plus large areas of diffuse touching. This may represent the handling of many priests over dozens or hundreds of years, but, given the diffusion of the smears, these marks indicate that multiple handlers touched it from different angles. Perhaps for the anniversary of Michel du Bec's death, those gathered to hear his obituary were invited to participate in touching the represented body of the bishop. Maybe touching the book formed part of the requiem Mass, as a way to touch the deceased on the anniversary of his death date for years after his physical flesh had melted from his bones. Why they would touch Michel du Bec's image but not Simon Matifas de Bucy's is not clear. Perhaps Michel du Bec was thought to have healing powers, or he had a larger, more active group of bereaved, who continued to attend his anniversary Mass for years after his death. What is clear is that a specific set of rituals was carried out for these two men's anniversaries, that those rituals differed, and that the signs of wear on the manuscript itself both recorded and then prescribed habits of touching that extended across a long time.

What of the other images added to the manuscript? A painted obituary was added for Lord Henry de Sucy, or Henricus de Suciaco, dated 8 December 1310 (fol. 315r; Fig. 111). Unlike the miniatures for Simon de Bucy and Michel du Bec, this shows not the deceased lying in state, but Mass being said in his memory.[12] Perhaps the purpose of the miniature is to shape future behavior. The obituary states that Henry has left six denarios in perpetuity for Mass to be said in his honor, three for the deacon and three for the subdeacon. Like the other miniatures, this illumination has also been touched, and wet-touched at that. In particular, the user targeted the top of the frame with a wet finger and smeared the black ink on the chest of the officiating priest, the garments of the two assistants, and several places on the geometric background. Perhaps the officiating priest read Henry de Sucy's obituary, with his long list of donations to the church, and wet-touched the image of the Mass, which mirrored the very one he was celebrating. The image did not lend itself to being touched by the gathered mourners, since it probably did not represent the deceased.

Similar in composition to the miniature for Henry de Sucy is the one heading the added obit for Hugues de Besançon, cantor, who died in 1320. A column-wide miniature depicts him celebrating (or possibly assisting at) Mass (Fig. 112).[13] This image has not been touched in the same way as the other ones. There are some small areas of abrasion on the curtain and the altar cloth, and perhaps one wet fingerprint on the

---

12   Stanford p. 671 n. 19, describes this image as depicting Henry de Sucy celebrating Mass.
13   Fols 214–15 form an added bifolio, filled with a single obituary.

Fig. 111 Mass being celebrated for Lord Henry de Sucy, from the Grand Obituary, entry for December 8, 1310. Bibliothèque Nationale de France, Paris, MS lat. 5185 CC, fol. 315r

red chasuble, but it was not touched extensively and systematically, nor was the diaper background touched, nor the gold border decoration. In other words, the ritual enacted around some of the previous images was not enacted here.

Fig. 112 Obituary for Hugues de Besançon, on an added folio. Bibliothèque Nationale de France, Paris, MS lat. 5185 CC, fol. 214r

An obituary for Girardus (Gérard) de Courlandon (d. 1319) made on an added bifolium was furnished with a column-wide miniature that was touched many times (Fig. 113). To emphasize his gifts, the miniature shows the deceased presented by a bishop-saint gifting a golden model of a church (or a chapel) to the Virgin and Child. Christ extends his arm as if eagerly accepting this munificence. This time, a constellation of wet fingermarks appears around and on the body of the Virgin, with a few additional wet marks on the body of the saint, and the area between Gérard and his gift. Additionally, one or more people has vigorously wet-touched the gold decoration emanating from the top of the frame, which has liquefied the black outlines of the gold and caused the paint to transfer to the facing folio (Fig. 114). Despite these enthusiastic wet-touchings, the fibers of the parchment do not bear heavy traces of use (Fig. 115), which suggests that the attention Gérard received came shortly after his death, after which his obituary fell into desuetude.

Fig. 113 Girardus (Gérard) de Courlandon before the Virgin and Child, from the Grand Obituary, entry for March 23, 1319. Bibliothèque Nationale de France, Paris, MS lat. 5185 CC, fol. 170r, detail with miniature

6. Performances Within the Church 203

Fig. 114 Opening in the Grand Obituary, with original material on the verso facing an added obituary on the recto. Bibliothèque Nationale de France, Paris, MS lat. 5185 CC, fols 169v-170r

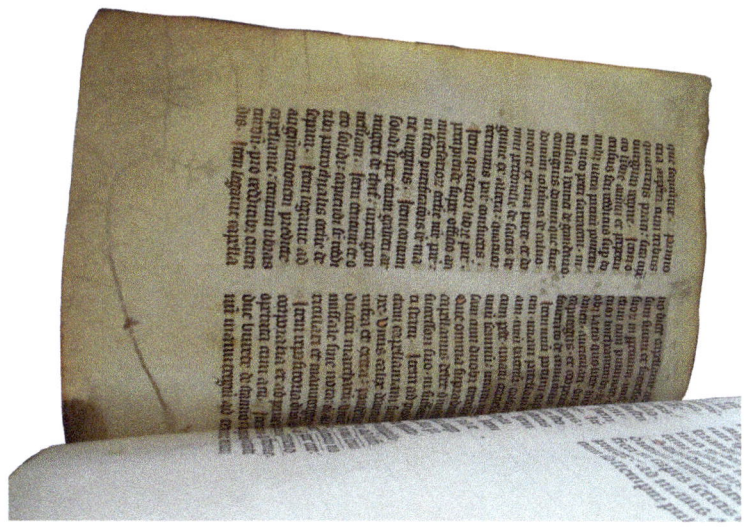

Fig. 115 Folio added to the Grand Obituary of Notre-Dame. Paris, BnF, Ms lat. 5185 CC, fol. 170v, photographed with backlighting

The added obituary of Simon de Guiberville, mentioned earlier, depicts the deceased, and provided several opportunities for touching. In the page-wide miniature (see Figs 107 and 108), he appears twice, first kneeling before the Virgin and Child, and then at a pulpit lecturing to a group of enraptured students.[14] Simon was a secular canon of Notre-Dame of Paris (1303–1309), and also chancellor of the University of Paris from c. 1301 until 10 December 1309. A public intellectual, as it were, Simon de Guiberville participated in the debate on the trial of the Templars.[15] Signs of wear reveal that his image, like that of Michel du Bec, was touched heavily with a diffuse pattern, indicating many people touching various parts of the page once. Perhaps on the anniversary of Simon's death, an officiating priest located the decorated folio with his obituary and read it aloud. This may have happened every year from the first anniversary of Simon's death until the early sixteenth century, when the book ceased to be used ceremonially; however, I suspect that most of the touching took place during living memory of the deceased. When reading the obituary, the priest may have turned the book toward the assembled audience to show them the illumination and to interact with it. They were apparently invited to touch the image and did so.

Whereas a single individual is likely to touch an image in the same place with each iteration of the ritual (as with a book owner touching a cult image in her book), and multiple people are likely to touch, say, an oath-swearing image in haphazard ways, here we find a third pattern: a few places on the miniature have been touched and have therefore attracted further touching. Previous priests (or mourners) set the finger tracks for future ones. Consequently, constellations of finger marks appear on the Virgin's hem, in the diaper background above where Simon's praying hands nearly touch Jesus's, on Simon's blue mantle, and on the bodies of the six students (especially the one clad in orange closest to the picture plane), on the diaper background in the very middle of the image, and on the gold border decoration, especially the boss and tri-petals near the lower right corner, and especially on the black-clad figure of Simon as a teacher. It seems, then, that various people who interacted with the

---

14 Simon also demonstrates his dedication to the Virgin in his seal matrix, which shows the Annunciation (London, British Museum, inv. 1872,0620.1).

15 Jochen Burgtorf, Paul Crawford, and Helen J. Nicholson, *The Debate on the Trial of the Templars (1307–1314)* (Routledge, 2016).

image chose different areas to touch. Some of these people were priests, who touched the image in the course of animating the image before an audience, but some may have comprised Simon's students, who were invited to touch the image. And what part of the image did they touch? The area showing their master preaching, in order to remember him as a teacher, and images of his students, in effect self-identifying with that element of the image.

This would explain why there are different patterns of wear for each of the figures: that a micro-culture of touching was present but subtly different for each obituary. In the case of Simon de Guiberville, perhaps the high degree of wear on his death-portrait was incurred by his many adoring students, who attended their teacher's anniversary funeral Mass for a decade or more. This would also explain why many of them touched the image of Simon as a teacher, rather than Simon as a worshipper of Mary, and why some elected to touch the representation of his students.

More than 100 years passed before the final two images were added to the Grand Obituary. A quire inscribed around 1472 contains obituaries for two people: Lady Margaret of Roche-Guyon (Margareta de Rupe Guidonis) and Guillaume Chartier, the Bishop of Paris (1386–1 May 1472).[16] These texts were written in one campaign of work on added parchment that now comprises fols 189–93. Margaret's date of death is not recorded in the manuscript, because it is likely that she commissioned the quire herself some time after 1472, when Guillaume Chartier died.[17] One of the few women commemorated in the Grand Obituary, she had her coat of arms painted into the otherwise empty space at 190r.

The section commences with her undated obituary, headed by a column miniature, which shows the Christ Child sitting on his mother's lap and holding a set of scales (Fig. 116). With his other hand Jesus grasps his mother's breast, reminding the viewer that he has received the greatest gift of all from her body. This extraordinary image emphasizes two things that Lady Margaret deemed essential for her

---

16 Molinier, *Obituaires de la Province de Sens*, Première Partie, I, pp. 121ff.
17 Margaret may have commissioned the quire from a scribe and illuminator in the Southern Netherlands rather than in Paris. The style of painting and depiction of the dress is consistent with those painted in Bruges around 1472.

obituary—motherhood and gift-giving. Lady Margaret places a sack full of offerings on one side of the balance, while two men—a bishop and a monk—place sacks on the other. The obituary text explains the story: the bishop and monk represent the chapter of Notre-Dame, and their gift bags represent the spiritual rewards and physical privileges that balance out Lady Margaret's concessions. She sold "the weight of the wax of Paris" to the chapter. This may refer to actual wax, which the church continually burned as candles (in fact, Chartier left money for a candle to burn in perpetuity at the altar of the Trinity in Notre-Dame), or it may refer to an item weighed on one of the two official scales of Paris. In Paris from the twelfth century onwards, there were two royal scales, with one weighing wax (in *poids de la cire*), and the other weighing everything else (called *poids de la roy*).[18] Of Lady Margaret's sale, worth 2175 Tours pounds, the chapter only paid her a portion of the agreed sum; however, Lady Margaret relinquished the remainder of this sum to the chapter. In other words, she sold them a large amount of something, possibly wax, at a steep discount. In exchange, the chapter celebrated Masses for her soul, and those of her father, mother, and daughter. In the image Margaret, in ceremonial garb patterned with the fleur-de-lis, appears with her daughter, who is wearing a tall pointed hennin fashionable in the early 1470s and may be proffering a sack. This highly unusual iconography thematizes the church weighing its gifts, and patrons calculating their rewards.[19] She was alive in 1472 to commission the quire and may have outlived the fashion for conical hats.

Patterns of wear in this image differ considerably from those witnessed elsewhere in the manuscript. Here, one or more people have lavished attention on all of the figures. Lady Margaret's face has been so heavily rubbed that it has been obliterated; all that remains is her body, draped with an armorial robe, and her daughter beside her, who has also been heavily fingerprinted along her face and torso. Those performing the ritual also touched the image of the Virgin, whose blue dress has been

---

18   Ruth A. Johnston, *All Things Medieval: An Encyclopedia of the Medieval World*, 2 vols. (Greenwood, 2011), Vol. II, p. 734.
19   One could compare it to a miniature depicting Duke Jean V on a balance fulfilling his pledge to give his weight in gold to the Carmelite brothers of Nantes in 1420, which is depicted in Princeton University Library, Garrett 40, fol. 121r. See Diane E. Booton, *Manuscripts, Market, and the Transition to Print in Late Medieval Brittany* (Ashgate, 2010), pp. 1–2.

Fig. 116 Miniature depicting Christ holding scales, on a folio from an added obituary for Lady Margaret of Roche-Guyon, Paris, ca. 1472. Paris, BnF, Ms lat. 5185 CC, fol. 189r, detail

rubbed down to the underdrawing in two areas. Some of this involved wet-touching, for the liquefied blue paint has migrated to the opposite folio. Christ's face, the gifts, and the faces of the two men have also been touched. The bishop's robes have also been wet-touched, resulting in paint transfer. Someone has even wet-touched Margaret's coat of arms, so that the red paint has adhered to the facing page. Mourners clearly interacted with her obituary on several occasions.

A few folios later, on 190v, the pattern of wear is completely different (Fig. 117). Guillaume's obituary commences with a column-wide miniature, made in the same campaign of work as Margaret's (Fig. 118). The image shows the bishop at a Mass at which an image of the Virgin—either as a sculpture or as an apparition—adorns the altar. Guillaume kneels in prayer while a choir sings behind him. His illumination has barely been touched, with perhaps only the Christ Child's face and the hem of the priest at the altar wet-touched (a glob of the blue hem has stuck to the facing folio), but the image of Guillaume himself is utterly unscathed. If an officiating priest touched this image, he limited himself to the portions with which he self-identified. Why, then, was such an elaborate illuminated obituary deemed necessary?

As women in this obituary book form a minority,[20] a mechanism for the commission might be that sons ordered obituaries for their fathers and wives for their deceased husbands, but there were fewer sons, daughters, and widowers who commissioned them for their dead wives and mothers. Here, the mechanism seems to have been that Margaret used the occasion of Guillaume's death to commission a double obituary; however, hers, not his, was the quire's raison d'être. An explanation for the difference in treatment between Guillaume's and Margaret's portraits might be this: the priest or church official who was performing the Mass for the Dead, therefore the one operating the book, was only one of the people doing the touching. The others were the gathered mourners. Margaret died some time after 1482, and the quire with two obituaries may have been added shortly thereafter, at a time when Margaret's memory was still fresh. Mourners may have avidly touched the book during the annual Masses in the few years after she died; however, there were fewer people who remembered Guillaume in the 1480s, as he had died in 1472. If my hypothesis is correct, then lay mourners, rather than priests, were responsible for much of the image-touching. Again, if this scenario is correct, then mourners at events such as commemorative Masses may have learned to use their bodies in performances involving manuscripts and thereby developed a "performance literacy" that they could have applied in other devotional

---

20 Another woman mentioned is Helysabeth, mother of Rainalclus, who founded a hospital dedicated to St Christopher (fol. 271r). Their joint obituary is not dated but is inscribed in the original thirteenth-century hand.

Fig. 117 Folio from an added obituary for Guillaume Chartier, with a miniature depicting a miraculous mass, Paris, ca. 1472. Paris, BnF, Ms lat. 5185 CC, fol. 190v

settings. For example, they could have applied similar gestures to their private prayer books.

Continual use of the Grand Obituary from the 1240s until the early sixteenth century degraded the parchment, with the oldest material the most worn. The added obituaries with portraits may have been designed to play a physical role in commemoration ceremonies. Those

Fig. 118 Miniature at the obituary for Guillaume Chartier depicting a miraculous mass, Paris, ca. 1472. Paris, BnF, Ms lat. 5185 CC, fol. 190v, det.

who attended Masses in Notre-Dame would have seen how priests interacted with the book, and if my hypothesis is correct, they would have had the opportunity to touch the image of the deceased. Such interactions would have played a role in how additional obituaries were conceived: as loci for touch. It is also likely that the way in which the book was touched changed over time. Perhaps in the thirteenth century, officiants had touched only words and letters. For example, on fol. 311, which is written on original, thirteenth-century parchment, someone has repeatedly wet-touched the KL (for kalens, meaning calendar) at the top of the page (Fig. 119). Although it is not possible to determine whether this wet-touching took place in the thirteenth, fourteenth, or fifteenth centuries, one possibility is that the marks were in fact made shortly after the manuscript's genesis, and that this wet-touching gesture was expanded for use on the imaged obituaries. As with the story of the missal told earlier, what had first been a ritual involving the word turned into one involving the image. The commemorated ones wanted to be remembered—and touched—far into the future. If we think about the layers in chronological order, we may be witnessing the beginnings of a ritual, which automatically inscribes itself on the page and develops over the course of the fourteenth and fifteenth centuries. Whereas the mourners for Simon de Bucy (who died in 1304) barely touched the manuscript, the practice gained momentum shortly thereafter, in the next decade. Given the extent of her gifts, Lady Margaret may have had access to this manuscript and decided to resurrect the elaborate ceremonies around it in the late fifteenth century. She saw this as a viable route to self-commemoration.

Fig. 119 Page on which the "Kalens" has been touched with a wet finger. Paris, BnF, Ms lat. 5185 CC, fol. 311r, det

As this chapter has shown, manuscripts participated in ceremonies. Those who handled them used the books to choreograph rituals in which the books themselves played a physical role. They were touched by audience members, including singers and funeral attendees, in such a way that people wanted to register their presence in the book and at the event. The ways in which books participated in the theatrics will be taken up in the next volume.

Conclusion

The Gloves Are Off

Manuscripts are part of a network of objects whose emotional connection was predicated upon their being handled. Given their size—which is an intimate nod to the animals that provided their raw material—the parchment surfaces of manuscripts only functioned as complex objects with multiple, changing surfaces if they were less than an arm's length away and bracketed by two hands that turned their pages, not inanimately standing on a shelf or lying in a chest. I have shown how gestures by readers—including choirmasters, priests, university proctors, and aldermen—could enlarge the images and decoration so that they became more visible to audiences.

During the period covered by this study—from the twelfth to the early sixteenth century—literacy grew considerably, as did book production. People learned not only how to read, but also how to handle the books they read. Certain physical gestures enacted with manuscripts in the late Middle Ages—including kissing or laying hands on certain images and rubbing out the faces of others—imparted a ritual significance to them. Using manuscripts created the possibility for certain physical habits that changed people's haptic and cognitive spaces. Just as our modern culture of ever smaller electronic screens has created a set of gestures and habits that did not exist previously (speed-typing with two thumbs, scrolling, clicking, tapping, pinching to zoom in), books also gave people a new set of gestures, of rubbing, wet-touching, and scraping, to name a few. By imagining how books incurred their indelible signs of wear, we can figure out how the objects were used, what habits created the wear, and what emotions or rituals lay behind those habits. (Volumes 2 and 3 will delve into more contexts and meanings of wet-touching.) Residue in manuscripts demonstrates how ritualized reading conditioned gestures that then left marks.

The durability of parchment has allowed traces of these gestures to be preserved. This means that parchment manuscripts are especially good at recording habit and ritual: traces of wear are self-documenting. I have looked for signs of wear that help reconstruct book rituals and their permutations. The very act of turning the pages can break the fibers of parchment, and I have shown how backlighted photography might begin to document these transformations, with respect to the Grand Obituary of Notre-Dame. By measuring the darkness of backlighted pages (which indexes broken fibers) within a single volume, one can measure differential use.[1] Two folios in different parts of the book might have corners that look equally clean and unfingerprinted; yet backlighting will show that one of those folios has been more handled than the other because the fibers of the parchment have been creased and broken. Backlighted, the creases show up as dark shadows.

Moreover, dry-touching might only register on the surface of the parchment after multiple events, while wet techniques, because they are more damaging, are likely to be evident after a single event, and their traces can sometimes record separate events. The evidence presented above suggests that wet- and dry-touching were appropriate in different contexts, with wet-touching sometimes serving as a substitute for kissing with the mouth, and dry-touching appropriate for oath-swearing. In Volume 3 we will see that some of the wet-touching introduces dampness at scenes of extreme sadness, as if the beholder were adding real or imitation tears to the image.

In studying the embodied beholding of late-medieval manuscripts, I have considered a variety of manuscript genres, each used in a different context. Book handling took place in social environments, where particular architectural settings contextualized users' actions. I have concluded, however, that these contexts often overlapped, that rituals from one domain borrowed from other domains. As I have shown in this book, oath-taking rituals borrowed from the mass, and images

---

1   In this way, the premises behind the use of a densitometer to measure fingerprints could be extended to large-format manuscripts, which do not reveal their dirt the way that octavo-sized manuscripts do, which have to be held continuously to keep them open. I refer to Rudy, "Dirty Books."

in oath-taking books are often indistinguishable from the Crucifixion images used in missals. Its presence further demonstrates that official rituals, like swearing-in laws, borrow components from the liturgy. Such actions trickle into other forms of public life (to be discussed in Volume 2), and then even into private devotion (to be discussed in Volume 3). Religious rituals shaped events far beyond the altar.

In the end, these book-touching habits were performed by people who had roles in civic, ecclesiastic, and domestic spheres and carried knowledge between them. One of the most significant gestures—the kiss—spread from the missal to these other spheres. These service books were developed in the twelfth century just as the Mass became more theatrical, and the rituals in the constellation of the Mass likewise became more theatrical.

Overall, these sites and patterns suggest five models for transmission, which operate in this and in the subsequent volumes of this study:

1. Someone is required, by the script of the ritual, to carry out particular actions (vertical)

2. A person in authority models behavior that others follow (vertical)

3. A person in authority (for example, a teacher or confessor) actively shapes the behavior through instruction (vertical)

4. Individuals apply haptic habits from one realm into another (horizontal)

5. Peer groups forge and copy behavior as a route to group formation (horizontal)

Some of these forms of transmission can be expected in a rule-bound, hierarchical society that was permeated and held together by religious practices. Interdisciplinary studies may reveal that these moments of transmission were motivated by humans imitating social behavior by means of mirror neurons.[2]

---

2   See Antony D. Passaro, "A Cautionary Note from a Neuroscientist's Perspective," *Postmedieval: A Journal of Medieval Cultural Studies* 3 (2012), pp. 355–60; Jill Stevenson, *Performance, Cognitive Theory, and Devotional Culture: Sensual Piety in Late Medieval York* (Palgrave Macmillan, 2014); John Onians, *European Art: A Neuroarthistory* (Yale University Press, 2016).

In making these claims, I am not precluding other forms of behavioral transmission that would have had a bottom-up structure. In particular, exemplars may include wandering minstrels and players, who were socially marginalized but worked in a living literary culture, and may have had an effect on their audience's behavior; or the behavior of pilgrims at shrines, which may have been partially controlled by shrine keepers but probably involved rituals invented and normalized by pilgrims, such as touching relics, images, and relic-proxies—to have some kind of tangible climax after expending considerable effort to get there. Likewise, certain medical treatments involving relics and images, which may have been spread by cure-seekers at shrines, may not have been strictly class-bound nor imposed from the top down. I leave it to others to pursue these forms of gestural transmission, which will require material evidence beyond the scope of this study.

How precisely one touches the image is directly related to the purpose of the touch. Touching a detail of the infant Christ in a small historiated initial requires great tenderness and care, the displaced tenderness of holding an actual baby. Touching an oath-image while the book is closed—under the very hand performing the touching—shows that physical contact with the image (and not necessarily looking at it) was instrumental for the oath. If my hypotheses are correct, then patterns of wear in oath books can reveal varying levels of literacy of the oath-swearers: perhaps the Cambridge University Statutes and the Arenberg Gospels in the Morgan Library were both touched at the bottom because the oath-swearer could read, whereas the book of statutes in den Bosch was touched at the side because the oath-swearer could not necessarily read, and instead, the relevant oath was read aloud to him by someone oriented toward the text, while the oath-swearer himself stood at the side. One implication of this study is that facsimiles of these manuscripts—even inexpensive ones made with a color printer—can help to enact the physical treatment that books have undergone, and thereby specify the role they played in rituals and in participants' emotional lives.

This study would have been impossible 20 years ago for two reasons. First, that world was still embroiled in iconographic studies and arguments about "masters" and "hands." Such questions of course persist, but other questions and perspectives have also become possible, shepherded in by material culture theory. Such studies inform my current book, although I have decided to tell the story through the lens of previously unpublished medieval manuscripts rather than of recent theorists. Secondly, this study has been made possible by the advent of cheap digital photography, which makes visible thousands of manuscripts that were previously sequestered in the darkness of remote libraries. As I have demonstrated, what is photographed and how it is photographed have consequences for the types of arguments one can make about the past. Twenty years ago, many of the items in this study would have been deemed unworthy of being photographed. Damaged miniatures continue to be suppressed on some institutional websites, and they are often eschewed in printed catalogues (as noted earlier) when the author wants to reproduce a representative example of a particular illuminator.

Simple but underutilized techniques, such as photography with backlighting, have the potential to reveal aspects of an object's biography. Whereas traditionally, documentary photography of manuscripts has endeavored to show the quality of the painting in the clearest possible light, other modes of photography will be necessary as art historians' and book historians' research shifts toward books' material culture. Photographing fore-edges can reveal areas of concentrated wear, and photographs of the backs of kissed miniatures can reveal when users' facial oils have soaked through the parchment.[3] I look forward to a time when such non-standard photography is available to those other than conservators.

As my study of some 500 examples so far indicates, intentional damage to manuscripts falls into several categories, which are categories of method, of motivation, and of audience: gestures can be made with the hand, with the mouth, with another body part, or with an instrument. They can be made with a full hand or just a finger, and that finger can be wet or dry. Motivation could be veneration, destruction, making a physical connection, or simply pointing out a figure or detail to onlookers. The audience for ritualized acts of touching can never just be the reader, for that person's acts are indelible and will be visible to any future reader of the book. Thus, the audience could include many people over time (including future readers), or they could include

---

3   Nicholson Baker, "Discards," *New Yorker*, April 4, 1994, pp. 83–84, applied similar thinking to libraries' card catalogues.

onlookers at this moment of ritualized touching, or both. Furthermore, a book can be touched by one person many times, or by many people once, and those resulting patterns of wear will look completely different. Thus, there is no single context for ritualized touching, but many, as my summative visualization shows (Fig. 120).

Fig. 120 Overview of ways a medieval manuscript is degraded. Diagram made by Kathryn M. Rudy.

http://hdl.handle.net/20.500.12434/74886711

Of all these actions that degrade the manuscript, only a few of them involve the willful destruction motivated by hate or fear. In other words, few fall into the category of "iconoclasm." The others resulted from strong feelings such as the desire to be part of a group, the desire to connect with the supernatural, the desire to be moved by texts and images, the desire to entertain an audience, or the desire for the public recognition of one's gravitas, as when swearing an oath.

The ritual of swearing oaths on Gospel manuscripts persisted into the twentieth century, most visibly in court rooms across Anglo-American courts, where witnesses were "sworn in" on a Bible before giving testimony. Although in the United States witnesses now promise to tell the truth by while raising a hand, with no book present, in my lifetime this process required that they place one hand on a Bible and raise their other hand in the air while audibly promising to tell "the truth, the whole truth, and nothing but the truth." This recently obsolete touching ritual, in turn, replaces an earlier one involving kissing the book, a practice borrowed from England. Doctors in the British Medical Journal of 1892 report:

> We are glad to see that the uncleanly practice of kissing the greasy covers of the much-thumbed Bible on which witnesses have usually been sworn is beginning to be dispensed with since the publication of our recent note on the subject. It cannot be too widely known that any witness can be sworn, on demand, with uplifted hand. At the inquest at Haileybury this week we notice that Dr. C. E. Shelly was so sworn, and so also Mr. Herbert Durham at an inquest at Guy's. If the doctors set the example

of rejecting this risky and disagreeable process, the practice of swearing with the uplifted hand may soon come into general use.[4]

In short, the practice of authorized book-kissing persisted through the Enlightenment and was only laid to rest due to a medical campaign. The doctors' palpable disgust was no doubt fueled by discoveries made by Louis Pasteur (1822–1895) about the microbial causes of disease. If germ theory motivated the shift from kissing the book to touching it, then pluralism and waxing atheism rendered the Gospel irrelevant.

The "greasy covers of the much-thumbed Bible" can tell a story. Even when they were discarded and their book blocks rebound, that, too can tell a story. Bindings protected their contents and also presented a social skin for the book. An avenue for further inquiry involves studying bindings in order to uncover aspects of a book's utility. For example, when manuscripts were rebound, they were often trimmed, so that the dark, damaged patches could be excised. Another reason to rebind books was that their bindings were no longer firm enough to protect the contents. Systematically studying how manuscripts are trimmed and when they were rebound (in part because their original bindings wore out from hard use) could be a fruitful way to track when their use occurred. Many heavily worn manuscripts survive in pristine sixteenth-century bindings, which suggests that their wear occurred before the Reformation, after which they were seldom opened. For example, the Rood Privilegeboek discussed in Chapter 5 is in a binding dated 1580, a date that also corresponds to the final tranche of documents added to the end of the book, and also to the final date when the book was in active use.

While others have shown that ecclesiastical officials ritualistically touched gospels and missals, I hope to have shown that these codified ways of handling books spread into rituals far beyond the church. Laying a hand on the image of Christ on the cross could refer to the Mass and thereby borrow its gravitas, just as touching the image of Christ in Judgment could impose a promise-keeping force onto those who submitted to these rituals and those who witnessed them. When manuscripts were made to record rules and obligations and to ensure that people heeded them, they often included Last Judgment imagery

---

4   *The British Medical Journal*, 2.1666 (Dec. 3, 1892), p. 1247.

of the sort displayed on church portals where judgments took place to buttress the authority of the book, as if to impress the gravity of obligation that they recorded.

At what point did an image become so degraded that it could no longer function? I have suggested that Canon pages in missals, which took the brunt of wear during the course of Mass, had a finite use before their keepers deemed them too worn to function and therefore swapped them, sometimes replacing an entire quire.[5] This situation invites further research: at what point did a Crucifixion image cease having utility within a missal? What happened to the images that were removed? Were they discarded, or held in some kind of elevated position and retained, like the items in a genizah? Indeed, at least some of them might have been taken from their manuscripts and retained as relics of performance. That might be the case with a damaged Crucifixion painting on parchment, which is now separate and glazed (Fig. 121).[6] Dating from ca. 1425–1450, it may have been deemed too damaged to function in its missal and was therefore taken out and framed. A backlighted photograph reveals the extent of the damage, with the parchment weakened by handling (Fig. 122).

In the story I have told here, the Gospel, and later the missal, were religiously charged objects that mediated between God and human Christian believers. The Gospel was a tangible form of God the way that dry ice is a tangible form of carbon dioxide: a powerful, seething entity, employed in the theater of the supernatural. Various speech acts drew on this charged property, and on the Gospel's need-to-be-touched, and they call upon books to play the role of props in theatrical spectacles. Whereas legal frameworks became more secularized in the later middle ages, the "magic" element of books—the fundamental idea that they bind people to God through their divine authority—left its large residue in the new, increasingly secular legal frameworks, which retained the idea of swearing on not just a book (which might contain laws)

---

5 An example is Paris, Bibl. Sainte-Geneviève, Ms. 1259, a thirteenth-century missal from the Abbey of Sainte-Geneviève in Paris, which has two fourteenth-century quires in the center of the book (fols 161–78), which include a new, clean full-page miniature with a Crucifixion and a highly idiosyncratic *bas-de-page* image. Although the catalogue describes this volume as containing parts of two different missals, one could also see the two newer quires as an act of medieval conservation.

6 Collection Huis Bergh Castle, 's-Heerenberg, The Netherlands, fr 40 (inv. 244); see A. S. Korteweg, *Catalogue ... at Huis Bergh Castle*, p. 151.

Conclusion: The Gloves Are Off 221

Fig. 121 Crucified Christ between Mary and John, single sheet, glazed. 's-Heerenberg, The Netherlands, Collection Dr. J. H. van Heek, Huis Bergh Foundation, Ms. Fr 40 (inv. 244). Image © The Huis Bergh Foundation, CC BY 4.0

but on the image of Christ crucified, Christ as Judge, or the Gospel writers whose hands had been guided by God. It's not difficult to get people to embrace the new, but it's difficult to get them to shed the old. Supernatural habits are hard to shake.

Fig. 122 Crucified Christ between Mary and John, single sheet, glazed. 's-Heerenberg, The Netherlands, Collection Dr. J. H. van Heek, Huis Bergh Foundation, Ms. Fr 40 (inv. 244). Amateur photograph with backlighting

Coda

This volume has offered an approach to reception theory, in that the user/viewer/reader co-produces meaning by creating a performance around, with, and in response to, the book and its contents. Insofar as the user/viewer/reader leaves a trace on the page, he or she is also co-producing the surface design alongside the illuminator and scribe, sometimes adding marks, sometimes rubbing them away, sometimes smearing or flattening surface detail. The method I have exemplified in these pages, unlike traditional art history, does not assume that the images in books will be experienced primarily optically, but that manuscripts (as opposed to just images) will be experienced in tactile, proprioceptive, auditory, olfactory, and gustatory ways, as well. It is my sincere hope that readers who have made it this far will close their screens and make their way to the nearest library with staff who will allow them to leaf through a medieval manuscript. Where is *your* nearest manuscript? French regional libraries are my favorites. When you arrive, avoid the urge to request their most famous manuscript, and ask for something grungy and neglected instead.

Ask this manuscript: How were you held, used, handled? Who interacted with you, and who was your audience? Who, if anyone, read you aloud, and how did they hold their audience's attention? Who touched you, and where?

By asking such questions, you are developing a more intimate approach to history. Please email me and tell me about what you learned by thinking about the physical material in this way.

Index

altar 10, 15, 17, 26, 41, 45–46, 54–55, 60, 63, 66, 66, 69, 73, 83, 78, 85, 80, 87, 82, 89, 94, 106, 117–119, 160, 185, 193, 199, 206, 208, 205
Angers Missal = Angers, Archives départementales de Maine-et-Loire, Ms. J(001) 4138 1–2, 22, 102, 106
Aratea 23
Arenberg Gospels = New York, Morgan Library, M.869) 61–63, 67–68, 118, 206

blood 83, 94, 119, 163
book of hours 17, 40, 183, 185

canon (of the Mass) 1, 46, 51, 63, 66, 71, 94–95, 117, 120, 122, 137, 161, 163, 204
choir psalter 157, 168, 194
Clermont Missal = Clermont-Ferrand, Bibliothèque municipale (Bibliothèque du Patrimoine), 0065 (64.-A. 5) 71–73, 79, 144
conservation 114, 188, 210
coutumiers (customs books) 138, 144, 156
coronation 48, 52–55, 60, 66, 69
Coronation Book of Charles V = London, British Library, Cotton MS Tiberius B. viii 69, 72, 77, 84
Crucifixion (cross) 22, 37, 63, 62, 65, 64, 67–68, 71–73, 85, 90, 84–85, 92, 94–96, 98–99, 94, 101–102, 96, 104, 107–108, 111, 113, 115, 118–119, 121–122, 143, 147, 149–155, 163, 165–166, 205, 210–211, 222
curtain 12, 21–22, 39–40, 118, 199

damp breath 158
degradation, abrasion 1–9, 13, 23–25, 27, 31–32, 71–72, 79, 95, 90, 98, 101, 108, 116, 135, 150, 154, 156, 160, 188, 199, 209, 208, 210
digitization 1–2, 37, 94, 147, 154, 161, 178
dry-touching 6, 19, 36, 40, 65, 101, 144, 150, 204, 207

evangelist 74–75, 106, 135, 139, 154
fingernail 32, 72
funeral 195, 198, 205, 212

gold 6, 36, 46, 53, 100–101, 108, 125, 129, 132, 182, 197, 200–202, 204, 206
Gospel manuscripts (evangeliary) 5, 18, 26, 39, 45–46, 51–55, 58, 61, 59–61, 70–71, 73–74, 78, 106, 113, 137, 139, 142, 145, 147, 152, 156, 163, 178, 208–210, 221
Grand Obituary of Notre-Dame = Paris, BnF, Ms. lat. 5185 CC 5, 187, 189, 191–192, 195–196, 198, 200, 202–203, 205, 209, 204

heretic / heresy 70, 160–161, 163–164
holes in parchment 1, 22, 39–40, 101, 110, 145
holy water 8, 32, 60, 160, 166, 168, 180, 182–183, 185, 193

ink 27, 32, 35–36, 94, 108, 116, 132, 162–163, 178, 168, 187, 199
inquisitors' manuals 161
ivories 13

kissing (osculation) 6, 8–9, 12, 17–18, 34–35, 37, 60, 79, 75–76, 83, 77–79, 85–86, 82, 88, 90, 92–95, 90, 96, 98–100, 102, 97, 104, 106–110, 115–116, 118–120, 151, 178, 186, 195, 203–205, 207–209

Last Judgment 17, 51, 119, 131–133, 135, 137, 153, 209
leather 1, 11–12, 40, 110, 119, 153–154, 161
legal manuscript 113, 133
Life of St Edmund = New York, Morgan Library, Ms. M.736 75
liturgy 45, 47, 83, 81, 88, 83, 94, 113, 205

Mass 5, 15, 17–18, 20–21, 45, 48, 50, 66, 83, 85, 80, 86, 81, 87–88, 82, 89–90, 92–93, 87, 94, 100, 108, 114, 135, 137, 151, 157, 169, 163, 175, 180, 186–190, 192–194, 199–200, 205–206, 208, 210, 205, 209–210, 220–222, 225
missal 1, 5, 18, 20–23, 25, 34–35, 37, 41, 45, 52, 67, 71, 69, 73–74, 79, 85, 80, 87, 81, 88–93, 87, 94–102, 106–108, 111–115, 109, 116–118, 120–121, 137, 147, 149, 151–152, 154, 163, 157–158, 193, 211, 205, 209–210
museum 1–2, 24–25

oath iv, 5, 12, 15–16, 35–36, 45, 49–55, 58–60, 63, 66, 64, 67, 65, 68, 66, 69, 67, 70, 68, 71, 69, 72, 70, 73–74, 78, 113, 125–126, 116–117, 128–129, 120–121, 132–133, 137, 127, 139, 142–144, 138, 150–156, 158–161, 163, 165, 204, 204–206, 208
obituary manuscript 187, 193

paint 6, 8, 25–27, 29, 32, 35–36, 58, 69, 72, 74, 79, 85, 92, 95, 99–102, 105–106, 108, 115, 109, 116–120, 129, 132, 142, 156, 168, 163, 175, 180, 195, 197, 199, 202, 205, 207, 207, 210
paper 1, 6, 118–119, 145, 158

photography 3–4, 33, 101, 112, 119, 132, 168, 170–171, 187, 189–191, 203–204, 207, 210–211, 222
  backlighted 189, 204
pontifical 69, 166, 177–178
psalm 32–34

rainwater 32
relic 12, 26, 38–39, 46, 49–55, 60, 74, 76, 85, 113, 129, 133, 160, 170, 184, 186, 193, 206, 210

Sachsenspiegel 50, 115–116, 126–133, 137–138
Sainte-Chapelle missal = London, British Library, Harley Ms 2891 94, 96
saliva 101–102, 108, 120, 147
sewing 1, 12, 21, 39–40, 110
St Amand Gospels = Cologne, Schnütgen Museum, Hs. G 531 58–59

Te igitur 89, 84, 90–91, 108–109, 112, 114, 116, 119
theatricality 5, 18, 61, 59, 73, 79, 78, 85, 81, 88, 83, 205, 210
Tower of Babel 42–43

university 155–156, 203

Waldensians 160–161, 164–166
wax 1, 8, 10, 32–34, 114, 125, 206
wet-touching 6, 9, 19, 35, 37, 40, 42, 97, 105–108, 110, 129, 132, 136, 163, 195, 199, 201–202, 207–208, 211, 203–204, 207
wine 10, 32

York Gospels = York Minster, Ms. Add. 1 61

Bibliography

Aceto, Maurizio, Angelo Agostino, Gaia Fenoglio, Ambra Idone, Fabrizio Crivello, Martin Grießer, Franziska Kirchweger, Katharina Uhlir, and Patricia Roger Puyo, "Analytical Investigations on the Coronation Gospels Manuscript," *Spectrochimica acta. Part A, Molecular and Biomolecular Spectroscopy* 171 (2017), 213–21.

Adams, Morgan Simms, "Identifying Evidence of Textile Curtains in Medieval Manuscripts in the Morgan Library & Museum," *Suave Mechanicals: Essays on the History of Bookbinding* (Vol. 6), edited by Julia Miller (The Legacy Press, 2020), pp. 2–61.

Akehurst, F.R.P., "Illustration and Decoration in Agen Archives Départementales de Lot-et-Garonne 42," in *"Li Premerains Vers": Essays in Honor of Keith Busby*, edited by Catherine M. Jones and Logan E. Whalen (Rodopi, 2011), pp. 1–11.

Albiero, Laura, and Eleonora Celora, eds., "Décrire le manuscrit liturgique: Méthodes, problématiques, perspectives," *Bibliologia* 64 (Brepols, 2021).

Anderson, Christy, Anne Dunlop, and Pamela H. Smith, eds., *The Matter of Art Materials, Practices, Cultural Logics, c.1250–1750* (Manchester University Press, 2016).

Angheben, Marcello, *Les portails romans de Bourgogne: Thèmes et programmes* (Brepols, 2021).

Anjou—Sevilla, *Tesoros de arte, Exposicion organizada por la Comisaria de la Ciudad de Sevillla para 1992 y el Conseil Général de Maine-et-Loire, Real Monasterio de San Clemente, 25 de Junio—2 de Agosto* (Tabapress, 1992).

Assmann, Jan, *Cultural Memory and Early Civilization: Writing, Remembrance, and Political Imagination* (Cambridge University Press, 2011).

Austin, J. L., *How to Do Things with Words* (The William James Lectures) (Clarendon Press, 1962).

Avril, François, *Manuscript Painting at the Court of France: The Fourteenth Century (1310–1380)* (George Braziller, 1978).

Babois-Auboyneau, Agnès, *L'Illustration des Sacramentaires et Missels de l'An 1000 aux Années 1150. I: Synthèse. II: Annexes et Catalogue. III: Illustrations* (3 vols) (University of Poitiers, unpublished MA thesis, 1995).

Baker, Nicholson, "Discards," *New Yorker* (4 April 1994), pp. 83–84.

Bartholeyns, Gil, Pierre-Olivier Dittmar, and Vincent Jolivet, "Des Raisons de Détruire une Image," *Images Revues* 2 (2006), http://imagesrevues.revues.org/248.

Becker, Peter Jörg, and Eef Overgaauw, eds., *Aderlass und Seelentrost. Mittelalterliche Handschriften und Inkunabeln aus Berliner Sammlungen*, exh. cat. (Mainz Zabern, 2003).

Bell, Peter, Joseph Schlecht, and Björn Ommer. "Nonverbal Communication in Medieval Illustrations Revisited by Computer Vision and Art History," *Visual Resources* 29.1–2 (2013), pp. 26–37.

Billoré, Maïté and Esther Dehoux, "The Judge and the Martyr: Images of Power and Justice in Religious Manuscripts from the Twelfth to the Fifteenth Centuries," *Textual and Visual Representations of Power and Justice in Medieval France: Manuscripts and Early Printed Books*, edited by Rosalind Brown-Grant, Anne D. Hedeman, and Bernard Ribémont (Ashgate, 2015), pp. 171–90

Binski, Paul, P. N. R. Zutshi, and Stella Panayotova, *Western Illuminated Manuscripts: A Catalogue of the Collection in Cambridge University Library* (Cambridge University Press, 2011).

Blick, Sarah, and Laura Deborah Gelfand, eds. *Push Me, Pull You: Imaginative and Emotional Interaction in Late Medieval and Renaissance Art* (2 vols) (Brill, 2011).

Booton, Diane E., *Manuscripts, Market, and the Transition to Print in Late Medieval Brittany* (Ashgate, 2010).

Borland, Jennifer, "Violence on Vellum: St. Margaret's Transgressive Body and Its Audience," *Representing Medieval Genders and Sexualities in Europe: Construction, Transformation, and Subversion, 600–1530*, edited by Elizabeth L'Estrange and Alison More (Ashgate, 2011), pp. 67–87.

Bradin, Cormack and Carla Mazzio, *Book Use Book Theory 1500–1700* (University of Chicago Library, 2005), http://pi.lib.uchicago.edu/1001/dig/pres/2011-0098.

Bredekamp, Horst, *Kunst als Medium Sozialer Konflikte: Bilderkämpfe von der Spätantike bis zur Hussitenrevolution* (Suhrkamp, 1975).

Brown, Elizabeth A. R., "The Tyranny of a Construct: Feudalism and Historians of Medieval Europe," *The American Historical Review* 79.4 (1974), pp. 1063–88.

Burgtorf, Jochen, Paul Crawford, and Helen J. Nicholson, *The Debate on the Trial of the Templars (1307–1314)* (Routledge, 2016).

Burke, Peter, *Eyewitnessing: The Uses of Images as Historical Evidence* (Cornell University Press, 2001, reprinted 2008).

Büttner, Andreas, *Der Weg zur Krone: Rituale der Herrschererhebung im spätmittelalterlichen Reich* (Jan Thorbecke Verlag, 2012).

Bynum, Caroline Walker, *Christian Materiality: An Essay on Religion in Late Medieval Europe* (Zone Books, 2011).

Calkins, Robert G., *Illuminated Books of the Middle Ages* (Thames and Hudson, 1983, reprinted Cornell University Press, 1986).

Callahan, Daniel F., "The Peace of God and the Cult of the Saints in Aquitaine in the Tenth and Eleventh Centuries," *Historical Reflections / Réflexions Historiques* 14.3 (1987), 445–66.

Camille, Michael, "Obscenity under Erasure: Censorship in Medieval Illuminated Manuscripts," *Obscenity: Social Control and Artistic Creation in the European Middle Ages*, edited by Jan M. Ziolkowski (Brill, 1998), pp. 139–54.

Carré, Yannick, *Le Baiser sur la Bouche au Moyen Âge: Rites, Symboles, Mentalités, à Travers les Textes et les Images, XIe-XVe Siècles* (Le Léopard d'Or, 1992).

Caspers, Charles, "The Western Church during the Late Middle Ages: *Augenkommunion* or Popular Mysticism?" In *Bread of Heaven: Customs and Practices Surrounding Holy Communion, Essays in the History of Liturgy and Culture* (Liturgia Condenda, Vol. 3), edited by Charles Caspers, Gerard Lukken, and Gerard Rouwhorst (Kok Pharos, 1995), pp. 83–98.

Caviness, Madeline Harrison, *Visualizing Women in the Middle Ages: Sight, Spectacle, and Scopic Economy* (University of Pennsylvania Press, 2001).

Ceulemans, Christina, and Robert Didier. "Les Processions et Le Char de La Châsse de Sainte Gertrude," *Un Trésor Gothique, La Chasse de Nivelles. Exhibition Catalogue. Cologne, Schnütgen-Museum, 24 Novembre 1995–11 Février 1996, Paris, Musée National du Moyen Age-Thermes de Cluny, 12 Mars-10 Juin 1996* (Réunion des Musées Nationaux, 1996), pp. 104–06.

Chen, Andrew H., *Flagellant Confraternities and Italian Art, 1260–1610: Ritual and Experience* (Amsterdam University Press, 2018).

Cohen, Esther, *The Crossroads of Justice: Law and Culture in Late Medieval France* (Brill, 1993).

Collins, Matthew, Matthew D. Teasdale, Sarah Fiddyment, Jiří Vnouček, Valeria Mattiangeli, Camilla Speller, Annelise Binois, Martin Carver, *et al.* "The York Gospels: A 1000-Year Biological Palimpsest," *Royal Society Open Science* 4.10 (2017), pp. 1–11.

Coleman, Joyce, *Public Reading and the Reading Public in Late Medieval England and France* (Cambridge University Press, 1996).

Connerton, Paul, *How Societies Remember* (Cambridge University Press, 1989).

Cushing, Kathleen G., *Reform and the Papacy in the Eleventh Century: Spirituality and Social Change* (Manchester University Press, 2005).

Cutler, Anthony, *The Hand of the Master: Craftsmanship, Ivory, and Society in Byzantium (9th-11th Centuries)* (Princeton University Press, 1994).

Daston, Lorraine, *Things That Talk: Object Lessons from Art and Science* (Zone Books, 2008).

de Hamel, Christopher, *A History of Illuminated Manuscripts* (D.R. Godine, 1986).

Deimling, Barbara, "From Church Portal to Town Hall," in *The History of Courts and Procedure in Medieval Canon Law*, edited by Wilfried Hartmann and Kenneth Pennington (Catholic University of America Press, 2016), pp. 30–50.

Dewick, E. S., ed., *The Coronation Book of Charles V of France; Cottonian Ms Tiberius B viii* (Vol. 16) (Henry Bradshaw Society, 1899).

Dix, Gregory, *The Shape of the Liturgy* (Dacre Press, 1945).

Dobozy, Maria and Ruth Mazo Karras, *The Saxon Mirror: A "Sachsenspiegel" of the Fourteenth Century* (University of Pennsylvania Press, 2014).

Doquang, Mailan S., "Status and the Soul: Commemoration and Intercession in the Rayonnant Chapels of Northern France in the Thirteenth and Fourteenth Centuries," *Memory and Commemoration in Medieval Culture*, edited by Elma Brenner, Mary Franklin-Brown and Meredith Cohen (Ashgate, 2013), pp. 93–118.

Dückers, Rob and Ruud Priem, *The Hours of Catherine of Cleves: Devotion, Demons and Daily Life in the Fifteenth Century* (Ludion, 2009).

Dumoutet, Edouard, *Le Désir de voir l'hostie et les origines de la dévotion au Saint-Sacrement* (Beauchesne, 1926).

[Durand] *The Rationale divinorum officiorum of William Durand of Mende: A New Translation of the Prologue and Book One*, trans. Timothy M. Thibodeau (Columbia University Press, 2007).

[Durand] *On the Clergy and Their Vestments: A New Translation of Books 2–3 of the Rationale divinorum officiorum*, trans. Timothy M. Thibodeau (University of Scranton Press, 2010).

[Durand] *Rationale IV: On the Mass and Each Action Pertaining to It* (Corpus Christianorum in Translation (CCT 14)), trans. Timothy M. Thibodeau (Brepols, 2013).

Elkins, James, "On Some Limits of Materiality in Art History" *31: Das Magazin des Instituts für Theorie* [Zürich] 12 (2008), pp. 25–30.

Els, Josef, "Das Aachener Liuthar-Evangeliar. Zur Bedeutung des Aachener Evangeliars Ottos III," *Rheinische Heimatpflege* 48 (2011), pp. 181–94.

Freedberg, David, "The Fear of Art: How Censorship Becomes Iconoclasm," *Social Research* 83.1 (2016), pp. 67–99.

Freedberg, David, *The Power of Images: Studies in the History and Theory of Response* (University of Chicago Press, 1989).

Frijhoff, Willem, "The Kiss Sacred and Profane: Reflections on a Cross-Cultural Confrontation," *A Cultural History of Gesture: From Antiquity to the Present Day*, edited by Jan N. Bremmer and Herman Roodenburg, pp. 210–36 (Polity, 1994).

Fullagar, Richard, and Rhys Jones, "Usewear and Residue Analysis of Stone Artefacts from the Enclosed Chamber, Rocky Cape, Tasmania," *Archaeology in Oceania* 39.2 (2004), pp. 79–93.

Fulton, Rachel, "'Taste and See That the Lord Is Sweet' (Ps. 33:9): The Flavor of God in the Monastic West," *The Journal of Religion* 86.2 (2006), pp. 169–204.

Fulton, Rachel, *From Judgment to Passion: Devotion to Christ and the Virgin Mary, 800–1200* (Columbia University Press, 2002).

Gameson, Richard, "Manuscript Art at Christ Church, Canterbury, in the Generation after St Dunstan," *St Dunstan: His Life, Times, and Cult*, edited by Nigel Ramsay, Margaret Sparks and Tim Tatton-Brown (Boydell Press, 1992).

Ganz, David, "Giving to God in the Mass: The Experience of the Offertory," *The Languages of Gift in the Early Middle Ages*, edited by Wendy Davies and Paul Fouracre (Cambridge University Press, 2010), pp. 18–32.

Ganz, David, "Touching Books, Touching Art: Tactile Dimensions of Sacred Books in the Medieval West" *Postscripts* 8.1–2 (2017), pp. 81–113.

Ganz, David, *Buch-Gewänder: Prachteinbände im Mittelalter* (Dietrich Reimer Verlag, 2015).

Giraud, Cédric, ed., *Notre-Dame de Paris, 1163–2013: Actes du Colloque Scientifique Tenu au Collège des Bernardins, à Paris, du 12 au 15 Décembre 2012 / Actes Réunis par Cédric Giraud* (Brepols, 2013).

Gittos, Helen, *Liturgy, Architecture, and Sacred Places in Anglo-Saxon England. Medieval History and Archaeology* (Oxford University Press, 2013).

Green, Johanna, "Digital Manuscripts as Sites of Touch: Using Social Media for 'Hands-On' Engagement with Medieval Manuscript Materiality," *Archive Journal* (September 2018), http://www.archivejournal.net/?p=7795.

Griffiths, Fiona and Kathryn Starkey, eds., *Sensory Reflections: Traces of Experience in Medieval Artifacts* (Sense, Matter, and Medium, 1) (De Gruyter, 2019).

Gruber, Christiane, "In Defense and Devotion: Affective Practices in Early Modern Turco-Persian Manuscript Paintings," *Affect, Emotion, and Subjectivity in Early Modern Muslim Empires: New Studies in Ottoman, Safavid, and Mughal Art and Culture*, edited by Kishwar Rizvi (Brill, 2017), pp. 95–123.

Guérard, Benjamin Edme Charles, *Cartulaire de l'Église Notre Dame de Paris* (Collection de Documents Inédits sur l'Histoire de France. Sér. 1, Collection des Cartulaires de France. Tom. 4–7) (Imprimerie de Crapelet, 1850).

Hahn, Cynthia, "Peregrinatio et Natio: The Illustrated Life of Edmund, King and Martyr," *Gesta* 30.2 (1991), pp. 119–39.

Hennessy, Marlene Villalobos, "The Social Life of a Manuscript Metaphor: Christ's Blood as Ink," *The Social Life of Illumination: Manuscripts, Images, and Communities in the Late Middle Ages* (Medieval Texts and Cultures of Northern Europe), edited by Joyce Coleman, Mark Cruse and Kathryn A. Smith (Brepols, 2013), pp. 17–52.

Hill, Derek, *Inquisition in the Fourteenth Century: The Manuals of Bernard Gui and Nicholas Eymerich* (Heresy and Inquisition in the Middle Ages) (York Medieval Press, 2019).

Hofmeister, Philipp, *Die christlichen Eidesformen. Eine liturgie- und rechtsgeschichtliche Untersuchung* (Zink, 1957).

Hughes, Andrew S., *Medieval Manuscripts for Mass and Office: A Guide to Their Organization and Terminology* (University of Toronto Press, 1995).

Jackson, Deirdre, "Virgin, Devil, Bishop, King: Nicola Pisano's Pulpit in Siena and Alfonso X's Cantigas de Santa Maria," in *Illuminating the Middle Ages: Tributes to Prof. John Lowden from His Students, Friends and Colleagues* (Library of the Written Word, Vol. 79), edited by Laura Cleaver, Alixe Bovey and Lucy Donkin (Brill, 2020), pp. 259–75.

Johnston, Ruth A., *All Things Medieval: An Encyclopedia of the Medieval World* (2 vols) (Greenwood, 2011).

Jungmann, Josef A., *The Mass of the Roman Rite: Its Origins and Development* (2 vols), trans. Francis A. Brunner (Benziger, 1951), Rev. and abridged ed. *Notre Dame, Ind.: Christian Classics*, [2012].

Katzenstein, Ranee and Emilie Savage-Smith. *The Leiden Aratea: Ancient Constellations in a Medieval Manuscript* (J. Paul Getty Museum, 1988).

Kisch, Guido, "A Fourteenth-Century Jewry Oath of South Germany," *Speculum* 15.3 (1940), pp. 331–37.

Kisch, Guido, *Sachsenspiegel and Bible* (Publications in Mediaeval Studies, Vol. 5) (The University of Notre Dame Press, 1941).

Klápste, Jan, *The Czech Lands in Medieval Transformation* (East Central and Eastern Europe in the Middle Ages, 450–1450), trans. Sean Mark Miller and Katerina Millerová (Brill, 2012).

Koldeweij, Jos, "Gezworen op het Kruis of op Relieken," *Representatie. Kunsthistorische Bijdragen over Vorst, Staatsmacht en Beeldende Kunst, Opgedragen aan Robert W. Scheller*, edited by Johann-Christian Klamt and Kees Veelenturf (Nijmegen: Valkhof Pers, 2004), pp. 158–79.

Kolmer, Lothar, *Promissorische Eide im Mittelalter* (Regensburger historische Forschungen) (M. Lassleben, 1989).

Korteweg, Anne S., *Catalogue of Medieval Manuscripts and Incunabula at Huis Bergh Castle in 's-Heerenberg* (Stichting Huis Bergh, 2013).

Korteweg, Anne S., *Liturgische Handschriften uit de Koninklijke Bibliotheek* (Rijksmuseum Meermanno-Westreenianum, 1983).

Kwakkel, Erik, "Decoding the Material Book: Cultural Residue in Medieval Manuscripts," in *The Medieval Manuscript Book: Cultural Approaches*, edited by Michael Van Dussen and Michael Johnston (Cambridge University Press, 2015), pp. 60–76.

Lehmann, Ann-Sophie, "Taking Fingerprints: The Indexical Affordances of Artworks' Material Surfaces," *Spur der Arbeit: Oberfläche und Werkprozess*, edited by Magdalena Bushart and Henrike Haug (Böhlau Verlag, 2018 (2017)), pp. 199–218.

Leroquais, V., *Les Sacramentaires et les Missels Manuscrits des Bibliothèques Publiques de France* (4 vols) (Tiip. Macon, 1924).

Lowden, John, "Treasures Known and Unknown in the British Library" (Keynote address at a conference "Treasures Known and Unknown," held at the British Library Conference Centre, 2–3 July 2007), http://www.bl.uk/catalogues/illuminatedmanuscripts/TourKnownA.asp.

Magin, Christine, "So dir Gott Helfe: Der Erfurter Judeneid im historischen Kontext," *Erfurter Schriften zur Jüdischen Geschichte* 4 (2017), pp. 14–28.

Malafouris, Lambros, *How Things Shape the Mind: A Theory of Material Engagement* (The MIT Press, 2013).

Mann, Jacob, "Oaths and Vows in the Synoptic Gospels," *The American Journal of Theology* 21.2 (1917), pp. 260–74.

Marcus, Jacob Rader, *The Jew in the Medieval World: A Source Book, 315–1791* (Hebrew Union College Press, 1990).

Mauss, Marcel, "Techniques of the Body," *Incorporations*, edited by Jonathan Crary and Sanford Kwinter (Zone, 1992), pp. 455–77.

McGerr, Rosemarie Potz, "Guyart Desmoulins, the Vernacular Master of Histories, and is Bible Historiale," *Viator* 14 (1983), pp. 211–44.

Meier, Esther, "Turning Toward God and Outward Actions: The Priest in the *Te Igitur* Initials of the Middle Ages," *Iconography of Liturgical Textiles in the Middle Ages*, edited by Evelin Wetter and Michael Bangert (Abegg-Stiftung, 2010), pp. 79–88.

Miegroet, Hans J. van, "Gerard David's 'Justice of Cambyses': Exemplum Iustitiae or Political Allegory?" *Simiolus: Netherlands Quarterly for the History of Art* 18.3 (1988), pp. 116–33.

Molinier, Auguste, *Obituaires de la Province de Sens, Première Partie* (Imprimerie Nationale, 1902).

Moore, R. I., *The Formation of a Persecuting Society: Authority and Deviance in Western Europe, 950–1250* (2nd ed.) (Blackwell, 2007).

Moullié, Amédée, "Coutumes Priviléges et Franchises de la Ville d'Agen *Recueil des travaux de la société d'agriculture, sciences et arts d'Agen* 5 (1850), pp. 237–343.

Nees, Lawrence, "Prolegomenon to a Study of the Vienna Coronation Gospels: Common Knowledge, Scholarship, Tradition, Legend, Myth," in Garver, Valerie L., and Owen M. Phelan, eds. *Rome and Religion in the Medieval World: Studies in Honor of Thomas F.X. Noble* (Ashgate, 2014), pp. 253–74; republished as an unpaginated ebook, Routledge, 2016, Chapter 12, https://doi.org/10.4324/9781315607030

Nelson, Robert S., "The Discourse of Icons, Then and Now," *Art History* 12 (1989), pp. 144–57.

Neuheuser, Hanns Peter, "Die Kanonblätter aus der Schule des Moerdrecht-Meisters," *Wallraf-Richartz-Jahrbuch* 64 (2003), pp. 187–214.

Newhauser, Richard G., "The Senses, the Medieval Sensorium, and Sensing (in) the Middle Ages," in *Handbook of Medieval Culture* (Vol. 3), edited by Albrecht Classen (De Gruyter, 2015), pp. 1559–75.

O'Daly, Irene, "Leiden, UB, GRO 22: The Art of Reasoning in Medieval Manuscripts" (Dec. 2020), https://art-of-reasoning.huygens.knaw.nl/gro22.

O'Meara, Carra Ferguson, *Monarchy and Consent: The Coronation Book of Charles V of France: British Library Ms Cotton Tiberius B.viii* (Harvey Miller, 2001).

Orchard, Nicholas, *The Leofric Missal* (Boydell Press for the Henry Bradshaw Society, 2002).

Overbey, Karen Eileen and Jennifer Borland, "Diagnostic Performance and Diagrammatic Manipulation in the Physician's Folding Almanacs," in *The Agency of Things in Medieval and Early Modern Art: Materials, Power and Manipulation*, edited by Grazyna Jurkowlaniec, Ika Maryjaszkiewicz and Zuzanna Sarnecka (Routledge, 2018), pp. 144–56.

Pächt, Otto and J. J. G. Alexander, *Illuminated Manuscripts in the Bodleian Library Oxford*, edited by J. J. G. Alexander (Clarendon Press, 1966–1973).

Palazzo, Éric, "Art and Liturgy in the Middle Ages: Survey of Research (1980–2003) and Some Reflections on Method," *The Journal of English and Germanic Philology* (Vol. 105.1 of The State of Medieval Studies) (Jan. 2006), pp. 170–84.

Palazzo, Éric, "Performing the Liturgy," *Early Medieval Christianities, c.600-C.1100*, edited by Thomas F. X. Noble and Julia M. H. Smith (Cambridge University Press, 2008), pp. 472–88.

Pallasmaa, Juhani, *The Eyes of the Skin: Architecture and the Senses* (Academy Editions, 1996).

Pallasmaa, Juhani, *The Thinking Hand: Existential and Embodied Wisdom in Architecture* (Wiley, 2009).

Paquay, Valentijn, "Het Rood Privilegeboek (1): Kroonjuweel van de stad," and "Het Rood Privilegeboek (2): Kroonjuweel van de stad," *Bossche Bladen* (n.p. [2009]), pp. 84–89 and 117–22, reproduced in *Bossche Encyclopedie*, edited by A.F.A.M. (Ton) Wetzer, https://www.bossche-encyclopedie.nl/.

Passaro, Antony D., "A Cautionary Note from a Neuroscientist's Perspective," *Postmedieval: A Journal of Medieval Cultural Studies* 3 (2012), pp. 355–60.

Petkov, Kiril, *The Kiss of Peace: Ritual, Self, and Society in the High and Late Medieval West* (Cultures, Beliefs, and Traditions) (Brill, 2003).

Pinner, Rebecca, *The Cult of St Edmund in Medieval East Anglia* (Boydell Press, 2015).

Plummer, John, *Liturgical Manuscripts for the Mass and the Divine Office* (The Pierpont Morgan Library, 1964).

Poleg, Eyal, "The Bible as Talisman: Textus and Oath-Books," *Approaching the Bible in Medieval England* (Manchester Medieval Studies) (Manchester University Press, 2013), pp. 59–107.

Prinet, Max, "L'Illustration du Grand Obituaire de Notre-Dame de Paris," *Mémoires de la Société des Antiquaires de France* 77 (1924–1927), pp. 109–24.

Radding, Charles M. and Antonio Ciaralli, *The Corpus Iuris Civilis in the Middle Ages: Manuscripts and Transmission from the Sixth Century to the Juristic Revival* (Brill, 2007).

Randolph, Adrian W. B., *Touching Objects: Intimate Experiences of Italian Fifteenth-Century Art* (Yale University Press, 2014).

Renier, Gustaaf Johannes, *History, Its Purpose and Method* (Allen and Unwin, 1950).

Richardson, H. G., "The English Coronation Oath," *Speculum*, 24.1 (1949), pp. 44–75.

Rogers, Nicholas, "From Alan the Illuminator to John Scott the Younger: Evidence for Illumination in Cambridge," in *The Cambridge Illuminations: The Conference Papers*, edited by Stella Panayotova (Harvey Miller, 2007), pp. 287–99, fig. 4a.

Rogers, Nicholas, "The Old Proctor's Book: A Cambridge Manuscript of c. 1390," *England in the Fourteenth Century: Proceedings of the 1985 Harlaxton Symposium*, edited by W.M. Ormrod, pp. 213–23 (Boydell Press, 1986).

Rosenthal, Jane E., *The Historiated Canon Tables of the Arenberg Gospels* (Columbia University, PhD dissertation, 1974).

Rubin, Miri, *Corpus Christi: The Eucharist in Late Medieval Culture* (Cambridge University Press, 1991).

Rudy, Kathryn, "Dirty Books: Quantifying Patterns of Use in Medieval Manuscripts Using a Densitometer," *Journal of Historians of Netherlandish Art* 2, 1 (2010), unpaginated.

Rudy, Kathryn, "Kissing Images, Unfurling Rolls, Measuring Wounds, Sewing Badges and Carrying Talismans: Considering Some Harley Manuscripts through the Physical Rituals They Reveal," *eBLJ* (the electronic journal of the British Library) *special volume: Proceedings from the Harley Conference, British Library, 29–30 June 2009* (2011).

Rudy, Kathryn, *Piety in Pieces: How Medieval Readers Customized Their Manuscripts* (Cambridge: Open Book Publishers, 2016), https://doi.org/10.11647/OBP.0094.

Rudy, Kathryn, *Postcards on Parchment: The Social Lives of Medieval Books* (Yale University Press, 2015).

Scherer, J. E., *Die Rechtsverhaeltnisse der Juden in den Deutsch- Oesterreichischen Ländern. Mit einer Einleitung über die Principien der Judengesetzgebung in Europa während des Mittelalters* (Duncker and Humblot, 1901).

Schnusenberg, Christine, *The Relationship Between the Church and the Theatre: Exemplified by Selected Writings of the Church Fathers and by Liturgical Texts until Amalarius of Metz (775–852 A. D)* (University Press of America, 1988).

Scholten, Frits, "Een Nederlandse ivoren pax uit de late middeleeuwen," *Bulletin van het Rijksmuseum* 52.1 (2004), pp. 2–23.

Schramm, Percy Ernst, *A History of the English Coronation* (Clarendon Press, 1937).

Schreiner, Klaus, "Litterae Mysticae. Symbolik und Pragmatik heiliger Buchstaben, Texte und Bücher in Kirche und Gesellschaft des Mittelalters," *Pragmatische Dimensionen mittelalterlicher Schriftkultur*, edited by Christel Meier, et al. (Wilhelm Fink, 2002), pp. 277–337.

Sciacca, Christine, "Raising the Curtain on the Use of Textiles in Manuscripts," *Weaving, Veiling, and Dressing: Textiles and Their Metaphors in the Late Middle Ages* (Medieval Church Studies), edited by Kathryn M. Rudy and Barbara Baert (Brepols, 2007), pp. 161–90.

Serbat, Louis, "Tablettes à écrire du XIVe siècle," *Mémoires de la Société nationale des Antiquaires de France* 73 (1913, published 1914), 301–13.

Simader, Friedrich, "Das so genannte 'Reiner Musterbuch'—Notizen zum Forschungsstand," in *Zisterziensisches Schreiben im Mittelalter—Das Skriptorium der Reiner Mönche: Beiträge der Internationalen Tagung im Zisterzienserstift Rein, Mai 2003* (Jahrbuch FüR Internationale Germanistik., Reihe A: Kongressberichte), edited by Anton Schwob and Karin Kranich-Hofbauer (Peter Lang, 2005), pp. 141–50.

Simons, Patricia, "Women in Frames: The Gaze, the Eye, the Profile in Renaissance Portraiture," *History Workshop* 25 (Spring, 1988), pp. 4–30.

Stanford, Charlotte A., "The Body at the Funeral: Imagery and Commemoration at Notre-Dame, Paris, About 1304–1318," *The Art Bulletin* 89.4 (2007), pp. 657–73.

Stevenson, Jill, *Performance, Cognitive Theory, and Devotional Culture: Sensual Piety in Late Medieval York* (Palgrave Macmillan, 2014).

Stobbe, Otto, *Die Juden in Deutschland während des Mittelalters* (L. Lamm, 1923).

Stones, Alison, and François Avril, *Gothic Manuscripts, 1260–1320: Part Two* (2 vols) (Harvey Miller Publishers, 2014).

Välimäki, Reima, *The Awakener of Sleeping Men: Inquisitor Petrus Zwicker, the Waldenses, and the Retheologisation of Heresy in Late Medieval Germany* (University of Turku, PhD thesis, 2016).

Van Dijk, S.J.P., *Handlist of Latin Liturgical Manuscripts in the Bodleian Library* (8 vols), typescript created 1957–1960.

Velden, Hugo van der, "Cambyses for Example: The Origins and Function of an Exemplum Iustitiae in Netherlandish Art of the Fifteenth, Sixteenth and Seventeenth Centuries," *Simiolus: Netherlands Quarterly for the History of Art* 23.1 (1995), 5–62.

Vogel, Cyrille, Reinhard Elze, and Michel Andrieu, eds., *Le Pontifical Romano-Germanique du Dixième Siècle* (vols 1–3) (Biblioteca apostolica vaticana, 1963–1972).

Ward, P. L. "The Coronation Ceremony in Mediaeval England," *Speculum* 14.2 (1939), pp. 160–78.

Wijsman, Hanno, "Een eed zweren op een miniatuur," *Handschriften voor het hertogdom. De mooiste verluchte manuscripten van Brabantse hertogen, edellieden, kloosterlingen en stedelingen* (Veerhuis, 2006).

Zammit Lupi, Theresa, "Books as Multisensory Experience," *Tracing Written Heritage in a Digital Age*, edited by Ephrem Ishac, Thomas Casandy and Theresa Zammit Lupi (Harrassowitz, 2021), pp. 21–31.

Illustrations

Fig. 1	Opening from a Missal for the Use of Angers at the Canon, 1439? Angers, Archives départementales de Maine-et-Loire, J(001) 4138, fol. 196v (quater)-196r (quinquies). Cliché: IRHT-CNRS	2
Fig. 2	Folio from a missal, with a Mass for St Elizabeth added in a fifteenth-century hand. Paris, Bibliothèque Sainte-Geneviève, Ms 97, fol. 241r. Cliché: IRHT-CNRS	21
Fig. 3	Opening in a missal for the Use of Angers, before the Canon, 1439(?). Angers, Archives départementales de Maine-et-Loire, J(001) 4138, fols 195v-196r. Cliché: IRHT-CNRS	23
Fig. 4	Heavily worn folio in a choir breviary, at the incipit Beatus vir. Oxford, Bodleian Library, Ms. Lat. Liturg. d. 7, fol. 41r.	30
Fig. 5	Opening in a choir breviary, with replaced corners. Oxford, Bodleian Library, Ms. Lat. Liturg. d. 7, fol. 88v-89r.	31
Fig. 6	Folio of Augustine's commentary on Psalms from Reading Abbey, with wax stains, photographed in raking light. Oxford, Bodleian Library, Ms. Bodl. 241, fol. 33v	33
Fig. 7	Folio of Augustine's commentary on Psalms from Reading Abbey, with wax stains. Oxford, Bodleian Library, Ms. Bodl. 241, fol. 24r	34
Fig. 8	Folio from a Missal, with the Ascension of Christ, ca. 1380–1420. Ljubliana, The National and University Library of Slovenia, Ms. 162, fol. 102r. Public domain image provided by Narodna in univerzitetna knjižnica	38
Fig. 9	Margin in a missal with a repair, from a missal from the Knights Hospitallers, Southern Germany, 1469. 's-Heerenberg, The Netherlands, Collection Dr. J. H. van Heek, Huis Bergh Foundation, Ms. 15. Image © The Huis Bergh Foundation, CC BY 4.0	41
Fig. 10	Tower of Babel, from *Guiard des Moulins*, *Grande Bible Historiale Complétée*, written and illuminated in Paris, 1371–1372. The Hague, Meermanno Museum, Ms. 10 B 23, fol. 19r	43

Fig. 11	Incipit of the *Constitutiones feudorum cum glossis*. France, 14th century. Vienna, Österreichische Nationalbibliothek, cod. 2262, fol. 174v.	49
Fig. 12	Opening at the beginning of the Book of Matthew, Evangeliarium, St. Amand, c. 860–880. Cologne, Schnütgen Museum, Hs. G 531, fol. 11v-12r.	58
Fig. 13	Opening at the beginning of the Book of Mark. Evangeliarium, St. Amand, c. 860–880. Cologne, Schnütgen Museum, Hs. G 531, fols 62v-63r.	58
Fig. 14	Opening at the beginning of the Book of Luke. Evangeliarium, St. Amand, c. 860–880. Cologne, Schnütgen Museum, Hs. G 531, fols 97v-98r.	59
Fig. 15	Opening at the beginning of the Book of John. Evangeliarium, St. Amand, c. 860–880. Cologne, Schnütgen Museum, Hs. G 531, fols 151v-152r.	59
Fig. 16	Second opening in the Book of Luke. Evangeliarium, St. Amand, c. 860–880. Cologne, Schnütgen Museum, Hs. G 531, fols 98v-99r.	61
Fig. 17	Evangelist portrait of John, full-page drawing, *Arenberg Gospels*, Canterbury, ca. 1000–1020. New York, The Morgan Library & Museum, Ms. M.869, fols 126v.	64
Fig. 18	Crucifixion page, full-page drawing with painted elements. *Arenberg Gospels*, Canterbury, ca. 1000–1020. New York, The Morgan Library & Museum, Ms. M. 869, fol. 9v.	65
Fig. 19	Added oaths. *Arenberg Gospels*. New York, The Morgan Library & Museum, Ms. M. 869, fol. 4r.	67
Fig. 20	Scraped inscription on the back of the Crucifixion miniature. *Arenberg Gospels*. New York, The Morgan Library & Museum, Ms. M. 869, fol. 9r.	68
Fig. 21	Charles V swearing an oath on an open book being held by a bishop, Paris, 1365. London, British Library, Cotton Ms. Tiberius B VIII/2, fol. 46v.	70
Fig. 22	Christ Crucified, and God in Majesty, full-page miniatures in a missal for the Use of Clermont, 1455–1474. Clermont-Ferrand, Bibliothèque municipal, Ms. 65, fols 216v-217r. Cliché: IRHT-CNRS	71
Fig. 23	Opening folio of *Guiard des Moulins, Bible Historiale Complétée*, with God in Majesty surrounded by the evangelists' symbols. Paris, ca. 1370–1380. The Hague, Koninklijke Bibliotheek, Ms. 78 D 43, fol. 1r.	75

Fig. 24	Presentation scene: Petrus Comestor presenting his book to Archbishop Guillaume of Sens, in Guiard des Moulins, *Bible Historiale Complétée*. Paris, ca. 1370–1380. The Hague, Koninklijke Bibliotheek, Ms. 78 D 43, fol. 2r.	76
Fig. 25	God measuring the Universe with a compass, in Guiard des Moulins, *Bible Historiale Complétée*. Paris, ca. 1370–1380. The Hague, Koninklijke Bibliotheek, Ms. 78 D 43, fol. 3r, detail	76
Fig. 26	Creation: division of the waters, in Guiard des Moulins, *Bible Historiale Complétée*. Paris, ca. 1370–1380. The Hague, Koninklijke Bibliotheek, Ms. 78 D 43, fol. 3v, detail	77
Fig. 27	Creation: sun and moon, in Guiard des Moulins, *Bible Historiale Complétée*. Paris, ca. 1370–1380. The Hague, Koninklijke Bibliotheek, Ms. 78 D 43, fol. 4r, detail	77
Fig. 28	Creation: beasts of the field and Adam, in Guiard des Moulins, *Bible Historiale Complétée*. Paris, ca. 1370–1380. The Hague, Koninklijke Bibliotheek, Ms. 78 D 43, fol. 5r, detail	78
Fig. 29	Monks kneeling and grasping the feet of St Edmund and kissing them, in a Miscellany on the life of St Edmund. England, Bury St Edmunds, c. 1130. New York, The Morgan Library & Museum, Ms. M.736, fol. 22v	82
Fig. 30	Osculation, in the *Coronation Book of Charles V*, Paris, 1365. London, British Library, Cotton Ms. Tiberius B VIII/2, fol. 64r.	84
Fig. 31	*Te igitur* folio from a missal for the use of the abbey of Saint-Desle de Lure, made before 1073. Besançon, Bibliothèque municipale, Ms. 72, fol. 13v. Cliché: IRHT-CNRS	91
Fig. 32	Opening at the Canon from a missal, France, thirteenth century. Paris, Bibliothèque Mazarine, Ms. 422, fols 125v-126r. Cliché: IRHT-CNRS	92
Fig. 33	Opening of a missal at the Canon, from the abbey of Notre-Dame in Belval, twelfth century. Charleville-Mézières, Bibliothèque municipale [Médiathèque Voyelles], Ms. 3, fols 44v-45r. Cliché: IRHT-CNRS	93
Fig. 34	Opening of a missal at the Canon, Paris in 1317 or 1318. London, British Library, Harley Ms. 2891, fols 145v-146r.	95
Fig. 35	Crucifixion in a missal at the Canon. Southern Germany (Augsburg?), 1469. Ms. 15, Inv. nr. 281, fol. 70v. 's-Heerenberg, The Netherlands, Collection Dr. J. H. van Heek, Huis Bergh Foundation, Ms. 15. Image © The Huis Bergh Foundation, CC BY 4.0	96

Fig. 36	Opening of a missal within the Canon. Southern Germany (Augsburg?), 1469. Ms. 15, Inv. nr. 281, fols 70v-71r. 's-Heerenberg, The Netherlands, Collection Dr. J. H. van Heek, Huis Bergh Foundation, Ms. 15. Image © The Huis Bergh Foundation, CC BY 4.0	97
Fig. 37	Opening of a missal within the Canon. Southern Germany (Augsburg?), 1469. Ms. 15, Inv. nr. 281, fols 78v-79r. 's-Heerenberg, The Netherlands, Collection Dr. J. H. van Heek, Huis Bergh Foundation, Ms. 15. Image © The Huis Bergh Foundation, CC BY 4.0	97
Fig. 38	Opening of a missal at the Canon. Paris ca. 1315. Paris, Bibliothèque national de France, Ms. lat. 861, fol. 147v-148r.	98
Fig. 39	Opening of a missal at the Canon, missal of the Nijmegen Bakers' Guild, 1482–1483. Nijmegen, Museum Het Valkhof, Ms. CIA 2, fols 125v-126r.	99
Fig. 40	Opening of a missal at the Canon, for the use of Amiens, ca. 1490–1500. Amiens, Bibliothèque Municipale, Ms. 163, fol. 155v-156r. Cliché: IRHT-CNRS	100
Fig. 41	Opening of a missal, with a Crucifixion, thirteenth century, use of Arras. Arras, Bibliothèque Municipale, Ms. 888, fol. 175v-176r. Cliché: IRHT-CNRS	101
Fig. 42	Opening of a missal at the Canon, early fifteenth century, made for Paris. Paris, Bibliothèque Sainte-Geneviève, Ms. 97, fols 136v–137r. Cliché: IRHT-CNRS	102
Fig. 43	Canon page shot with backlighting, made for Paris, early fifteenth century. Paris, Bibliothèque Sainte-Geneviève, Ms. 97, fols 136v. Photograph: author	103
Fig. 44	Back of the folio with the Crucifixion, made for Paris, early fifteenth century. Paris, Bibliothèque Sainte-Geneviève, Ms. 97, fol. 136r. Cliché: IRHT-CNRS	104
Fig. 45	Back of the folio with God the Father, made for Paris, early fifteenth century. Paris, Bibliothèque Sainte-Geneviève, Ms. 97, fol. 137v. Cliché: IRHT-CNRS	105
Fig. 46	Opening of a missal within the Canon, Use of Angers, 1439? Angers, Archives départementales de Maine-et-Loire, J(001) 4138, fol. 196v (quarter) – 196r (quinquies). Cliché: IRHT-CNRS	106
Fig. 47	Crucifixion (Delft, ca. 1460–1480) mounted in a missal (South Holland, ca. 1440–1450). The Hague, Koninklijke Bibliotheek, Ms. B 76 E 2, fol. 101v	107

Fig. 48	*Te igitur* page from a missal, fourteenth century, Use of Chartres. Oxford, Bodleian Library, Canon Liturg. 344, fol. 105r (*cvi* in the original foliation)	109
Fig. 49	Detail from previous image: fingerprint and wet-touched baguette. Oxford, Bodleian Library, Ms. Canon Liturg. 344, detail of 105r.	110
Fig. 50	Crucifixion in a missal at the Canon, twelfth century with later additions, Augsburg. Oxford, Bodleian Library, Ms. Canon. Liturg. 354 fol. 67r (which is fol. Lxfij in the original foliation)	111
Fig. 51	Back of the Canon page (which faces the *Te igitur*) in a missal, twelfth century with later additions, Augsburg. Oxford, Bodleian Library, Ms. Canon. Liturg. 354, fol. 67v	112
Fig. 52	Crucifixion in a missal at the Canon, twelfth century with later additions, Augsburg. Oxford, Bodleian Library, Ms. Canon. Liturg. 354 fol. 67r (which is fol. Lxfij in the original foliation). Photographed in its material context	113
Fig. 53	Back of the Canon page (which faces the *Te igitur*) in a missal, twelfth century with later additions, Augsburg. Oxford, Bodleian Library, Ms. Canon. Liturg. 354, fol. 67v. Photographed in its material context	114
Fig. 54	Added office of the crown of thorns in a twelfth-century missal, Augsburg. Oxford, Bodleian Library, Ms. Canon. Liturg. 354, fols 61v-62r.	115
Fig. 55	Folio from a missal for the Use of Utrecht, with a historiated initial depicting David at prayer for the first Sunday of Advent in the Temporal, ca. 1400–1410 with added sections, Northern Netherlands. The Hague, Koninklijke Bibliotheek, Ms. 128 D 29, fol. 7v.	116
Fig. 56	Opening of a missal at the Canon, Use of Utrecht, ca. 1400–1410 with added sections, Northern Netherlands. The Hague, Koninklijke Bibliotheek, Ms. 128 D 29, fols 128v-129r.	117
Fig. 57	Opening of a missal at the Canon in a printed missal, Switzerland or Germany (Basel?), c.1487. Oxford, Bodleian Library, Auct. 6 Q 1.15, unf.	120
Fig. 58	Folio from a manuscript missal depicting God in Majesty (Paris, 1370–1380) bound into *Eusebius Historia Ecclestica*, printed by Nicholas Ketelaert and Gerardus Leempt of Nijmegen in 1473 with hand-flourished initials. Oxford, Bodleian Library, Auct. 7 Q 2.13.	121

Fig. 59 Folio from a manuscript missal depicting Christ Crucified 121 (Paris, 1370–1380) bound into *Eusebius Historia Ecclestica*, printed by Nicholas Ketelaert and Gerardus Leempt of Nijmegen in 1473 with hand-flourished initials. Oxford, Bodleian Library, Auct. 7 Q 2.13.

Fig. 60 Erfurt Jewish Oath, parchment and a wax seal, ca. 1200, 124 Erfut. Erfurt, Old Synagogue. Photo kindly supplied by the Municipal Archive Erfurt, 2006

Fig. 61 Opening folio of the *Sachsenspiegel* by Eike von Repgow, 127 copied in 1336, Rastede (Lower Saxony). Oldenburg, Landesbibliothek, Ms. CIM I 410, fol. 6r

Fig. 62 Folio from the *Sachsenspiegel* by Eike von Repgow, 128 copied in 1336, Rastede (Lower Saxony). Oldenburg, Landesbibliothek, Ms. CIM I 410, fol. 18r.

Fig. 63 Folio from the *Sachsenspiegel* by Eike von Repgow, early 130 fourteenth century, central-eastern Germany. Heidelberg, University Library, Cod. Pal. germ. 164, fol. 15r. Reproduced under a CC-BY-SA 4.0 license

Fig. 64 Folio from the prologue of the *Sachsenspiegel* by Eike von 131 Repgow, translated into Middle Dutch, with a miniature depicting the Last Judgment, copied ca. 1405, Utrecht. The Hague, Koninklijke Bibliotheek, Ms. 75 G 47, fol. 6r

Fig. 65 Amateur photograph showing the opening of the 132 *Sachsenspiegel* by Eike von Repgow, translated into Middle Dutch, with a miniature depicting the Last Judgment, copied ca. 1405, Utrecht. The Hague, Koninklijke Bibliotheek, Ms. 75 G 47, fols 5v-6r

Fig. 66 Opening and dedicatory image of Ulrich IV von Albeck's 134 *Promptuarium iuris*, copied and illuminated in 1429. Graz, University Library, Ms 23, vol. 1, fol. 1r

Fig. 67 Opening folio of the register for the *dismeesters* (stewards) 141 of the Cathedral of Sint-Salvator, Bruges, 1457, Bruges. © KIK-IRPA, Brussels (Belgium), cliché z011761

Fig. 68 Swearing ceremony, with a lord seated before standing 140 crowd. From the *Livre des statuts et coutumes de la ville d'Agen*, ca. 1300. Agen Archives départementales de Lot-et-Garonne, Ms. 42, fol. 14v.

Fig. 69 Newcomer swearing on a book. From the *Livre des statuts* 141 *et coutumes de la ville d'Agen*, ca. 1300. Agen Archives départementales de Lot-et-Garonne, Ms. 42, fol. 53v.

Illustrations 245

Fig. 70 Incipit of the Gospel of John. From the *Livre des statuts* 142
et coutumes de la ville d'Agen, ca. 1300. Agen Archives
départementales de Lot-et-Garonne, Ms. 42, fol. 10r.

Fig. 71 Opening bifolio, with the Throne of Mercy in a Mandorla 143
with the Evangelists' Symbols, and the Virgin and Child
Flanked by Angels, full-page miniatures in the *Livre des
statuts et coutumes de la ville d'Agen*, ca. 1300. Agen Archives
départementales de Lot-et-Garonne, Ms. 42, fols 7v-8r.

Fig. 72 Front cover dated 1580, Roodt Privilegieboeck. 146
's-Hertogenbosch, Stadsarchief, oudarchief inv. nr A 525.

Fig. 73 Opening in the Roodt Privilegieboeck, with the beginning 148
of the Book of John, and the beginning of the Charter.
's-Hertogenbosch, Stadsarchief, oudarchief inv. nr A 525,
fols iii (verso) – iiii (recto).

Fig. 74 Full-page miniature depicting Christ crucified between 148
Mary and John bound into the book of civic statutes for the
city of 's-Hertogenbosch, called the Roodt Privilegieboeck,
ca. 1430. 's-Hertogenbosch, Stadsarchief, oudarchief inv. nr
A 525, fols 55v-56r.

Fig. 75 Opening of a missal at the Canon, made in Utrecht and 149
exported to Bruges. Bruges, Sint-Salvatorkathedraal,
treasury. © KIK-IRPA, Brussels (Belgium), cliché Z011681

Fig. 76 Roodt Privilegieboeck,'s-Hertogenbosch, Stadsarchief, 150
oudarchief inv. nr A 525, fols LX verso– LX bis recto

Fig. 77 Folio in the Old Proctors' Book of Cambridge with an image 157
depicting St. Christopher. Cambridge, University Archives,
Collect. Admin. 3, fol. 6r. Reproduced by kind permission of
the Syndics of Cambridge University Library.

Fig. 78 Folio in the Old Proctors' Book of Cambridge with the 158
beginning of a series of oaths. Cambridge, University
Archives, Collect. Admin. 3, fol. 6v. Reproduced by kind
permission of the Syndics of Cambridge University Library.

Fig. 79 Folio in the Old Proctors' Book of Cambridge with an 159
image depicting Virgin and Child in an architectural
niche. Cambridge, University Archives, Collect. Admin. 3,
fol. 8r. Reproduced by kind permission of the Syndics of
Cambridge University Library.

Fig. 80	Front cover of a compilation of texts about inquisition and heresy, fourteenth century. Linz, Oberösterreichische Landesbibliothek (OÖLB), Cod. 177. [to cite this according to the library's standards: Linz, AT-OOeLB, Hs.-177 (Sammelhandschrift zu Themen von Inquisition und Umgang mit Häresie, Saec. XIV). 1300]	162
Fig. 81	Folio from a compilation of texts about inquisition and heresy, with incipits of the four Gospels. Linz, Oberösterreichische Landesbibliothek (OÖLB), Cod. 177, fol. 1r.	164
Fig. 82	Folio from a compilation of texts about inquisition and heresy, with a drawing of Christ Crucified. Linz, Oberösterreichische Landesbibliothek (OÖLB), Cod. 177, fol. 10r.	165
Fig. 83	Folio in a noted ferial choir Psalter, possibly for St Lawrence's, Trau (Dalmatia), ca. 1450–1475. Oxford, Bodleian Library, Ms. Canon. Liturg. 395, fol. vii recto	169
Fig. 84	Opening in a noted ferial choir Psalter, possibly for St Lawrence's, Trau (Dalmatia), ca. 1450–1475. Oxford, Bodleian Library, Ms. Canon. Liturg. 395, fol. vi verso – vii recto. Amateur photograph.	170
Fig. 85	Folio in a noted ferial choir Psalter, possibly for St Lawrence's, Trau (Dalmatia), ca. 1450–1475. Oxford, Bodleian Library, Ms. Canon. Liturg. 395, fol. 190v.	171
Fig. 86	Opening in a noted ferial choir Psalter, possibly for St Lawrence's, Trau (Dalmatia), ca. 1450–1475. Oxford, Bodleian Library, Ms. Canon. Liturg. 395, fol. 190v-191r. Amateur photograph	171
Fig. 87	First folio of an antiphonary, with a small miniautre depicting the Virgin and Child flanked by founders, Abbey of Marchiennes, ca. 1450–1475. Douai, Bibliothèque municipale, Ms. 117, fol. 1r. Cliché: IRHT-CNRS	172
Fig. 88	Detail of previous figure. Douai, Bibliothèque municipale, Ms. 117, fol. 1r. Cliché: IRHT-CNRS	173
Fig. 89	Trinity, Historiated initial cut from a Venetian antiphonary, mounted at the end of the manuscript. Oxford, Bodleian, Ms. Douce a. 1, fol. 155, item d.	174
Fig. 90	Opening in an antiphonary, with a historiated initial depicting St Augustine, fifteenth century, Venice. Oxford, Bodleian, Ms. Douce a. 1, fols 70v-71r	175
Fig. 91	St Augustine, fifteenth century, Venice. Oxford, Bodleian, Ms. Douce a. 1, fol. 70v.	176

Illustrations 247

Fig. 92   Cutting fron an antiphonary made in Venice, mounted at the end of the manuscript. Oxford, Bodleian, Ms. Douce a. 1, fol. 148r   177

Fig. 93   Master of Catherine of Cleves, Hand of God holding book into the margin, Pontifical, ca. 1450, Chapter of St. Mary in Utrecht. Utrecht, Universiteitsbibliotheek Ms. 400, fol. 34r   179

Fig. 94   Folio in a Pontifical Master of Catherine of Cleves, the blessing of the vestements. Utrecht, Universiteitsbibliotheek Ms. 400, fol. 99r   180

Fig. 95   Detail of previous image. Utrecht, Universiteitsbibliotheek Ms. 400, fol. 99r   181

Fig. 96   Instructions for performing a Baptism, in a rubricated noted ritual, England, fifteenth century. Oxford, Bodleian Library, Ms. Laud. Misc. 267, fols 13v–14r   181

Fig. 97   Master of Heiligenkruz (Bohemian?), Death of the Virgin, ca. 1400–1401. Tempera and oil with gold on panel. Gift of the Friends of the Cleveland Museum of Art in memory of John Long Severance 1936.496   182

Fig. 98   detail of previous image   183

Fig. 99   Instructions for performing last rites, in a rubricated noted ritual, England, fifteenth century. Oxford, Bodleian Library, Ms. Laud. Misc. 267, fols 85v-86r   184

Fig. 100   Burial of the Dead, full-page miniature in a book of hours made in the Southern Netherlands. Chicago, University Library, Ms. 347, fol. 98v   185

Fig. 101   Processional cart for the relics of Gertrude of Nijvel, ca. 1500. The cart is 412 cm long. Kept in the Church of St Gertrude in Nijvel   186

Fig. 102   Noted Mass for the dead, in the Grand Obituary of Notre-Dame. Paris, BnF, Ms lat. 5185 CC, fols 130v-131r   189

Fig. 103   Noted Mass for the dead, in the Grand Obituary of Notre-Dame. Paris, BnF, Ms lat. 5185 CC, fols 130v-131r photographed with backlighting   190

Fig. 104   Obituary from the original production of the Grand Obituary of Notre-Dame. Paris, BnF, Ms lat. 5185 CC, fol. 311r, photographed with backlighting   191

Fig. 105   Folio added after 1492 to the Grand Obituary of Notre-Dame. Paris, BnF, Ms lat. 5185 CC, fol. 235r, photographed with backlighting   191

Fig. 106   Opening with original and added material, including the added obituary of Simon de Guiberville (d. 1320). Paris, BnF, Ms lat. 5185 CC, fols. 242v–243r   193

Fig. 107	Simon de Guiberville preaching to an audience. Paris, BnF, Ms lat. 5185 CC, fol. 243r (detail)	194
Fig. 108	Funeral of Bishop Simon Matifas de Bucy, on an added folio in the Grand Obituary, entry for June 22, 1304. Bibliothèque Nationale de France, Paris, MS lat. 5185 CC, fol. 224r (detail)	195
Fig. 109	Added folio with the obituary of Bishop Simon Matifas de Bucy, in the Grand Obituary, entry for June 22, 1304. Bibliothèque Nationale de France, Paris, MS lat. 5185 CC, fol. 224r	196
Fig. 110	Funeral of Cardinal Michel du Bec, on an added folio in the Grand Obituary, entry for August 22, 1318. Bibliothèque Nationale de France, Paris, MS lat. 5185 CC, fol. 265r	198
Fig. 111	Mass being celebrated for Lord Henry de Sucy, from the Grand Obituary, entry for December 8, 1310. Bibliothèque Nationale de France, Paris, MS lat. 5185 CC, fol. 315r	200
Fig. 112	Obituary for Hugues de Besançon, on an added folio. Bibliothèque Nationale de France, Paris, MS lat. 5185 CC, fol. 214r	201
Fig. 113	Girardus (Gérard) de Courlandon before the Virgin and Child, from the Grand Obituary, entry for March 23, 1319. Bibliothèque Nationale de France, Paris, MS lat. 5185 CC, fol. 170r, detail with miniature	202
Fig. 114	Opening in the Grand Obituary, with original material on the verso facing an added obituary on the recto. Bibliothèque Nationale de France, Paris, MS lat. 5185 CC, fols 169v-170r	203
Fig. 115	Folio added to the Grand Obituary of Notre-Dame. Paris, BnF, Ms lat. 5185 CC, fol. 170v, photographed with backlighting	203
Fig. 116	Miniature depicting Christ holding scales, on a folio from an added obituary for Lady Margaret of Roche-Guyon, Paris, ca. 1472. Paris, BnF, Ms lat. 5185 CC, fol. 189r, detail	207
Fig. 117	Folio from an added obituary for Guillaume Chartier, with a miniature depicting a miraculous mass, Paris, ca. 1472. Paris, BnF, Ms lat. 5185 CC, fol. 190v	209
Fig. 118	Miniature at the obituary for Guillaume Chartier depicting a miraculous mass, Paris, ca. 1472. Paris, BnF, Ms lat. 5185 CC, fol. 190v, det.	210
Fig. 119	Page on which the "Kalens" has been touched with a wet finger. Paris, BnF, Ms lat. 5185 CC, fol. 311r, det	211
Fig. 120	Overview of ways a medieval manuscript can be degraded. Diagram made by Kathryn M. Rudy	218

Fig. 121 Crucified Christ between Mary and John, single sheet, glazed. 's-Heerenberg, The Netherlands, Collection Dr. J. H. van Heek, Huis Bergh Foundation, Ms. Fr 40 (inv. 244). Image © The Huis Bergh Foundation, CC BY 4.0   221

Fig. 122 Crucified Christ between Mary and John, single sheet, glazed. 's-Heerenberg, The Netherlands, Collection Dr. J. H. van Heek, Huis Bergh Foundation, Ms. Fr 40 (inv. 244). Amateur photograph with backlighting   222

About the Team

Alessandra Tosi was the managing editor for this book.

Rosalyn Sword performed the copy-editing and proofreading.

Jeevanjot Kaur Nagpal designed the cover. The cover was produced in InDesign using the Fontin font.

Luca Baffa typeset the book in InDesign and produced the paperback and hardback editions. The text font is Tex Gyre Pagella; the heading font is Californian FB. Luca produced the EPUB, AZW3, PDF, HTML, and XML editions — the conversion was made with open-source software such as pandoc (https://pandoc.org/), created by John MacFarlane, and other tools freely available on our GitHub page (https://github.com/OpenBookPublishers).

This book has been anonymously peer-reviewed by experts in their field. We thank them for their invaluable help.

This book need not end here...

Share

All our books — including the one you have just read — are free to access online so that students, researchers and members of the public who can't afford a printed edition will have access to the same ideas. This title will be accessed online by hundreds of readers each month across the globe: why not share the link so that someone you know is one of them?

This book and additional content is available at:

https://doi.org/10.11647/OBP.0337

Donate

Open Book Publishers is an award-winning, scholar-led, not-for-profit press making knowledge freely available one book at a time. We don't charge authors to publish with us: instead, our work is supported by our library members and by donations from people who believe that research shouldn't be locked behind paywalls.

Why not join them in freeing knowledge by supporting us: https://www.openbookpublishers.com/support-us

Follow @OpenBookPublish

Read more at the Open Book Publishers **BLOG**

You may also be interested in:

Image, Knife, and Gluepot
Early Assemblage in Manuscript and Print
Kathryn M. Rudy

https://doi.org/10.11647/OBP.0145

Piety in Pieces
How Medieval Readers Customized their Manuscripts
Kathryn M. Rudy

https://doi.org/10.11647/OBP.0094

 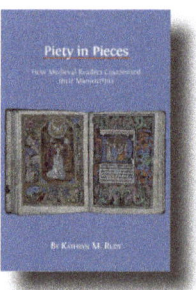

The Juggler of Notre Dame and the Medievalizing of Modernity
Volume 1: The Middle Ages
Jan M. Ziolkowski

https://doi.org/10.11647/OBP.0132

 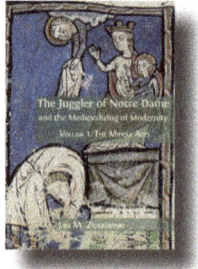

www.ingramcontent.com/pod-product-compliance
Lightning Source LLC
Chambersburg PA
CBHW061251230426
43664CB00025B/2930